SALAD AS A MEAL

We've Always Had Paris . . . and Provence (with Walter Wells)

Vegetable Harvest

The Provence Cookbook

The Paris Cookbook

L'Atélier of Joël Robuchon

Patricia Wells at Home in Provence

Patricia Wells' Trattoria

Simply French

Bistro Cooking

The Food Lover's Guide to France

The Food Lover's Guide to Paris

SALAD AS A MEAL

HEALTHY MAIN-DISH SALADS FOR EVERY SEASON

Patricia Wells

PHOTOGRAPHY BY JEFF KAUCK

WILLIAM MORROW

An Imprint of HarperCollins*Publishers*

NOTE: Please be advised that people with compromised immune systems, children,
and the elderly should check with their physician before eating raw foods.

HarperCollins books may be purchased for educational, business, or sales promotional use.
For information please write: Special Markets Department, HarperCollins Publishers,
10 East 53rd Street, New York, NY 10022.

FIRST EDITION

Designed by Lorie Pagnozzi

Library of Congress Cataloging-in-Publication Data

Wells, Patricia.
    Salad as a meal : healthy main-dish salads for every season / Patricia Wells.—1st ed.
        p. cm.
    Includes index.
    ISBN 978-0-06-123883-3
    1. Salads. I. Title.
    TX740.W36 2011
    641.8'3—dc22   2010027043

11   12   13   14   15   ID4/QG   10   9   8   7   6   5   4   3   2   1

WITH GRATITUDE TO ALL MY STUDENTS, WHO HAVE SUSTAINED AND INSPIRED ME OVER THE YEARS: WE HAVE FORMED DEEP AND LASTING FRIENDSHIPS, YOU'VE KEPT ME ON MY TOES, AND YOU DO HELP ME STAY YOUNG. THE TEACHER IS ALWAYS THE ONE WHO LEARNS THE MOST!

CONTENTS

SALAD AS A MEAL: AN INTRODUCTION

The original inspiration for this, my twelfth, book comes from the simple, old-fashioned menu at Brasserie Lipp on Paris's Left Bank. In big, bold red letters at the top of the French menu it proclaims in clear English: NO SALAD AS A MEAL.

The folks at Lipp are simply trying to prevent the ladies who lunch from considering a simple tossed green salad a meal. But how times change. Today, with heightened concern about nutrition as well as the great wealth of choice in what we eat—ultra-fresh seasonal produce, an ever-growing variety of greens, sparkling fish and shellfish, all manner of cheeses, oils, vinegars, nuts, and seeds—I find that at home (if not at Lipp) we are more likely to fashion a salad as an entire meal. That ultimate backup, the pantry, can provide a large palette to choose from, allowing us to shop for just one or two fresh items to create a satisfying, fulfilling, healthy meal.

Salads have always conjured up fresh, healthy, youthful thoughts, and when one considers the expression "salad days" (in French *les années de jeunesse)* it makes us all want to consume more salads to remain eternally fresh and youthful. The word "salad," in fact, comes from the Latin word for salt, *sal,* and to salt, or *salare.* Originally a salad was just greens tossed with salt; later it moved on to include all manner

of greens and additions, with an unlimited number of dressings. (Speaking of salt, my favorites come from Brittany, where the sun-dried salt provides natural sources of potassium, calcium, magnesium, copper, and zinc. I use fine sea salt in baking and everyday cooking, add coarse salt to water for blanching vegetables or cooking pasta, and reserve the rare *fleur de sel* as a "finishing" salt at the table.)

The French have always been huge salad fans and are fanatical about how a salad is dressed. In fact they have a great expression, *fatiguer la salade,* meaning that the salad must be carefully tossed and tossed until the greens are *fatigué,* or exhausted—until they have absorbed all the dressing that they can. (Our good friend Jean-Claude Viviani holds court as the house salad is tossed, and insists that the salad greens must be turned thirty-three times to create a properly dressed salad!)

The inspiration for the recipes here come from all over: from meals with friends and in restaurants, from trips around my garden, and from such excellent salads as a meal as those from Greece, the American Cobb and Caesar salads, the French *frisée aux lardons,* and the classic goat cheese wrapped in bacon and set on a sturdy bed of greens.

Whatever the salad, its success depends upon super-fresh and flavorful ingredients and plenty of crunch, a sound that satisfies. The crunch can come in the form of truly crisp young greens such as baby spinach or even the traditional iceberg lettuce, but a shower of toasted pumpkin seeds, spicy nuts, corn flour tortilla chips, and cubes of tasty Parmesan croutons can also add the essential crisp edge.

In my own personal definition, a salad as a meal does not need to include lettuce or greens; it can simply be a light and refreshing salad-related entity. A creamy chilled ricotta terrine, a protein-rich poached turkey breast dressed with herbs, a pasta flavored with a vinaigrette-like sauce of spicy mustard, a favorite chicken and tarragon terrine glistening in a sturdy gelatin, or such Middle Eastern classics as chickpea fritters—or falafel—teamed up with a gorgeous heirloom tomato salad and a healthy dose of tahini dressing are all salads as a meal in my book.

I have offered a chapter of appetizers that one might pair with other salads, as well as a healthy dose of soups, both hot and cold, that can be served ahead of or alongside a variety of salads.

My own personal taste is for salads with a good hit of protein, so here I have plenty of fish and shellfish carpaccio and ceviche dishes, a number that include home-smoked fish and poultry, lots of meat, and a recipe for poached chicken that can serve as the base of many a salad. Eggs and cheese can add that needed protein to any meal, and so easy egg crepes, frittatas, and my treasured ricotta terrine fit into that category.

Bread is an integral part of any salad I plan to enjoy, so I include several pizza-style flatbreads, easy bread crisps made from your favorite breads, and homemade flatbreads as well as my much-loved homemade sourdough bread, one that requires a bit of attention and discipline but pays you back in spades in terms of enjoyment and raves from family and friends.

I offer a collection of my favorite dressings but am not rigid about which dressing must go with which salad, except in the case of such classics as the revered Caesar and Cobb salads. In most cases, if one is enjoying a wine with the salad as a meal, the less vinegar in the dressing the better, since vinegar can kill the flavor of even the most modest of wines. Rather, go for a light salad dressing with a lemon, buttermilk, yogurt, or light cream base.

The extensive pantry section focuses on some of my favorite homemade foods: home-cured capers and cornichons, homemade vinegar, as well as a quick lemon confit, pickled figs, a favored series of flavored salts, brine-cured black olives, and pickled peppers.

In a perfect world we would all grow our own herbs, lettuces, and vegetables. In the summer months I am blessed with a voluptuous garden that I

Espelette *pepper*

experiment with each year, adding varieties that we love and that do well and omitting those that don't produce or please. But even if you don't have a patch of soil, try to grow at least a few treasured herbs—mint and rosemary come to mind—in pots to instantly perk up and vary your salads.

For the past few years I have experimented endlessly with growing salad greens, planting a packet of seeds every few weeks during the summer, and find that some greens grow like weeds and keep delivering week after week as "cut and come again" stars. Others never develop into much or even if they do, they don't seem to fit into my world. So I anticipate that I will have to balance the thrills with the disappointments.

A WORD ON SUGGESTED WINES

Wine is one of the world's greatest pleasures, and I am endlessly in search of best buys, wines that offer great flavor and simple pleasure for less. I have been careful to research each of the wines suggested here, and at this writing they are all imported into the United States. If you don't find the wine at a favorite wine store, ask the owner if he can't bring it in.

A WORD ON THE PHOTOS IN THE BOOK

I first met photographer Jeff Kauck when his wife, Sue, and daughter, Dana, came one sunny week in June as students in our regular cooking weeks in Provence. We built a friendship and a mutual admiration and the trio returned to our home in Provence to photograph this book. We spent two marvelous weeks creating the photos. All the bowls and dishes shown here are French handmade and artisanal pottery, and all the photographs were taken in natural light. We captured as many as possible outdoors, except when the pesky Mistral wind moved us inside.

I present this book with the hope that you will enjoy it as much as I loved creating it.

Vaison-La-Romaine, France

October 2010

APPETIZERS AND SIDES

EVERY SALAD LOVES A SIDEKICK, A QUICK ADDITION THAT OFFERS TEXTURAL CONTRAST AND EXTRA FLAVOR. MY FAVORITES INCLUDE FLAVORED NUTS, MARINATED OLIVES, AND BAY-LEAF-SCENTED BABY ARTICHOKES MARINATED IN OIL. THIN SLICES OF BREAD OR TOAST SLATHERED WITH BLACK OLIVE TAPENADE, WITH A LIGHT AND MILDLY SPICED GUAMACOLE, OR WITH EITHER CHICKPEA OR EGGPLANT DIP PAIR BEAUTIFULLY WITH ANY SALAD AS A MEAL.

SPICY BASQUE MIXED NUTS

I have a snack drawer in my kitchen, always stocked with healthy treats to snack on: nuts, seeds, dried fruits, and candied ginger. I created this recipe to add to my growing collection! Buy the best quality organic nuts you can find: I buy mine at the Sunday morning organic farmer's market in Paris. The nuts are perfect for showering on any salad for added crunch and punch.

3 CUPS

EQUIPMENT: A BAKING SHEET.

1 teaspoon ground *piment d'Espelette* or other ground mild chile pepper

1/4 teaspoon hot-smoked *pimentón de la Vera* or other hot-smoked paprika

1/4 teaspoon mild paprika

1/2 teaspoon fine sea salt

2 teaspoons extra-virgin olive oil

1 cup (4 ounces) freshly cracked walnut halves

1 cup (4 ounces) shelled almonds

1 cup (4 ounces) whole hazelnuts

1. Preheat the oven to 350°F.

2. In a large bowl, combine the *piment d'Espelette, pimentón de la Vera,* paprika, salt, and oil. Stir to blend. Add the nuts and toss to coat them evenly with the spices and oil. Spread the nuts in a single layer on the baking sheet. Place in the oven and toast, shaking the pan from time to time, until the nuts are fragrant, are beginning to pop, and are crisp and golden, 10 to 12 minutes. (Store in an airtight container at room temperature for up to 2 weeks.)

   NOTE: *Piment d'Espelette,* a mildly spicy pepper from France's Basque region, and smoked *pimentón* from Spain can be found on my Amazon Store on the home page of PatriciaWells.com.

CURRIED PUMPKIN SEEDS

These mildly spicy, properly salty seeds can double as a snack and as a garnish for all manner of salads. I like to keep them on hand for the moment when hunger strikes during the day and for embellishing a salad.

2 CUPS

EQUIPMENT: A BAKING SHEET.

2 cups (8 ounces) hulled pumpkin or squash seeds

1 tablespoon Homemade Curry Powder (page 292)

2 tablespoons tamari or other Japanese soy sauce

1. Preheat the oven to 350°F.

2. In a large bowl, combine the seeds, curry powder, and tamari, tossing to evenly coat the seeds. Spread the seeds in a single layer on the baking sheet. Place in the oven and toast, shaking the pan from time to time, until the seeds change color from steel-gray to toasty brown, begin to pop and puff up, and are crisp, 8 to 12 minutes. (Store in an airtight container at room temperature for up to 2 weeks.)

Spicy Basque Mixed Nuts (left) and Curried Pumpkin Seeds

VARIATION: I also make these with the Japanese sesame-seasoned salt known as *gomasio* in place of the curry powder. While one can find the salt in health food stores, I find it easier to make my own (see page 304). You can make it in small batches so it remains fresher and livelier.

CHICKPEA AND SESAME DIP: HUMMUS

A farmer near us in Provence grows wonderfully rich-tasting chickpeas, which I turn into tangy, lemon-flecked dips, accompaniments to poultry dishes, or I prepare our favorite falafel (see page 54). For the most delicious hummus, cook your own dried chickpeas; the canned ones can taste tinny and are not nearly as flavorful.

2 CUPS

EQUIPMENT: A FOOD PROCESSOR OR A BLENDER.

2 1/2 cups Home-Cooked Chickpeas (page 12), drained (reserve liquid)

2 plump, moist garlic cloves, peeled, halved, and green germ removed

4 tablespoons freshly squeezed lemon juice (or to taste)

3 tablespoons tahini (sesame paste)

1 teaspoon fine sea salt

2 tablespoons best-quality sesame oil (such as Leblanc), see Note

1/4 cup cilantro leaves

1/8 teaspoon paprika

Set aside 1/2 cup of the chickpeas for garnish. In the bowl of a food processor or a blender, mince the garlic. Add the remaining 2 cups of chickpeas, the lemon juice, tahini, salt, and 1 tablespoon of the oil. Blend until smooth, adding the reserved cooking liquid if necessary to make a smooth puree. Taste for seasoning. Spoon the dip into a large, shallow bowl, and garnish with the reserved 1/2 cup of chickpeas, a drizzle of oil, cilantro, and paprika. Serve. (The dip can be stored, without the garnish, covered and refrigerated, for up to 3 days.)

NOTE: I prefer the fresh, high-quality flavor of the nut seed oils from the small French family producer Leblanc. Many of their oils can be found on my Amazon store via patriciawells.com. I do not use toasted Asian sesame oils for I find them too harsh and often not fresh.

HOME-COOKED CHICKPEAS

3 CUPS

A scant 3 cups (1 pound) dried chickpeas

2 tablespoons extra-virgin olive oil

1 medium onion, peeled, halved lengthwise, and thinly sliced

8 plump, moist garlic cloves, crushed and peeled

1 teaspoon fine sea salt

1 quart cold water, Homemade Chicken Stock (page 310), or Homemade Vegetable Stock
(page 312)

1 bouquet garni: several fresh parsley sprigs and several bay leaves encased in a wire mesh tea
infuser or bound in a piece of cheesecloth

1. Rinse and drain the chickpeas, picking through them to remove any pebbles. Place the
chickpeas in a large bowl and add cold water to cover. Set aside at room temperature for
12 to 24 hours. This will help speed up the cooking time.

2. In a large saucepan combine the oil, onion, garlic, and salt and stir to coat with the oil.
Sweat—cook, covered, over low heat without coloring until soft and translucent—for
about 5 minutes. Drain and rinse the soaked chickpeas and add them to the saucepan.
Stir to coat them with the oil, and cook for 1 minute more. Add the water or stock and
the bouquet garni. Simmer, covered, until the chickpeas are tender. The cooking time
will vary—from 30 minutes to 2 hours—depending upon the freshness of the beans.
Younger beans will cook more quickly; beans more than 1 year old will take longer.
Taste for seasoning. (Store in the cooking liquid in an airtight container in the freezer
for up to 3 months.)

SMOKY EGGPLANT DIP: BABA GHANOUSH

There are few aromas that can compete with the smoky richness of eggplant being cooked over a hot fire. I set these on a grate directly over a gas flame, but hot coals or an outdoor grill is an excellent alternative. Cooking the eggplant over an open flame imparts a depth of flavor and aroma that cannot be achieved with simple oven roasting. I enjoy a smoky eggplant dip that has a good lemony tang and a healthy hit of fresh garlic. Serve this with Falafel (page 54), Crispy Flatbread (page 260), or Homemade Pita Bread (page 268) or as one of several appetizers. Sometimes I think that the purpose of a salad is to shake up the palate, and this combination sure does that!

2 CUPS

EQUIPMENT: A TWO-PRONGED MEAT FORK; A SMALL, SHARP KNIFE OR A SERRATED GRAPEFRUIT SPOON; A FOOD PROCESSOR OR A BLENDER.

2 small, fresh eggplants (each about 8 ounces), rinsed (do not peel)

2 plump, moist garlic cloves, peeled, halved, and green germ removed

3 tablespoons tahini (sesame paste)

3 tablespoons freshly squeezed lemon juice (or to taste)

1/2 teaspoon fine sea salt

Mild paprika, for garnish

2 tablespoons minced fresh parsley leaves

2 teaspoons best-quality sesame oil (such as Leblanc) or extra-virgin olive oil

1. With a two-pronged meat fork, prick the eggplants all over. Place them directly over an open gas flame, hot coals, or an outdoor grill. Cook for 10 minutes, turning the eggplants constantly with tongs, until the entire skin is blackened, blistered, and has collapsed in on itself. Remove the eggplants from the heat and place in a plastic bag. Let the eggplants cool for 10 minutes.

2. Gently peel the eggplant skin away from the flesh with a small, sharp knife or a serrated grapefruit spoon. Be careful not to let any pieces of the skin remain. (Use paper towels to wipe away any recalcitrant bits of skin.) Place the eggplant pulp in a colander and let it drain for 5 minutes.

3. In a food processor or blender, chop the garlic. Add the tahini, lemon juice, and salt and process to blend. Add the eggplant pulp and process just for a few seconds, to blend the ingredients. Taste for seasoning. The mixture should remain rather chunky. Spoon the dip into a shallow bowl and garnish with paprika, the parsley, and the oil. Serve at room temperature. (Store in an airtight container in the refrigerator for up to 3 days.)

PARMESAN BABY CAKES: SAVORY *CANNELÉS*

Classic cannelés *are popular rum-and-vanilla-flavored cakes from the Bordeaux region of France. Traditional* cannelés *are baked in beautiful individual tin-lined copper molds. The problem was never the recipe—just the ability to unmold, one by one, the sweet and fragrant cakes. Now that single sheets of silicone molds—holding anywhere from 18 to 28 to 54 miniature cakes—can be readily found on the market, the sweet treats are child's play. And once you have invested in the molds, there is no reason not to move* cannelés *into the savory side of cuisine. Here is my version, filled with cheese and bits of cured meat, making them perfect accompaniments to any salad.*

18 *CANNELÉS*

EQUIPMENT: A PASTRY BRUSH; A SILICONE MINIATURE
***CANNELÉS* MOLD, SHEET OF 18; A BAKING SHEET.**

1 cup whole milk

1 1/2 tablespoons unsalted butter, plus 1 tablespoon melted butter for the molds

1 cup unbleached, all-purpose flour

1 cup freshly grated Parmigiano-Reggiano cheese

1 large egg, lightly beaten

1/4 teaspoon fine sea salt

1/4 teaspoon ground *piment d'Espelette* or other ground mild chile pepper

1/4 cup cooked diced bacon, pancetta, or coppa (optional)

1. Preheat the oven to 375°F.

2. In a medium saucepan, combine the milk and butter. Bring to a boil over high heat. Remove from the heat and whisk in the flour, cheese, egg, salt, and *piment*

d'Espelette. The batter will be lumpy. Set aside to rest for 30 minutes, whisking from time to time.

3. Brush the molds with the melted butter. Place the silicone sheet on a baking sheet. Carefully spoon the batter into the buttered molds, filling them just to the top. If using the meat, drop a few pieces into each mold. Place the baking sheet in the oven and bake until the *cannelés* have puffed up and are a very deep golden brown, about 45 minutes.

4. Remove from the oven and let cool for about 5 minutes. Then turn the cakes out of the molds onto a clean, flat surface. Let cool and firm up before serving, at least 20 minutes. The *cannelés* are best served the day they are baked.

MARINATED OLIVE QUARTET

If a single variety of olives can be good, can't three or four be better? There is something special about the tang of this mixture that takes the dish beyond a recipe for simple cured olives. Combine as many different varieties as you like. The additions of fennel seeds, a touch of hot pepper flakes, and tiny cubes of lemon confit help to round out the flavors. Serve these scattered over a green salad or as part of an appetizer platter. You do not need to pit the olives.

2 CUPS

1/2 cup extra-virgin olive oil

1/4 cup best-quality red-wine vinegar

1 teaspoon fennel seeds

1/2 teaspoon Red Hot Salt (page 307), or hot red pepper flakes to taste

3 fresh or dried bay leaves

1/4 cup finely minced Quick Lemon Confit (page 297)

2 cups mixed olives, preferably a mix of best-quality French Brine-Cured Black Olives (page 302), green Picholine olives, green pimiento-stuffed olives, and tiny black Niçoise olives

In a large saucepan, combine the oil and vinegar. Heat over low heat just until warm. Remove from the heat and add the fennel, Red Hot Salt or pepper flakes, bay leaves, and lemon confit. Add the olives and toss to coat them with the liquid. Transfer to a large, airtight container. Refrigerate, shaking the container regularly to redistribute the liquid, for at least 2 hours and up to 2 weeks.

BLACK OLIVE TAPENADE WITH LEMON CONFIT

This is one recipe that does not withstand mediocre ingredients. Gather the finest ingredients you can and you will be rewarded with a salty, pungent, jet-black classic spread for slathering on toast, tomatoes, or eggplant or for using simply as a dip with crunchy toast shards. I love the addition of homemade lemon confit, adding a touch of crunch as well as a bit of zest.

1 1/2 CUPS

EQUIPMENT: A FOOD PROCESSOR OR A BLENDER.

10 anchovy fillets in olive oil, drained

2 cups best-quality French Brine-Cured Black Olives (page 302), pitted

1 tablespoon Capers in Vinegar (page 289), drained

1 teaspoon Dijon mustard

1 plump, moist garlic clove, peeled, halved, and green germ removed

1/4 teaspoon fresh thyme leaves

6 tablespoons extra-virgin olive oil

Coarse, freshly ground black pepper

1/4 cup finely minced Quick Lemon Confit (page 297)

In a food processor or a blender, combine the anchovies, olives, capers, mustard, garlic, and thyme. Process to form a thick paste. With the food processor running, add the oil in a steady stream until it is thoroughly incorporated. Season with pepper. Taste for seasoning. Fold in the lemon confit. (Store in an airtight container in the refrigerator for up to 1 week.)

NOTE: It is natural that the oil will separate. At serving time, simply whisk to redistribute the oil.

PICHOLINE OLIVES WITH TOASTED CUMIN AND PAPRIKA

Picholine olives are meaty, green, torpedo-shaped olives from Provence. They are cured in brine and often found seasoned with various herbs and spices. This is my creation, with the delicate, earthy flavor of toasted cumin seeds and the haunting smokiness of Spanish paprika.

2 CUPS

EQUIPMENT: A COVERED JAR LARGE ENOUGH TO FIT THE OLIVES SNUGLY.

2 cups best-quality Picholine olives, drained

1/2 cup extra-virgin olive oil

1/4 cup best-quality red-wine vinegar

1 teaspoon cumin seeds, toasted and bruised (see Note)

1 teaspoon hot-smoked *pimentón de la Vera* or other hot-smoked paprika

Place the olives in the jar. In a large saucepan, combine the olive oil, vinegar, cumin, and paprika. Bring just to a boil over high heat. Pour the mixture over the olives. Cover securely and shake the jar. Serve at room temperature. (Store in an airtight container in the refrigerator for up to 2 weeks.)

NOTE: To toast cumin seeds, place the seeds in a small, dry skillet over moderate heat. Shake the pan regularly until the grains of cumin are fragrant and evenly toasted, about 2 minutes. Watch carefully! They can burn quickly. Transfer the cumin to a large plate to cool. Then bruise the seeds with a mallet, or grind them to a coarse powder in a spice grinder or a coffee mill.

TAPENADE "TOASTS"

When baked, the simple combination of tapenade, cheese, egg whites, and herbs is transformed into firm golden rounds that resemble toast. These salty, thin "toasts" lend themselves to endless variations. They can be sampled as appetizer crisps, mounded with fresh goat cheese and garnished with herbs, spread with mashed avocado, or even topped with cubes of marinated fish. Think of these as croutons, adding crunch to any salad.

12 "TOASTS"

EQUIPMENT: A BAKING SHEET.

1/2 cup Black Olive Tapenade with Lemon Confit (page 20)

3 tablespoons freshly grated Parmigiano-Reggiano cheese

2 large egg whites

2 tablespoons cold water

1/2 teaspoon fresh lemon thyme or summer savory leaves

1. Preheat the oven to 425°F.

2. In a small bowl, combine the tapenade, cheese, egg whites, and cold water. Whisk to blend. Drop the mixture by tablespoons, spaced well apart, onto a baking sheet. The mixture will spread out to about 3-inch rounds. Sprinkle with the thyme or summer savory leaves. Bake until the rounds are firm and brown on the bottom but still a bit moist in the center, about 5 minutes. Transfer to a cake rack to cool completely. Plan to consume these the day they are made.

GUACAMOLE LIGHT

I first tasted a lightened version of this popular avocado mixture at the Golden Door Spa in California. This is a snap to make, and feel free to season to taste: if you like a touch of spice, go for it! I like to spread it on thin slices of toasted whole wheat bread and serve it as a side to salads. The peas do not need to be cooked here: even raw, they remain bright and green, making for a perky spread.

1 1/2 CUPS

EQUIPMENT: A FOOD PROCESSOR OR A BLENDER.

1 cup fresh or frozen peas (no need to thaw)

1 small spring onion or scallion, white part only, trimmed, peeled, and cut into thin rings

1 large ripe avocado, halved, pitted, peeled, and cubed

1 tablespoon freshly squeezed lime or lemon juice

1/4 teaspoon Red Hot Salt (page 307), or hot pepper sauce to taste

2 tablespoons minced fresh cilantro

1/2 teaspoon fine sea salt

In a food processor or a blender, combine the peas, onion, avocado, citrus juice, Red Hot Salt or pepper sauce, cilantro, and salt. Pulse for just a few seconds, crushing to a rather chunky puree. Taste for seasoning. (Store in an airtight container in the refrigerator for up to 2 days.)

BABY ARTICHOKES MARINATED IN OLIVE OIL

I don't know where my addiction to marinated artichokes came from, but I consider that the refrigerator is bare if there is not a jar of these tangy marinated vegetables waiting to be showered on bread tarts or pizzas, served as is in an antipasto platter, and added to salads and pastas. This is one time I endorse frozen vegetables, for I find no loss of flavor with frozen baby artichokes, and they are a true time-saver.

20 ARTICHOKE HALVES
EQUIPMENT: A STERILIZED **2**-CUP CANNING JAR, WITH A LID,
OR SEVERAL SMALLER JARS.

1 cup water

1 cup cider vinegar

1 teaspoon fine sea salt

8 fresh or dried bay leaves

10 frozen baby artichoke hearts (about 10 ounces), halved (no need to thaw)

About 1/2 cup extra-virgin olive oil

1. In a large saucepan, combine the water with the vinegar, salt, and 4 bay leaves. Add the artichokes and bring to a simmer over medium heat. Simmer until the artichokes are tender but still offer a bit of resistance when pierced with a knife, about 5 minutes. (Cooking time will vary according to the size of the artichokes.) Drain the artichokes, discarding the vinegar mixture and bay leaves.

2. While the artichokes are still warm, arrange them in layers in the canning jar. Arrange the remaining 4 bay leaves around the sides of the jar. Cover the artichokes completely with oil. Set aside, uncovered, until the artichokes are completely cool.

The artichokes can be consumed as soon as they are cool, but will have even greater depth of flavor if allowed to marinate for at least 24 hours. (Store in an airtight container in the refrigerator for up to 2 months, making sure that the artichokes are always covered in oil.)

VARIATION: To turn these delicious marinated artichokes into a flavorful spread or dip, drain the artichokes, reserving the oil, and place them in a food processor or a blender; then blend to a smooth puree, adding as much of the reserved oil as necessary. Any leftover liquid can be used as a base for a vinaigrette or as a vinaigrette itself.

SOUP SIDES

THINK OF SOUPS AS LIQUID SALADS. IN THE SUMMER MONTHS, I KEEP A BAT-
TERY OF CHILLED SOUPS IN THE REFRIGERATOR AND LOVE TO SIP THEM FOR
BREAKFAST OR SNACKS AS WELL AS WITH MEALS. IN MY COOKING CLASSES OR
WHEN ENTERTAINING, WE OFTEN PAIR A TINY GLASS OF SOUP WITH THE
MAIN MEAL SALAD, OFFERING TEXTURAL VARIATION TO ROUND OUT THE
FEAST.

CILANTRO-FLECKED HEIRLOOM TOMATO SOUP

In the summer months, I keep a batch of this soup on hand in the refrigerator, and I often sip a glassful for breakfast. Light, refreshing, and full of flavor, it hits the spot any time of the day. It matches beautifully with a salad as a meal made up of nothing but chunks of fresh garden tomatoes drizzled with a touch of Basil-Lemon Dressing (page 319). Yes, tomato soup with tomato salad. When they are ripe and ready, never too many tomatoes in my book!

12 SERVINGS
EQUIPMENT: A BLENDER OR A FOOD PROCESSOR;
12 CHILLED SHALLOW SOUP BOWLS.

1 1/2 pounds ripe heirloom tomatoes, cored and quartered (do not peel)

1/2 cup imported Italian tomato paste

2 teaspoons fine sea salt

1 teaspoon ground *piment d'Espelette* or other ground mild chile pepper

2 tablespoons best-quality sherry-wine vinegar

1 cup fresh cilantro leaves, plus extra for garnish (I use a variety of cilantro called Delfino)

Combine all the ingredients, except the extra cilantro leaves, in a a blender or a food processor. Add 1 2/3 cups water and puree to a smooth liquid. Taste for seasoning. The soup can be served immediately, but the flavors benefit from ripening for at least 3 hours and up to 24 hours, refrigerated. Serve in soup bowls, garnished with cilantro leaves. (Store without the garnish in an airtight container in the refrigerator for up to 2 days. Reblend at serving time.)

Food processor or blender? In most cases, the food processor and blender can be used interchangeably. But for many soups—especially those that are made in quantity, such as this tomato soup—I find the blender is more accommodating. Even large food processors tend to overflow with a larger volume of liquid. And while the food processor purees, the blender can turn soups into a thicker, emulsified liquid.

Selecting the best tomato paste: Be sure to read the ingredients label when purchasing tomato paste. Many domestic brands contain sugar and other sweeteners. Brands from Italy generally contain nothing but tomatoes and salt. In this recipe in particular, where a quantity of tomato paste is used, the pure version is a must.

BROCCOLI SOUP WITH MINT

Warm or chilled, this colorful soup finds a welcome place at our table. Broccoli and mint have an affinity for one another, as the herb introduces bright, assertive aromas as well as flavors.

6 SERVINGS

EQUIPMENT: A **10**-QUART PASTA POT FITTED WITH A COLANDER; A FOOD PROCESSOR OR A BLENDER; **6** WARMED OR CHILLED SHALLOW SOUP BOWLS.

3 tablespoons coarse sea salt

1 pound broccoli, cut into stems and florets (about 6 cups)

1 quart Homemade Chicken Stock (page 310) or Homemade Vegetable Stock (page 312)

Fine sea salt

About 2 tablespoons crème fraîche, for garnish

Fresh mint leaves, for garnish

1. Prepare a large bowl of ice water.

2. Fill the pot with 8 quarts of water and bring it to a rolling boil over high heat. Add the coarse sea salt and the broccoli. Blanch, uncovered, until the broccoli is crisp-tender, 3 to 4 minutes. Immediately drain the broccoli and plunge the stems and florets into the ice water so they cool down as quickly as possible and retain their crispness and bright green color. (The broccoli will cool in 1 to 2 minutes. After that, it will soften and begin to lose crispness and flavor.) Transfer the broccoli to a colander and drain.

3. Transfer the broccoli to a food processor or blender. Add the stock and puree to a smooth liquid. If serving the soup warm, transfer it to the pot in which the broccoli was cooked and heat it through. Season to taste with the fine sea salt. Serve in soup bowls, drizzled with crème fraîche and garnished with mint leaves. (Store without the garnish in an airtight container in the refrigerator for up to 3 days. Reblend at serving time.)

CHILLED EVERGREEN TOMATO VELOUTÉ

This quick and sublime summer soup is a picture postcard of my August garden in Provence. I grow two varieties of green tomatoes, Green Zebra and Evergreen. Each year I taste them side by side, and I still cannot decide which I like better. Green Zebra, yellowish green with yellow and white stripes, is sweet and tangy at the same time, while Evergreen (also known as Emerald Evergreen) is indeed emerald-colored, and along with tang and sweetness is a bit creamy as well. Of course this soup can also be made with red, orange, or yellow varieties. The gentle sweetness of the vanilla bean loves the company of tomatoes. Don't be afraid to let the mixture blend for a full 3 minutes, to create a thick emulsion. And use the best olive oil you can find, for the rich elegance of the oil really shines here.

12 SERVINGS
EQUIPMENT: A BLENDER OR A FOOD PROCESSOR; **12** CHILLED GLASSES.

1 plump, moist vanilla bean

2 pounds ripe Evergreen or Green Zebra tomatoes, cored and quartered (do not peel)

1/3 cup extra-virgin olive oil

1 teaspoon fine sea salt

1. Flatten the vanilla bean and cut it in half lengthwise. With a small spoon, scrape out the seeds. (Reserve the pod for another use. I dry the pods and bury them in a large glass jar of sugar to flavor it.)

2. Combine all the ingredients in a blender or a food processor. Add 1/3 cup water and blend for a full 3 minutes, to create a thick emulsion. Serve very cold in glasses. (Store in an airtight container in the refrigerator for up to 3 days. Reblend at serving time.)

GOLDEN ZUCCHINI AND BUTTERMILK SOUP

Soups do not get simpler, more versatile, healthier, or more satisfying than this golden zucchini and buttermilk soup. And it can be prepared in a snap, with many variations.

8 SERVINGS

EQUIPMENT: A FOOD PROCESSOR OR A BLENDER;

8 CHILLED SHALLOW SOUP BOWLS OR SMALL, CLEAR GLASSES.

2 plump, moist garlic cloves, peeled, halved, and green germ removed

1 pound golden zucchini or yellow summer squash, chopped

1 teaspoon fine sea salt

2 cups buttermilk, shaken to blend

1/4 cup minced dill or mint (or a combination of the two) or zucchini or squash blossoms,
cut into a chiffonade

In a food processor or a blender, mince the garlic. Add the zucchini, salt, and buttermilk and puree to a smooth liquid. Taste for seasoning. Serve in soup bowls or small, clear glasses, garnished with the dill, mint, or zucchini or squash blossoms. (Store without the garnish in an airtight container in the refrigerator for up to 3 days. Reblend at serving time.)

Variation: Use a 1-pound European cucumber in place of the zucchini or summer squash.

SHELLFISH VELOUTÉ WITH KAFFIR LIME DUST

This spicy, fragrant, and beautiful pale pink soup combines many of my favorite ingredients: the usually discarded shells of shrimp or langoustines, lemon, red pepper flakes, and yogurt. It is a variation on a shellfish soup I have been making for years. In this version, I whisk in yogurt to add a touch of body to what is usually a rather thin though vibrant soup. I have a small kaffir lime tree growing in my courtyard in Provence, and so have put the fragrant leaves to good use here. I often serve the soup in small portions as a cool and refreshing appetizer on warm summer evenings, but it is also ideal as an accompaniment to any fish salad.

16 SERVINGS

EQUIPMENT: A **5**-QUART STOCKPOT; A WOODEN MALLET; DAMPENED CHEESECLOTH; A SPICE GRINDER OR A COFFEE MILL; **16** CHILLED SHALLOW SOUP BOWLS.

2 tablespoons extra-virgin olive oil

8 ounces shrimp shells (not including heads), rinsed (from 1 1/2 pounds shrimp)

1 whole lemon, preferably organic, rinsed and quartered

1 tablespoon fennel seeds

2 segments star anise

2 quarts cold water

One 28-ounce can peeled Italian plum tomatoes in their juice

Several fresh or dried bay leaves

1 plump, moist garlic head, halved crosswise (do not peel)

1/4 teaspoon hot red pepper flakes (or to taste)

1 teaspoon fine sea salt

3 tablespoons imported Italian tomato paste

6 fresh or dried kaffir lime leaves, minced

1 quart plain nonfat yogurt

1. In the stockpot, heat the oil over moderate heat until hot but not smoking. Add the shells and sear until they turn bright pink and very fragrant, about 5 minutes. Add the lemon, fennel, star anise, cold water, and the tomatoes, bay leaves, garlic, pepper flakes, salt, and tomato paste. Bring to a boil, cover, and boil vigorously for 25 minutes. To extract the maximum flavor from the shells, use a wooden mallet to crush and break them up in the pot. Taste occasionally for seasoning and strength.

2. Line a large colander with a double layer of the dampened cheesecloth, and place over a large bowl. Ladle the broth and solids into the colander, pressing down hard on the solids to extract the maximum juices and flavor. Taste for seasoning. You should have about 1 quart broth. If you have more, reduce the broth over medium heat to 1 quart. Chill. (Store in an airtight container in the refrigerator for up to 1 day.)

3. In a spice grinder or coffee mill, grind the kaffir lime leaves to a fine powder.

4. At serving time, add the yogurt to the soup. Whisk to blend. Taste for seasoning. Serve chilled in soup bowls, sprinkled with the kaffir lime dust.

On kaffir limes: I have a thriving kaffir lime tree, and admire the leaves for their perfume and the slightly piquant touch they can add to any dish. Kaffir limes—also known as wild limes or Thai limes—are essential to Asian cooking, but Westerners are quickly discovering their virtues. The dark green, glossy kaffir lime leaves can be found fresh, dried, and frozen in many Asian food shops. Both fresh and dried leaves can be chopped or ground to a powder in an electric spice mill or coffee grinder. I find that frozen leaves, once thawed, are less versatile.

CHILLED PEA AND BUTTERMILK SOUP

I often serve this soup as an opening-night appetizer at my cooking school in Provence, always to raves and looks of pleasant surprise. I love the light, lactic tang of buttermilk, as well as its creamy thickness. Pair this with the Spring Salad: Asparagus, Peas, Beans, and Fennel (page 100).

8 SERVINGS

EQUIPMENT: A FOOD PROCESSOR OR A BLENDER; **8** CHILLED SHALLOW SOUP BOWLS OR SMALL, CLEAR GLASSES.

2 plump, moist garlic cloves, peeled, halved, and green germ removed

2 cups fresh or frozen peas (no need to thaw)

1 teaspoon fine sea salt

2 cups buttermilk, shaken to blend

1/4 cup finely minced fresh mint leaves; several zucchini or squash blossoms, cut into a chiffonade; or cilantro sprigs

In a food processor or a blender, mince the garlic. Add the peas, salt, and buttermilk and puree to a smooth liquid. Taste for seasoning. Serve in soup bowls or small, clear glasses, garnished with the mint, cilantro, or zucchini or squash blossoms. (Store without the garnish in an airtight container in the refrigerator for up to 3 days. Reblend at serving time.)

WATERCRESS SOUP WITH WARM OYSTERS

As winter approaches I begin to have a deep craving for the brilliant, peppery watercress leaf and use it liberally in salads and soups and as a vegetable all on its own. This soup was inspired by a version I had at Fish, our regular hangout in Paris's 6ᵗʰ arrondissement. To keep the watercress's bright green color, I blanch and refresh it and then heat it gently at serving time. At the last minute, plump Brittany oysters are warmed in the colorful soup.

8 SERVINGS

EQUIPMENT: A **10**-QUART PASTA POT FITTED WITH A COLANDER; A FOOD PROCESSOR OR A BLENDER; **8** WARMED SHALLOW SOUP BOWLS.

2 quarts Homemade Chicken Stock (page 310)

3 tablespoons coarse sea salt

2 bunches watercress, trimmed and washed

16 fresh oysters removed from their shells

1. Pour the stock into a saucepan and boil over high heat until reduced by half, about 25 minutes.

2. Prepare a large bowl of ice water.

3. Fill the pasta pot with 8 quarts of water and bring it to a rolling boil over high heat. Add the salt and the watercress. Blanch, uncovered, until the watercress is cooked through, 3 to 4 minutes. Immediately drain the watercress and plunge it into the ice water so it cools down as quickly as possible and retains its bright green color. (The watercress will cool in 1 to 2 minutes.) Transfer the watercress to a colander and drain, pressing down to release as much liquid as possible. Transfer it to a clean towel and wrap tightly to further release liquid.

4. Transfer the watercress to a food processor or blender. Add the stock and puree to a smooth liquid. Taste for seasoning.

5. At serving time, gently warm the soup and ladle it into soup bowls. Arrange 2 oysters in each bowl. Serve warm. (Store without the oysters in an airtight container in the refrigerator for up to 3 days. Reblend at serving time.)

VARIATION: If fresh oysters are not readily available, a simple garnish of sour cream and a touch of minced fresh mint leaves offers an excellent variation.

CHILLED YOGURT, HERB, AND JALAPEÑO SOUP

This chilled summer soup is a veritable garden in a bowl, with fresh mint, cilantro, peppers, and spring onions gathered from the potager *just seconds before the soup appears at the table. A cup of this soup is an ideal accompaniment to any summer salad; I particularly love it with the Crab, Avocado, and Quinoa Salad with Technicolor Tomatoes (page 126).*

4 SERVINGS
EQUIPMENT: A FOOD PROCESSOR OR A BLENDER;
4 CHILLED SOUP BOWLS.

2 cups plain whole-milk yogurt, well chilled

1 cup fresh mint leaves

1 cup fresh cilantro leaves

4 plump, moist garlic cloves, peeled, halved, and green germ removed

1 teaspoon minced fresh jalapeño pepper (or canned chopped jalapeño peppers)

2 small spring onions or scallions, white part only, trimmed, peeled, and thinly sliced

1 tablespoon freshly squeezed lime or lemon juice

Fine sea salt

1. In a food processor or a blender, combine the yogurt, half the mint, half the cilantro, the garlic, jalapeño, spring onions, and citrus juice. Puree to a smooth liquid. Season with salt to taste.

2. Finely chop the remaining mint and cilantro leaves. Serve the soup in soup bowls, garnished with the chopped herbs. (Store without the garnish in an airtight container in the refrigerator for up to 3 days. Reblend at serving time.)

ZUCCHINI AND FRESH GINGER VELOUTÉ

This magical five-ingredient soup is delicious hot or cold, and can be assembled in a matter of minutes. When fresh zucchini is in season, I always have a batch of this in my refrigerator, ready for welcoming sips to accompany a meal, or as a quick and healthy snack. I first sampled a version of this at La Villa Saint Victor outside of Uzès in Provence, where chef Stèphane Vieljeux creates wonderful, fresh fare. Even though the soup is called a velouté—because of its creamy, velvety smoothness—the only cream is an optional dollop anointed at serving time.

8 SERVINGS

EQUIPMENT: **A FOOD PROCESSOR, A BLENDER, OR AN IMMERSION BLENDER;**
8 WARMED OR CHILLED SHALLOW SOUP BOWLS.

3 tablespoons extra-virgin olive oil

6 small spring onions or scallions, white part only, trimmed, peeled, and thinly sliced

Fine sea salt

1 tablespoon minced fresh ginger

2 pounds firm zucchini, rinsed, trimmed, and cut into small pieces (do not peel)

1 1/2 quarts Homemade Chicken Stock (page 310) or Homemade Vegetable Stock (page 312)

Crème fraîche, for garnish (optional)

1. In a stockpot, combine the oil, spring onions, and salt, and sweat—cook, covered, over low heat until soft and translucent—for 3 to 5 minutes. Add the ginger and cook briefly. Add the zucchini and stock and bring to a low boil. Simmer, covered, for 10 minutes.

2. Remove from the heat and puree to a smooth liquid in a food processor or blender or with an immersion blender. Taste for seasoning. Serve, hot or chilled, in soup bowls and garnish with crème fraîche, if using. (Store without the garnish in an airtight container in the refrigerator for up to 3 days. Reblend at serving time.)

EGGS, CHEESE, BEANS, GRAINS, AND PASTA

A SALAD DOES NOT HAVE TO BE JUST GREENS AND A DRESSING! THIN, SPINACH-FILLED EGG CREPES; A CHILLED TERRINE OF RICOTTA AND PARMESAN; FRIT-TATAS; GRAIN SALADS; AND THOSE SPICY CHICKPEA BALLS KNOWN AS FALAFEL FIND THEIR WAY INTO MY REPERTOIRE. FOR SOME EATERS, THESE ITEMS MAY NOT FALL IN THE CATEGORY OF SALADS, BUT IN MY HOUSE, I LIKE A LOT OF DIFFERENT LITTLE ITEMS ON A PLATE, AND OFTEN A SIMPLE TOSSED GREEN SALAD LIKES TO HAVE SOME FRIENDS AROUND.

EGG CREPES WITH MUSHROOMS AND SPINACH

Accompanied by a fresh and lively green salad, these ultra-thin egg crepes make a perfect lunch. The egg crepe is quite simply a light envelope for whatever you want to put inside. Here I suggest mushrooms and spinach, but one could also dig into the pantry or refrigerator for all manner of herbs, vegetables, and cheese on hand.

2 SERVINGS

EQUIPMENT: A **10**-INCH NONSTICK CREPE PAN; **2** WARMED PLATES.

2 teaspoons extra-virgin olive oil

6 large mushrooms, cleaned, trimmed, and thinly sliced

Fine sea salt

8 ounces fresh spinach, stemmed and chopped

Freshly grated nutmeg

2 ultra-fresh large eggs, at room temperature

1 tablespoon minced fresh herbs (such as parsley, thyme, mint, and/or basil)

2 tablespoons freshly grated Parmigiano-Reggiano cheese

Coarse, freshly ground black pepper

Several handfuls of salad greens, tossed with dressing of choice

1. In a large nonstick skillet, heat 1 teaspoon of the oil over moderate heat. Add the mushrooms, season lightly with salt, and cook just until soft, 3 to 4 minutes. With a slotted spoon, transfer the mushrooms to a sieve to drain. Add the spinach and 2 tablespoons of water to the skillet. Cover and cook until wilted, 1 to 2 minutes. Drain the spinach and season with salt and freshly grated nutmeg.

2. Crack each egg into a small bowl. Lightly beat each egg with a fork (not a whisk), just enough to combine the yolk and the white well without incorporating any air bubbles, which might make the crepe dry out. Add 1 tablespoon of water to each bowl.

3. Warm the crepe pan for a few seconds over high heat. Add 1/2 teaspoon of the remaining oil and swirl to evenly coat the pan. Add 1 beaten egg, tilting the pan from side to side to evenly coat the bottom. Cook just until the egg is evenly set but still slightly liquid on top, about 1 minute. Remove the pan from the heat. Quickly spoon half the spinach, then half the mushrooms, herbs, and cheese in the center of the egg crepe to form a strip parallel to the pan's handle. With a fork, carefully fold the crepe over the filling from each side. Tip the pan up against the edge of a warmed plate so that the crepe rolls out browned side up. Season with salt and pepper. Repeat with the remaining ingredients to make a second filled crepe. Serve immediately, with a green salad alongside.

VARIATIONS: Wilted Swiss chard and feta; wilted lamb's lettuce and ricotta; salsa, cubed avocado, and grated cheese; morels in truffle cream with chives.

WINE SUGGESTION: Our winemaker, Yves Gras, makes one of the "best dry whites of the Southern Rhône," or so says wine expert Robert Parker. We agree, for his Sablet Blanc Le Fournas is crisp, chalky, elegant, and made for everyday drinking—perfect with this simple but sublime egg crepe.

RICOTTA, PARMESAN, AND LEMON ZEST TERRINE

This is a fabulous cheese-based terrine to have on hand anytime. A delicate mixture of fresh ricotta cheese, Parmigiano-Reggiano cheese, and eggs with a touch of lemon zest, it is a golden treasure. Serve it with a fresh tomato sauce and a tossed green salad and you have a marvelous meal. As garnish, you might add toast rounds, seared baby peppers, and roasted tomato halves topped with a basic puree. I like to call this a summer house recipe: you know, you rent a summer house with a plan to cook, but there is hardly a pot or a pan to be found. For this you need only bare-bones basics: a bowl, a fork, a loaf pan, a roasting pan, and an oven!

1 LOAF, 24 THIN SLICES

EQUIPMENT: A NONSTICK **1**-QUART RECTANGULAR LOAF PAN; A ROASTING PAN.

Vegetable oil for oiling the pan

1 pound buffalo-milk ricotta cheese

1/2 cup freshly grated Parmigiano-Reggiano cheese

4 large eggs, lightly beaten

Grated zest of 2 lemons, preferably organic

Fresh Tomato Sauce (page 308)

Several handfuls of salad greens, tossed with dressing of choice

1. Preheat the oven to 350°F.

2. Lightly brush the loaf pan with oil. Set aside.

3. In a large bowl, mash the ricotta and Parmigiano-Reggiano cheeses with a fork to blend. Add the eggs and lemon zest, and continue mashing until the eggs have been evenly incorporated. Pour the mixture into the prepared pan.

4. Fill a roasting pan with 1 inch of hot water and place the loaf pan in the water bath. Place the roasting pan in the oven and bake until the terrine is puffed, firm, and lightly browned, about 45 minutes. The water should just simmer gently; check it halfway through the cooking time and if necessary, add some hot water.

5. Remove the roasting pan from the oven and place the loaf pan on a wire rack. Let the terrine cool at for least 25 minutes before turning it out onto a rectangular cake plate. Serve the terrine chilled or at room temperature, cut into thin slices, with the tomato sauce and the green salad. (Store the terrine, covered, in the refrigerator for up to 3 days.)

WINE SUGGESTION: A chilled white, such as the offering from the Perrin brothers from Châteauneuf-du-Pape. Their Perrin et Fils Côtes-du-Rhône Réserve Blanc is super-crisp, a blend of Viognier, Grenache Blanc, and Roussanne, with citrus-like overtones and good acidity, perfect for this soothing terrine.

HOMEMADE YOGURT CHEESE

I eat yogurt is some form almost every day, and have come to rely on a battery of different yogurt cheeses to fulfill my lifelong passion for anything with a sharp, lactic tang. There is no secret or technique here: all you need is a good-quality, flavorful yogurt (I use only organic nonfat sheep's milk yogurt) and a cheese strainer, a piece of cheesecloth, or a reusable plastic mesh coffee filter. I make mine in antique French molds used for making goat cheese, but any mold with uniform holes can be used. The traditional heart-shaped porcelain molds used for making coeur à la crème *work well. In France, soft cheeses are sold in perforated molds called* faisselles, *and the firm plastic strainers can be reused. Short of a mold, the yogurt can be poured into a colander lined with several thicknesses of cheesecloth, though I find this method a bit messy. Sometimes I simply pour goat or sheep's milk yogurt or kefir into the strainer with no seasoning. For more forward flavors, I mix to taste a touch of salt, chopped fresh garlic, minced summer savory, minced rosemary, or finely chopped chives. Within 12 hours, you have a soft and supple cheese that can be used as a dip or a spread or rolled into little balls and drizzled with olive oil. In short, any way you would usually use a fresh cheese.*

ABOUT **6 OUNCES**

EQUIPMENT: A CHEESE STRAINER, A PERFORATED MOLD, A PLASTIC MESH COFFEE FILTER, OR DAMPENED CHEESECLOTH.

8 ounces plain nonfat yogurt

Fine sea salt, freshly minced garlic, summer savory, rosemary, chives (all optional)

1. Pour the yogurt—seasoned or not—into a strainer, a mold, or a colander lined with cheesecloth. Place the mold or colander in a container that will receive the liquid that drips. Cover with plastic wrap. Place in the refrigerator and drain for 12 to 24 hours.

2. Remove the cheese from the mold and taste for seasoning. Transfer to a bowl or roll into balls as appetizers. (I drink the liquid, or whey, that drains from the cheese, or use it in soups or breads.) Store in an airtight container in the refrigerator for up to 3 days.

ZUCCHINI BLOSSOM FRITTATA WITH GOAT CHEESE AND MINT

When zucchini and squash blossoms appear in my garden, I gather them just before lunch and quickly prepare this easy dish to serve with a simply dressed green salad, also from the garden. It is great to add to a Provençal salad buffet, which might include Socca (page 276), Picholine Olives with Toasted Cumin and Paprika (page 21), and Black Olive Tapenade with Lemon Confit (page 20).

4 SERVINGS

EQUIPMENT: A **10**-INCH ROUND BAKING DISH.

2 tablespoons extra-virgin olive oil

1 small onion, peeled, halved lengthwise, and thinly sliced

Fine sea salt

12 zucchini blossoms, rinsed

7 ounces mild, soft goat's milk cheese (or imported Greek feta cheese), cubed

2 tablespoons freshly grated Parmigiano-Reggiano cheese

6 ultra-fresh large eggs, lightly beaten

1/4 cup fresh mint leaves, cut into a chiffonade

Lemon wedges, for garnish

1. Preheat the oven to 425°F.

2. In a small skillet, combine the oil, onion, and salt, and sweat—cook, covered, over low heat until soft and translucent—for about 3 minutes. Transfer the onions to the baking dish. Arrange the zucchini blossoms like spokes on a wheel on top of the onions. Sprinkle with the goat cheese or feta and the Parmigiano-Reggiano cheese. Pour the eggs over all.

3. Place in the center of the oven and bake until the eggs are firm and the top is golden, about 20 minutes. Remove from the oven. Sprinkle with the mint chiffonade and serve with lemon wedges.

WINE SUGGESTION: This purely Provençal garden recipe deserves a local companion: I vote for the Lirac Blanc from the Domaine de la Mordorée, a *domaine* we have loved for decades. Their white Lirac is a complex and flattering blend of Grenache Blanc, Viognier, Roussanne, Bourboulenc, Marsanne, Picpoul, and Clairette.

CRISPY, SPICY CHICKPEA BALLS: FALAFEL

I like to use this delicious vegetarian salad to encourage my students to get over the fear of frying. Few people understand that when you deep-fry properly and judiciously at the correct temperature, ingredients absorb almost no oil at all. This recipe is proof: once you've cooked these crispy, spicy morsels, pour the used oil back in the bottle to see how little has been absorbed—usually just a few teaspoons for this recipe. I like to serve these with Tahini-Lemon-Yogurt Dressing and Dipping Sauce, Chickpea and Sesame Dip, and a quickly tossed salad of green and red baby pepper slices, tomatoes, and parsley.

4 SERVINGS

EQUIPMENT: A FOOD PROCESSOR OR A BLENDER; AN ELECTRIC DEEP-FAT FRYER; A
WIRE SKIMMER.

1 1/4 cups (7 ounces) dried chickpeas, rinsed

2 plump, moist garlic cloves, peeled, halved, green germ removed, and minced

1 medium onion, peeled and finely chopped

1 cup minced fresh cilantro

1 1/2 teaspoons fine sea salt

1 1/2 teaspoons toasted cumin seeds, ground

1/2 teaspoon ground coriander

1/2 teaspoon freshly ground black pepper

3/4 teaspoon ground cayenne pepper

Vegetable oil for deep-frying

1 recipe Tahini-Lemon-Yogurt Dressing and Dipping Sauce (page 332)

1 recipe Chickpea and Sesame Dip: Hummus (page 10)

Salad

4 ripe heirloom tomatoes, rinsed, cored, and quartered

Several baby peppers, sliced

1/4 cup fresh flat-leaf parsley leaves

Lemon and Olive Oil Dressing (page 330)

1. At least 12 hours and up to 24 hours before preparing the falafel, soak the chickpeas at room temperature in cold water to cover by 2 inches.

2. Drain the chickpeas and discard the water. In a food processor or a blender, combine the drained chickpeas, garlic, onion, cilantro, salt, cumin, coriander, black pepper, and cayenne. Puree as smooth as possible, about 2 minutes. With your hands, carefully form the mixture into sixteen 1-inch balls. (This can be done several hours in advance. Leave them uncovered at room temperature to dry out a bit.)

3. Pour the oil into a deep-fat fryer; the oil should be at least 2 inches deep. Place a wire skimmer into the oil, so that when you lift the falafel from the oil, they will not stick to the skimmer. Heat the oil to 375°F.

4. Gently drop the chickpea balls, a few at a time, into the hot oil and fry until firm and golden brown, about 3 minutes. (There is no need to turn them in the oil.) Remove from the oil with the skimmer, and drain on paper towels. Repeat for the remaining falafel.

5. Make the salad: Combine the tomatoes, peppers, and parsley in a salad bowl. Toss with just enough Lemon and Olive Oil Dressing to lightly and evenly coat the ingredients.

6. Arrange the falafel on a large plate and pierce each with a large toothpick for dipping into a bowl of Tahini-Lemon-Yogurt Dressing and Dipping Sauce. Serve with the salad and a bowl of Chickpea and Sesame Dip as an accompaniment.

WINE SUGGESTION: I would go with a rosé here, preferably a Tavel from Domaine de la Mordorée, a wine that is complex without being the least bit pretentious.

PENNE SALAD WITH TUNA AND SPICY MUSTARD

One sunny summer day my husband, Walter, and I visited good friends in the seaside village of Marseillan in the Languedoc. Former restaurateurs Alain Dumergue, Claude Udron, and Philippe Marquet were our hosts, and Claude prepared this quick, simple, and delicious pasta salad.

4 SERVINGS

EQUIPMENT: A **10**-QUART PASTA POT FITTED WITH A COLANDER; A STRAINER; **4** WARMED SHALLOW SOUP BOWLS.

1/4 cup coarse sea salt

1 pound Italian penne pasta

Two 6 1/2-ounce jars best-quality tuna in oil

1 tablespoon French Espelette pepper mustard (or other coarse-grain mustard)

1. Fill the pasta pot with 8 quarts of water and bring it to a rolling boil over high heat. Add the salt and the pasta, stirring to prevent the pasta from sticking. Cook until tender but still firm to the bite, about 11 minutes.

2. Meanwhile, set the strainer over a medium bowl. Pour the tuna into the strainer, reserving the tuna and the oil separately. Break up the tuna pieces. Transfer the oil to a large skillet, and add the mustard to it.

3. Gently warm the oil and mustard.

4. When the pasta is cooked, remove the pot from the heat. Remove the colander and drain the pasta over the sink, shaking the colander to remove the excess water. Immediately transfer the drained pasta to the skillet containing the oil and mustard. Toss to evenly coat the pasta. Add the tuna and toss once more. Taste for seasoning. Serve in shallow soup bowls. This dish can be served at room temperature if desired.

QUINOA SALAD WITH SPINACH, PARSLEY, AND SPRING ONIONS

This is perhaps my favorite grain salad, one that I can enjoy day after day. I often make up a batch and serve it for lunch or as an afternoon snack.

4 SERVINGS

EQUIPMENT: A SIEVE; A FOOD PROCESSOR OR A BLENDER.

1 1/2 cups quinoa

3 cups Homemade Vegetable Stock (page 312), Homemade Chicken Stock (page 310), or water

2 fresh or dried bay leaves

1 teaspoon fine sea salt

1 tablespoon freshly squeezed lemon juice

1 bunch fresh parsley, leaves only (2 cups loosely packed)

1 tablespoon extra-virgin olive oil

3 small spring onions or scallions, white part only, trimmed, peeled, and cut into very thin rings

5 ounces fresh spinach, stemmed, cut into a chiffonade (4 cups loosely packed)

Creamy Lemon-Chive Dressing (page 326)

1. In a large, dry, nonstick skillet, toast the quinoa over medium heat, stirring regularly, until it crackles and becomes aromatic, 3 to 5 minutes. Place the quinoa in a sieve and rinse under cold running water to remove the grain's coating, which can be bitter.

2. In a medium saucepan, bring the stock to a boil over high heat. Add the quinoa, bay leaves, and salt. Reduce the heat to low, cover, and simmer for 20 minutes, stirring from time to time to prevent the quinoa from sticking to the pan. Remove from the heat and let stand, covered, for 10 minutes. Remove and discard the bay leaves.

3. Meanwhile, in a food processor or a blender, combine the lemon juice, parsley leaves, and olive oil and process until the parsley is finely chopped.

4. Toss the vinaigrette with the quinoa and the spring onions. (Store in an airtight container in the refrigerator for up to 8 hours.)

5. At serving time, toss the spinach chiffonnade with just enough Creamy Lemon-Chive Dressing to lightly and evenly coat the greens. Add the quinoa and toss gently. Serve.

NOTE: Some brands of quinoa are already rinsed. Read the package directions.

WINE SUGGESTION: For no reason at all, this salad reminds me of Alsace, so I enjoy it with a light, dry, young Alsatian white, such as the offering from the house of Hugel, their Pinot Blanc Cuvée les Amours.

CLASSICS, WITH FRIENDS

MAKING A MEAL OUT OF A SALAD GOES WITH THE WAY WE LOVE TO LIVE TO-
DAY. HEALTHY AND QUICK TO COMPOSE, SALAD MEALS OFFER COLOR, TEX-
TURE, VARIETY. I NEVER TIRE OF THE CLASSICS: COBB, CURLY ENDIVE AND
BACON, THE EVER-LOVED CAESAR, AND THE LIST GOES ON. SOME NEWFOUND,
TOTALLY MODERN SALADS COULD BE ON THEIR WAY TO BECOMING CLASSICS,
SUCH AS BLANCHED GREEN BEANS; OR PEARS TEAMED UP WITH BLUE CHEESE
AND SALTED ALMONDS. NUTS, AVOCADOS, BITS OF CHEESE, AND NUT OILS
SUCH AS PISTACHIO OIL ARE PREFERRED TRICKS FOR "DOCTORING" ANY
SALAD.

MY CAESAR SALAD WITH POLENTA CROUTONS

Caesar salad could well be the number-one salad as a meal. If I had a dollar for every time I ordered the salad while traveling, I would be a deliriously wealthy woman! I've had some pretty dismal offerings, but by and large, most of the satisfying elements are there: crunch, a touch of piquancy from the dressing, the soothing quality of cheese, and sometimes the added protein from a few slices of poached or grilled chicken. The origin of the salad is disputed, but it is widely attributed to Caesar Cardini, an Italian who came to San Diego after World War I. He is thought to have created the salad in 1924 in his Tijuana restaurant. The success of a good Caesar rests with the dressing, the croutons, and the chilled romaine lettuce. Wash the lettuce and refrigerate it for an hour before tossing it with the dressing.

4 SERVINGS

EQUIPMENT: **4** CHILLED DINNER PLATES.

6 heads sucrine lettuce (see Note), or 1 head romaine lettuce

1 plump, moist garlic clove, peeled, halved, and green germ removed

Caesar Salad Dressing (page 323)

1/2 cup freshly grated Parmigiano-Reggiano cheese

3/4 cup Polenta Croutons (recipe follows) or Parmesan Croutons (page 281)

2 Poached Chicken Breasts (page 197), cut lengthwise into thin slices (optional)

1. Wash the greens. Tear the greens into small pieces. Chill well.

2. At serving time, rub the inside of a large salad bowl with the garlic halves. Discard the garlic. Arrange the chilled lettuce in the bowl. Toss with just enough dressing to lightly and evenly coat the greens. Add the cheese, croutons, and chicken, if using.

Toss with just enough dressing to coat the ingredients lightly and evenly. Arrange on the plates, and serve.

NOTE: In recent years tiny sucrine lettuce has arrived on the scene, with its buttery texture and soft, silky leaves. With its name rooted in the French word for sugar—*sucre*—the miniature head of greens has qualities of both romaine and butterhead. Sucrine's welcome touch of bitterness helps cut the fat in a dressing.

WINE SUGGESTION: This is easy: choose any good daily drinking red you have on hand. We love this with our own wine, Clos Chanteduc, a racy Côtes-du-Rhône that always brings a smile to our faces.

POLENTA CROUTONS

One Saturday at my favorite spa—Rancho La Puerta in Tecate, Mexico—my friend and trainer Mike Bee and I approached the generous lunchtime buffet as one of the waiters called out to Mike, "Be sure to try these polenta croutons!" We did, we loved them, so here they are. I love to toss them into a Caesar salad, but they will go fine with just about any salad or on their own as a "can't stop eating them" snack. You can gussy them up by adding a touch of Homemade Curry Powder (page 292) or Red Hot Salt (page 307) as they emerge from the oven.

3 CUPS

EQUIPMENT: AN 8-INCH SQUARE BAKING DISH; A NONSTICK BAKING SHEET OR A SILICONE MAT SET ON A BAKING SHEET

1 1/2 cups 1% milk

1/4 teaspoon freshly grated nutmeg

1/2 cup quick-cooking polenta

1/2 cup freshly grated Parmigiano-Reggiano cheese

1. Line the baking dish with foil to make it easier to remove the polenta.

2. Rinse a saucepan with water, leaving a bit of water clinging to the pan. (This will prevent the milk from sticking to the pan.) Add the milk and nutmeg to the pan and bring to a boil over high heat. (Watch carefully, for milk will boil over quickly.) Reduce the heat to medium and add the polenta in a steady stream, stirring constantly with a wooden spoon. Cook, stirring, until the polenta has thickened and leaves the side of the pan, about 1 minute.

3. Remove the pan from the heat. Stir in the cheese, blending thoroughly. Pour the polenta into the lined baking dish, smoothing the top with a spatula. Cover and refrigerate until firm, about 2 hours.

4. About 20 minutes before baking the croutons, center a rack in the oven. Preheat the oven to 375°F.

5. Remove the polenta from the refrigerator and invert it onto a cutting board and remove the foil. Cut it into 1/2-inch cubes. Transfer the cubes to the baking sheet and bake until the croutons are a deep golden brown, about 30 minutes. Remove the baking sheet from the oven and allow the croutons to cool.

NOTE: The croutons should be consumed the day they are prepared, for they will soften quickly.

MY COBB SALAD: ICEBERG, TOMATO, AVOCADO, BACON, AND BLUE CHEESE

Robert H. Cobb, owner of the Brown Derby restaurant in Hollywood, is said to have invented this salad in the 1930s as a late-night snack for himself. No wonder it has remained an American classic. With the crunch of the iceberg and onions, the soft richness of the avocado, the saltiness of the bacon, the sweetness of the tomato, and the bite of the blue cheese, this salad has it all! And it is beautiful to boot.

4 SERVINGS

2 1/2 ounces smoked bacon, rind removed, cut into matchsticks (3/4 cup)

1 head iceberg lettuce, chopped (4 cups)

2 ripe heirloom tomatoes, cored, peeled, seeded, and chopped

1 large ripe avocado, halved, pitted, peeled, and cubed

4 ounces chilled blue cheese (preferably Roquefort), crumbled (1 cup)

4 small spring onions or scallions, white part only, trimmed, peeled, and cut into thin rounds

Yogurt and Lemon Dressing (page 331)

Coarse, freshly ground black pepper

1. In a large, dry skillet, brown the bacon over moderate heat until crisp and golden, about 5 minutes. With a slotted spoon, transfer the bacon to several layers of paper towels to absorb the fat. Blot the top of the bacon with several layers of paper towels to absorb any additional fat. Set aside.

2. In a large, shallow bowl, combine the bacon, lettuce, tomatoes, avocado, cheese, and spring onions. Toss with just enough dressing to lightly and evenly coat the ingredients. Season generously with pepper, and serve.

WINE SUGGESTION: This is a special salad, one that seems to hit the spot with all my guests, so let's open a nice, special bottle of smoky-style Alsatian Riesling from the house of Léon Beyer, Trimbach, or Hugel. Neither you nor your guests will be disappointed.

HARD-COOKED EGGS

Hard-cooked eggs are a basic component of many salads, adding a nice hit of protein as well as color and texture.

2 EGGS

2 ultra-fresh large eggs, at room temperature

Place the eggs in a saucepan, and cover with water by 1 inch. Cook, uncovered, over medium-high heat until the first large bubbles rise steadily from the bottom of the pan. Reduce the heat so the water continues to simmer gently but never boils. Simmer for 10 minutes. The cooked eggs should now have a firmly set yolk and white. Pour off the hot water. Stop the cooking by running cold water over the eggs for 1 minute. When the eggs are cool, peel them.

CHEF'S SALAD: HAM, CHEESE, AND TENDER GREENS

This is one of the most classic Paris café salads, and one that does not allow for mediocrity. Use the finest ham and cheese, the freshest farm eggs, top-quality greens, and of course freshly squeezed lemon juice and extra-virgin olive oil, and you will be rewarded!

4 SERVINGS

5 ounces cooked ham, cubed (1 1/2 cups)

5 ounces aged Comté cheese, cubed (1 1/2 cups)

2 Hard-Cooked Eggs (page 69), quartered (optional)

1/4 cup minced fresh chives

4 cups torn soft greens, such as butterhead lettuce

Lemon and Olive Oil Dressing (page 330)

Fine sea salt

Coarse, freshly ground black pepper

In a large bowl, combine the ham, cheese, eggs, chives, and greens. Toss with just enough dressing to coat the ingredients lightly and evenly. Season lightly with salt and generously with pepper. Serve.

WINE SUGGESTION: If I am going to enjoy wine with a salad, I prefer a dressing made with lemon juice as opposed to vinegar, for too much vinegar can destroy the flavor of wine. Stay simple here—a light Chardonnay, a Chenin Blanc, or a fine rosé.

CURLY ENDIVE SALAD WITH BACON AND POACHED EGG: *FRISÉE AUX LARDONS*

I doubt that there is a more classic French salad than this one: curls of wintry endive, hearty chunks of salty bacon, a perfect poached egg, a faintly acidic vinaigrette with a touch of mustard, a shower of minced chives, plenty of freshly ground black pepper, and a glass of chilled Moulin à Vent to round it all out.

4 SERVINGS

EQUIPMENT: **4** RAMEKINS OR SMALL CUPS; A FLAT, FINE-MESH SIEVE OR A LARGE SLOTTED SPOON.

2 1/2 ounces smoked bacon, rind removed, cut into 1/4-inch cubes (3/4 cup)

1 plump, fresh garlic clove, peeled, halved, and green germ removed

6 cups (5 ounces) firmly packed curly endive (*frisée*), torn into bite-sized pieces

4 ultra-fresh large eggs

1 tablespoon distilled vinegar

1 shallot, trimmed, peeled, and finely minced

1/3 cup extra-virgin olive oil

3 tablespoons best-quality red-wine vinegar or sherry-wine vinegar

1 teaspoon imported French mustard

Fine sea salt to taste

1/4 cup finely minced fresh chives

Coarse, freshly ground black pepper

4 slices Thin Bread Crisps (page 274)

1. In a large, dry skillet, brown the bacon over moderate heat until crisp and golden, about 5 minutes. With a slotted spoon, transfer the bacon to several layers of paper

towels to absorb the fat. Do not discard the fat in the skillet. Blot the top of the bacon with several layers of paper towels to absorb any additional fat.

2. Rub the inside of a large salad bowl with the garlic halves. Discard the garlic. Add the endive. Set aside.

3. Break each egg into a ramekin or small cup. In a large, shallow saucepan, bring 2 inches of water to a boil. Add the distilled vinegar. One by one, bring the edge of a ramekin or cup level with the surface of the water and slide the egg in gently. Turn off the heat and cover the pan. Poach the eggs until the whites are firm but the yolks are still runny and are covered with a thin, translucent layer of white, about 3 minutes.

4. With the sieve or slotted spoon, carefully lift the eggs from the water and transfer them to several thicknesses of paper towels. Set aside.

5. Heat the bacon fat in the skillet and add the shallot. Sweat—cook, covered, over low heat until soft and translucent—for 2 to 3 minutes. Add the oil, vinegar, and mustard and heat through. Taste for seasoning and add salt if needed. While the dressing is still warm, pour it over the endive in the bowl, tossing to coat the greens lightly and evenly.

6. Divide the salad among 4 dinner plates. Scatter with the bacon. Carefully arrange a poached egg on top of each salad. Shower with the chives and plenty of pepper. Serve with the bread crisps.

WINE SUGGESTION: A light, white, chilled Sauvignon Blanc would pair nicely with this salad. The crisp acidity of the wine contrasts with the fat in the smoked bacon, creating a beautiful balance.

SALADE NIÇOISE

The modern salade Niçoise can be many things. I like mine with grilled fresh tuna, green beans and steamed potatoes, multicolored heirloom cherry tomatoes, a few nicely dressed greens, and a soft touch of anchovy.

4 SERVINGS

EQUIPMENT: A **10**-QUART PASTA POT FITTED WITH A COLANDER; A STEAMER;
A WOOD OR CHARCOAL FIRE.

9 quarts water

1/4 cup coarse sea salt

1 pound slim *haricot verts* (green beans), trimmed at both ends

1 pound yellow-fleshed potatoes (such as Yukon Gold)

Lemon and Olive Oil Dressing (page 330)

Four 6-ounce, 3/4-inch-thick tuna steaks

Fine sea salt

Coarse, freshly ground black pepper

4 cups firmly packed buttercrunch lettuce

8 ripe heirloom cherry tomatoes, preferably green, yellow, and red, halved

4 Hard-Cooked Eggs (page 69), quartered lengthwise

8 anchovy fillets in olive oil, drained

1/4 cup chives

1. Prepare a large bowl of ice water.

2. Fill the pasta pot with 8 quarts of water and bring it to a rolling boil over high heat. Add the salt and beans and cook until crisp-tender, about 5 minutes. (Cooking time will vary according to the size and tenderness of the beans.) Immediately remove the

colander from the water, allowing the water to drain from the beans. Plunge the beans into the ice water so they cool down as quickly as possible. (The beans will cool in 1 to 2 minutes. If you leave them longer, they will become soggy and begin to lose flavor.) Drain the beans and wrap them in a thick towel to dry. (Store the beans in the towel in the refrigerator for up to 4 hours.)

3. Prepare a wood or charcoal fire. Set the grill rack about 5 inches from the heat. The fire is ready when the coals glow red and are covered with ash.

4. Scrub the potatoes but do not peel them. Bring 1 quart of water to a simmer in the bottom of a steamer. Place the potatoes on the steaming rack. Place the rack over the simmering water, cover, and steam just until the potatoes are fully cooked, about 25 minutes. While still warm, place the potatoes in a small bowl and toss with just enough dressing to lightly and evenly coat them.

5. Season the tuna lightly with salt and pepper. Place the tuna at the 10 o'clock position on the hot grill rack. After 1 minute, rotate the tuna a quarter-turn to the right, to 2 o'clock. One minute later, flip the tuna over to the uncooked side, grill marks up, pointing to 10 o'clock. Grill for 1 minute and rotate to 2 o'clock again, cooking until the tuna is done to your liking. Transfer the tuna to a platter, season again with salt and pepper, and cover loosely with foil. Let rest for 5 minutes.

6. Place the lettuce in a large bowl. Toss with just enough dressing to lightly and evenly coat the lettuce. Place the tomatoes in another bowl and toss with just enough dressing to lightly and evenly coat them. Place the green beans in another bowl and toss with just enough dressing to lightly and evenly coat them.

7. Set a tuna steak at the edge of a large dinner plate. Arrange the lettuce, green beans, potatoes, eggs, and tomatoes alongside. Arrange the anchovies in a crisscross pattern on top and sprinkle with the chives. Serve.

WINE SUGGESTION: I never tire of one of our longtime favorite rosés, the legendary Bandol Rosé from the Domaine Tempier, a mineral-scented wine that is as versatile, and pleasing, as they come.

GREEK SALAD

In my salad memory, this classic stands out as perhaps the first salad as a meal I ever sampled. It's an ideal lunch any time of year, but especially when the garden or markets offer us their finest fresh oregano, ripe tomatoes, and crisp cucumbers. Serve this with toasted Homemade Pita Bread (page 268) or Tortilla Chips (page 263).

4 SERVINGS

1 tablespoon freshly squeezed lemon juice

1/2 teaspoon fine sea salt

3 tablespoons extra-virgin olive oil

3 tablespoons fresh oregano leaves, minced

10 small heirloom tomatoes, quartered lengthwise

1 European or hothouse cucumber (1 pound), halved lengthwise and cut into half-moons

20 best-quality French Brine-Cured Black Olives (page 302)

8 ounces Greek feta cheese, cubed (2 cups)

In a large, shallow bowl, combine the lemon juice and sea salt and whisk to blend. Add the olive oil and 1 tablespoon of the oregano, and whisk to blend. Add the tomatoes, cucumber, and olives, and toss to blend. Scatter with the feta and the remaining 2 tablespoons oregano. Serve on large dinner plates.

WINE SUGGESTION: Try this with a dry and appetizing Loire Valley white, a 100% Sauvignon Blanc Menetou-Salon from the vineyards of Philippe Gilbert.

A DECONSTRUCTED CLUB SANDWICH SALAD WITH PURPLE POTATO CHIPS

While lunching one day at our favorite wine bar in Avignon, Vinoe & Co., we sampled a truly delicious club sandwich accompanied by fabulously crispy paper-thin purple potato chips. For days I could not get the fine memory of the dish out of my head, and I decided to deconstruct the sandwich and turn the ingredients into a salad. Little did I know that fashion designer Sonia Rykiel had beaten me to it! On the menu at the Café Flore on Boulevard Saint Germain in Paris, there is a Club Sonia Rykiel, made without a gram of bread. And of course no potato chips! The one I sampled there was dreadful—not that I blame Sonia Rykiel. Make this salad at home and you'll be rewarded; it's so much easier to handle than a real club sandwich, which is always too thick and awkward to eat, and who needs food held together with toothpicks sprouting rainbow-colored plastic frills? I served this at a dinner party once and a guest described it as a Busted Up Club. Make this your own, using chicken, turkey, or beef, and be sure all the ingredients are first-rate. At home I serve this salad with homemade sourdough bread, thinly sliced and toasted.

4 SERVINGS

8 thin slices smoked bacon

4 firm ripe heirloom tomatoes, cored and quartered

1/2 head romaine lettuce, chopped (3 cups)

Creamy Lemon-Mustard Dressing (page 325)

4 thin slices sourdough bread, toasted (see page 270)

2 Poached Chicken Breasts (page 197), cut lengthwise into thin slices

1 recipe Purple Potato Chips (recipe follows)

1. In a large, dry skillet, brown the bacon over moderate heat until crisp and golden, about 5 minutes. With a slotted spoon, transfer the bacon to several layers of paper towels to absorb the fat.

2. In a large bowl, combine the tomatoes and chopped lettuce. Toss with just enough dressing to lightly and evenly coat the ingredients.

3. Place a slice of toast in the center of each dinner plate and drizzle with the dressing. Layer several slices of chicken on top of the toast. Arrange 2 slices of bacon on top of the chicken. Shower with the tomato salad. Serve with the potato chips.

A sandwich with a historic past: There are many theories about the history of the internationally loved club sandwich. Most link it to the Saratoga (N.Y.) Club in 1894, others to a late-night concoction born of necessity from leftovers found in the kitchen, and one story even suggests it was named after the 1930s double-decker "club cars" on trains that traveled between New York and Chicago.

WINE SUGGESTION: That day in Avignon we sampled a Fleurie, a cru Beaujolais that is often highly underrated. A favorite is the Fleurie les Garants from the Domaine du Vissoux, made with the fruity Gamay grape—a wine that is filled with smoke and spice.

PURPLE POTATO CHIPS

Even though purple potatoes have been around for a while, they're still always a surprise. These chips can be made with russet or Yukon Gold potatoes as well.

4 SERVINGS

EQUIPMENT: A MANDOLINE OR A VERY SHARP CHEF'S KNIFE; AN ELECTRIC DEEP-FAT FRYER FITTED WITH A BASKET.

4 ounces purple potatoes, peeled and sliced 1/16-inch thick (4 cups)

Vegetable oil for deep-frying

Fine sea salt

1. Wash the potato slices in warm water, and then drain thoroughly. Arrange the potatoes in a single layer on a large kitchen towel. Cover with another towel and pat the potatoes to dry them.

2. Pour the oil into the deep-fat fryer; the oil should be at least 2 inches deep. Heat the oil to 375°F. Slice by slice (so the potatoes do not stick together in the oil), carefully drop a small handful of potato slices into the frying basket in the fryer. Fry the potatoes until crisp, about 2 minutes. Transfer the potatoes to several thicknesses of paper towels to drain. Sprinkle with salt. Repeat until all the potatoes have been fried, being sure that the oil temperature returns to 375°F before continuing and that each batch is seasoned with salt. Transfer to a large serving platter and serve immediately.

BACON, LETTUCE, AND TOMATO *TARTINES*

The BLT salad is one of my preferred salads as a meal and one that can also be served in a smaller appetizer version. Is it that memorable taste from childhood—the crunch and saltiness of the bacon, the drip of the ripe tomato—that is so appealing? Probably a combination of all of these. Rather than mayonnaise, I dress this with a very light yogurt and lemon dressing. Tartine, *by the way, is just another word for an open-faced sandwich.*

4 SERVINGS

2 1/2 ounces smoked bacon, rind removed, cut into 1/4-inch cubes (3/4 cup)

3 heads sucrine lettuce (or 1/2 head iceberg lettuce), chopped

4 ripe heirloom tomatoes, cored, peeled, seeded, and chopped

Yogurt and Lemon Dressing (page 331)

4 thin slices sourdough bread, toasted (see page 270)

Coarse, freshly ground black pepper

1. In a large, dry skillet, brown the bacon over moderate heat until crisp and golden, about 5 minutes. With a slotted spoon, transfer the bacon to several layers of paper towels to absorb the fat. Blot the top of the bacon with several layers of paper towels to absorb any additional fat.

2. In a large, shallow bowl, combine the bacon, lettuce, and tomatoes. Toss with just enough dressing to lightly and evenly coat the ingredients. Arrange on the slices of toasted bread. Season generously with pepper, and serve.

VARIATION: To make it a Cobb *tartine*, add 1 small avocado, cubed, and 4 ounces best-quality blue cheese, crumbled.

WINE SUGGESTION: A fresh, mouth-filling red comes to mind here. Why not a young Burgundian Pinot Noir, such as Aubert de Villaine's Mercurey Les Montots?

BACON-WRAPPED GOAT CHEESE WITH DANDELION GREENS

This has been a family favorite ever since we moved to France in 1980. I like to wrap the slightly firm goat cheese in thin slices of smoked meat, such as coppa, bacon, pancetta, or smoked ham. The meat must be sliced as thin as possible so it cooks up quickly, before the goat cheese has time to melt and turn runny. So opt for a firm goat cheese. I like to serve this with an assertive salad, such as dandelion greens, or a sturdy spinach-like green from my garden, dressed with a simple, classic vinaigrette.

4 SERVINGS
EQUIPMENT: A LARGE NONSTICK SKILLET.

1 tablespoon minced mixed fresh herbs, such as chives, chervil, mint, and tarragon

4 small, firm rounds of goat's milk cheese (2 ounces each)

8 ultra-thin slices smoked bacon, pancetta, or smoked ham

6 cups firmly packed dandelion greens, torn into bite-sized pieces (or use baby spinach)

Classic Vinaigrette (page 324)

1. Sprinkle the herbs over both sides of each goat cheese round, pressing down lightly so they adhere. Wrap 2 slices of bacon, crisscross fashion, around each cheese.

2. Heat the skillet over moderate heat. Add the wrapped cheese and cook until the meat is browned, about 2 minutes per side. Transfer to a layer of paper towels to drain.

3. In a large salad bowl, toss the greens with just enough dressing to lightly and evenly coat them. Arrange the greens on large salad plates. Place a wrapped goat cheese on top of each salad and serve.

ASPARAGUS, HAM, AND POACHED EGG SALAD

On an afternoon in May, a favorite Provençal bistro served us this utterly delicious and totally beautiful spring salad of blanched asparagus, a perfect poached egg draped with a shiny, fragrant slice of ham from the French Basque region, and a tangle of soft greens. I like to serve this with toasted slices of my homemade Ham and Cheese Bread.

4 SERVINGS

EQUIPMENT: A **5**-QUART PASTA POT FITTED WITH A COLANDER; **4** RAMEKINS OR SMALL CUPS; A FLAT, FINE-MESH SIEVE OR A LARGE SLOTTED SPOON.

3 tablespoons coarse sea salt

16 green asparagus spears (1 pound), trimmed

4 ultra-fresh large eggs

1 tablespoon distilled vinegar

4 cups torn soft greens, such as buttercrunch lettuce

1/4 cup minced fresh chives

Lemon and Olive Oil Dressing (page 330)

4 thin slices top-quality ham

Fine sea salt

Coarse, freshly ground black pepper

Sliced Ham and Cheese Bread (page 266), toasted, for serving

1. Prepare a large bowl of ice water.

2. Fill the pasta pot with 3 quarts of water and bring it to a rolling boil over high heat. Add the coarse salt and the asparagus. Blanch, uncovered, until crisp-tender, about 3 minutes. (Cooking time will vary according to the size and tenderness of the

asparagus.) Immediately remove the colander from the water, letting the water drain from the asparagus. Plunge the asparagus into the ice water so they cool down as quickly as possible and retain their crispness and bright green color. (The asparagus will cool in 1 to 2 minutes. After that, they will soften and begin to lose crispness and flavor.) Drain the asparagus and wrap it in a thick kitchen towel to dry. (Do not cook the asparagus in advance or it will lose its crispness.)

3. Break each egg into a ramekin or small cup. Set aside. In a large, shallow saucepan, bring 2 inches of water to a boil. Add the vinegar. One by one, bring the edge of a ramekin or cup level with the surface of the water and slide the egg in gently. Turn off the heat and cover the pan. Poach the eggs until the whites are firm but the yolks are still runny and are covered with a thin, translucent layer of white, about 3 minutes.

4. With the sieve or slotted spoon, carefully lift the eggs from the water and transfer them to several thicknesses of paper towels.

5. Place the salad greens and chives in a large salad bowl. Toss with just enough dressing to coat the greens lightly and evenly.

6. Place the asparagus on a large plate and add just enough dressing to lightly coat the spears. Roll the asparagus in the dressing.

7. Arrange the dressed greens at one side of each of 4 large dinner plates. (Rectangular plates are particularly beautiful here.) Carefully place a poached egg alongside. Arrange 4 asparagus spears next to the eggs. Carefully drape a slice of ham over each of the poached eggs. Season the greens lightly with fine sea salt and generously with pepper. Sprinkle with chives. Serve with the toast.

WINE SUGGESTION: This salad calls out for a crisp white, a northern wine that will pair nicely with the egg, ham, and asparagus. One wine that can generally be found in our cellar in Paris is the Coteaux du Giennois, Domaine de Villargeau. It's a 100% Sauvignon Blanc and comes from very flinty soils near the Pouilly Fumé vineyards. It's a touch salty, chalky, and smoky and pairs nicely with the star ingredients in this salad.

CORN, BACON, FETA, TOMATO, AND AVOCADO SALAD

In France, really fresh corn appears intermittently in the market, so when I spy it, I score! I race to create a totally fresh salad with the day's harvest. This is one of my current favorites.

4 SERVINGS

EQUIPMENT: A LARGE, SHARP CHEF'S KNIFE.

2 1/2 ounces smoked bacon, rind removed, cut into 1/4-inch cubes (3/4 cup)

2 ears fresh corn, shucked

4 ripe multicolored heirloom tomatoes, cored, quartered, and chopped

2 ounces imported Greek feta cheese, crumbled (1/2 cup)

1 large ripe avocado, halved, pitted, peeled, and cubed

2 small spring onions or scallions, white part only, trimmed, peeled, and cut into thin rings

Yogurt and Lemon Dressing (page 331)

Coarse, freshly ground black pepper

1. In a large, dry skillet, brown the bacon over moderate heat until crisp and golden, about 5 minutes. With a slotted spoon, transfer the bacon to paper towels to absorb the fat. Blot the top of the bacon with paper towels as well.

2. Cut off the fat ends of the ears of corn, stand the ears on the flat end, and use the chef's knife to cut off the corn kernels. Place the kernels in a large bowl.

3. Add the tomatoes, bacon, feta, avocado, and spring onions to the corn. Toss with just enough dressing to coat the ingredients lightly and evenly. Season generously with pepper, and serve.

WINE SUGGESTION: This salad calls out for a young, balanced white: why not one from our winemaker Yves Gras, who makes a fabulously complex yet not showy white, a Sablet Blanc.

ICEBERG LETTUCE SALAD WITH BACON AND ROQUEFORT

We consider this the perfect Saturday lunch salad, one that is hearty enough to assuage one's hunger and that can be prepared in a flash, so there's no need to wait. I like to dress this with a light Buttermilk–Lemon Zest Dressing, but feel free to use your dressing of choice. And don't forget the freshly ground black pepper—it's essential here!

4 SERVINGS

2 1/2 ounces smoked bacon, rind removed, cut into 1/2-inch julienne (3/4 cup)

1 medium head iceberg lettuce, cut into wedges

1 tablespoon minced fresh chives

6 ounces chilled blue cheese (preferably Roquefort), crumbled (1 1/2 cups)

Buttermilk–Lemon Zest Dressing (page 322)

Fleur de sel

Coarse, freshly ground black pepper

1. In a large, dry skillet, brown the bacon over moderate heat until crisp and golden, about 5 minutes. With a slotted spoon, transfer the bacon to several layers of paper towels to absorb the fat. Blot the top of the bacon with several layers of paper towels to absorb any additional fat.

2. In a large salad bowl, combine the lettuce, chives, bacon, and cheese. Pour just enough dressing to lightly and evenly coat the ingredients. Season with *fleur de sel*. Divide the salad evenly among 4 plates. Season generously with pepper, and serve.

WINE SUGGESTION: It's time for a simple daily drinking white, such as a light, dry Alpine wine from the Savoie: try a Roussette from Pierre Boniface.

PROVENCE ON A PLATE: EGGPLANT, TOMATOES, GOAT CHEESE, AND TAPENADE

During my summer cooking classes this is a favorite Friday lunch dish, one that students dubbed Provence on a Plate, and the name has stuck. Who could not love the combination of perfectly cooked eggplant teamed up with garden-fresh tomatoes, homemade tapenade, soothing goat cheese. This is a dish that takes up quite a bit of room when preparing and plating this for fourteen people, so we move out into the courtyard, set up stations for peeling and slicing tomatoes, while indoors one or two students tend to cooking the tender, freshly harvested eggplant. I grow several varieties of eggplant each summer, including the white, egg-shaped eggplant that I often use in miniature versions of this stacked dish. This recipe is only a suggestion; all sorts of leftover cheese and vegetables could be added according to taste and whim.

4 SERVINGS
EQUIPMENT: A BAKING SHEET.

2 firm, fresh eggplants, washed but not peeled (about 8 ounces)

About 1 tablespoon extra-virgin olive oil, plus extra for drizzling

Fine sea salt

3 large, ripe heirloom tomatoes

12 slices soft goat's milk cheese or Greek feta cheese

Black Olive Tapenade with Lemon Confit (page 20)

About 24 large, fresh basil leaves

1. Center a rack in the oven. Preheat the oven to 475°F.

2. Trim and discard the ends of the eggplants. Cut each eggplant crosswise into slices about 1/2 inch thick. The eggplants should yield 16 slices. Place the eggplant slices side by side on the baking sheet. Brush them with the oil and season lightly with salt.

Place the baking sheet in the oven and roast until soft, about 5 to 7 minutes. Turn and brush the other side with oil and season with salt and return to the oven. Small eggplants should cook in 10 to 15 minutes; larger eggplants will take a little longer.

3. While the eggplant cooks, prepare the tomatoes. Core and peel the tomatoes. Cut each horizontally into 4 thick slices. The tomatoes should yield 12 slices.

4. Remove the eggplant from the oven. Arrange a slice of eggplant on each of 4 salad plates. Place a slice of tomato on top of the eggplant. Top with the cheese. Brush the cheese with the tapenade. Place a basil leaf on top of the tapenade. Repeat the stacking until each plate has 4 layers of eggplant and 3 layers of tomato, ending with the eggplant. Drizzle with olive oil and season with salt. Garnish with basil.

WINE SUGGESTION: There are actually wines that taste of black olives. We've found this in various tastings in Provence as well as Paris. The chef at Château de Beaucastel in Châteauneuf-du-Pape marries black olive dishes with their Vinsobres wine, finding that aromas and flavors of the wine echo the bounty of the groves of black olives that flank the vineyards near the village of Nyons.

PEAR, BLUE CHEESE, FENNEL, ENDIVE, AND SALTED ALMOND SALAD

This wintry salad combines some of my favorite foods: pears, blue cheese, fennel, Belgian endive, and salted almonds, preferably the incomparable Marcona almonds from Spain or the even rarer salted almonds from Provence. I toss these ingredients with a very light and creamy blue cheese dressing and pair it all with a crisp white Sauvignon Blanc.

4 SERVINGS

EQUIPMENT: A SMALL JAR WITH A LID; TWO **1**-QUART AIRTIGHT CONTAINERS; A MANDOLINE OR A LARGE, SHARP CHEF'S KNIFE.

Blue Cheese and Yogurt Dressing

1 cup plain nonfat yogurt

2 ounces chilled blue cheese (preferably Roquefort), crumbled (1/2 cup)

2 tablespoons freshly squeezed lemon juice

1/2 teaspoon fine sea salt

Salad

2 tablespoons freshly squeezed lemon juice

2 small bulbs fennel (8 ounces total), trimmed

2 medium-ripe pears

1/2 cup best-quality salted almonds, plus extra for garnish

6 ounces chilled blue cheese (preferably Roquefort), crumbled (1 1/2 cups)

2 Belgian endive heads, trimmed and cut lengthwise into a thin chiffonade

1/4 cup minced fresh chives

Coarse, freshly ground black pepper

1. Prepare the dressing: In the jar, combine the yogurt, blue cheese, lemon juice, and salt. Cover with the lid and shake to blend. Taste for seasoning. (Store in the jar in the refrigerator for up to 3 days.)

2. Fill one of the 1-quart airtight containers with cold water, and add 1 tablespoon of the lemon juice. With the mandoline or chef's knife, cut the fennel lengthwise into very thin slices, dropping the slices into the acidulated water. Cover the container and refrigerate. (Store in the refrigerator for up to 4 hours. The fennel will crisp up and the lemon juice will prevent it from darkening.)

3. Fill the second container with cold water and add the remaining 1 tablespoon lemon juice. Peel the pears, core them, and cut them lengthwise into 16 slices, dropping them into the acidulated water as you go. Cover the container. (Store in the refrigerator for up to 4 hours. The pears will crisp up and the lemon juice will prevent them from darkening.)

4. When you are ready to serve, drain the fennel and pears. In a large salad bowl, combine the fennel, pears, almonds, cheese, and endive. Toss with just enough dressing to coat the ingredients lightly and evenly. Arrange the salad on large dinner plates. Garnish with more almonds and the chives, and season with pepper.

WINE SUGGESTION: Pears always lead me to the Loire valley, a land of great white wines. I am a huge fan of the Sauvignon Blanc grape, and Sancerre from the Loire Valley is truly one of the world's great wines. I have several favorites to recommend with this dish, including offerings from the houses of Alphonse Mellot, Didier Dagueneau, and François Cotat.

RANCHO SALAD: CUCUMBERS, TOMATOES, COTTAGE CHEESE, AND FRILLS

I am not sure what an ingredient must do to get into the Comfort Food Hall of Fame, but cottage cheese is in mine. The creamy, lactic delicacy has carried me through since childhood, and even today the sight of a chilled, fresh, fragrant container of the light cheese makes me smile. On my regular visits to my "boot camp"—Rancho La Puerta in Tecate, Mexico—this is one of my favorite lunches. There is always a lunch buffet and it often includes giant bowls of their own garden-fresh tomatoes and cucumbers. I add cottage cheese and often a few spoonfuls of their spicy salsa. At home I add even more frills, such as thinly sliced spring onions, sliced celery, minced chives, and some of my Red Hot Salt to add spice to what might otherwise be a very quiet day. Since I don't drink wine with this salad at the Ranch, I don't at home, either.

4 SERVINGS

1 European or hothouse cucumber (about 1 pound), thinly sliced

4 ripe heirloom tomatoes, each cored and cut lengthwise into 8 slices

2 small spring onions or scallions, white part only, trimmed, peeled, and cut into thin rounds

2 celery ribs, cut crosswise into very thin slices

1/4 cup minced fresh chives

Red Hot Salt (page 307)

2 cups cottage cheese of choice

Avocado-Chile Salsa (page 337), optional

In a large bowl, combine the cucumber, tomatoes, onions, celery, and chives. Toss to combine, and season generously with the seasoned salt. Mound the mixture on large salad plates. Top each with a dollop of cottage cheese and the Avocado-Chile Salsa (if using) and serve.

FIG, SHEEP CHEESE, POMEGRANATE SEED, ARUGULA, AND KUMQUAT SALAD

In late September in our garden in Provence, there is a welcoming convergence of multitoned fruits as pomegranates burst open to reveal their shiny, colorful seeds, the purplish-black Ronde de Bordeaux figs begin dripping with honey-like juice, the kumquat tree in the courtyard remains laden with tangy orange fruit, and the lemons on the trees in front of the guest room call out to be harvested. Wild arugula grows between the grapevines in the vineyard, offering sturdy green leaves and clean white flowers that actually smell like honey! That's when this salad—which wins hands down on color alone—appears on our table.

4 SERVINGS

1/2 cup pomegranate seeds

8 fresh figs, stemmed and quartered

4 kumquats, stemmed, cut crosswise into very thin slices, and seeded

Best-quality aged balsamic vinegar to taste

Coarse, freshly ground black pepper

4 cups firmly packed arugula leaves and flowers

Lemon and Olive Oil Dressing (page 330)

Fine sea salt

4 ounces firm sheep's milk cheese, shaved with a vegetable peeler into very thin strips

1. In a large, shallow bowl, combine the pomegranate seeds, figs, and kumquats. Drizzle with the balsamic vinegar and season generously with pepper.

2. Place the arugula in a large salad bowl. Toss with just enough dressing to coat the greens lightly and evenly. Season with salt.

3. Divide the arugula among 4 large dinner plates. Arrange the dressed fig mixture on top of the greens. Scatter with the cheese, and serve.

VARIATIONS: Add, as desired, toasted walnuts, halved purple grapes, or strips of ham.

WINE SUGGESTION: A favorite local white wine comes from the nearby village of Cairanne, where Denis Alary makes a lovely Cairanne Blanc, a blend of 90% Clairette and 10% Roussanne. It's a perfect wine for this totally local salad.

Kumquat tree

CANTALOUPE, TOMATO, GOAT CHEESE, CUCUMBER, AND ONION SALAD

It took me a long time to come around to the idea of fruit in what is basically a vegetable salad, but the color, crunch, and gentle sweetness of cantaloupe melon is not to be resisted! This is a combination I come back to again and again.

4 SERVINGS

1 small, ripe cantaloupe melon, halved, seeded, cut into small wedges, and rind removed

2 pounds ripe heirloom tomatoes, cored and cut into wedges

4 ounces firm goat's milk cheese, crumbled (1 cup)

1 small cucumber, peeled and very thinly sliced

2 small spring onions or scallions, white part only, trimmed, peeled, and cut into thin rings

Yogurt and Lemon Dressing (page 331)

1/2 cup fresh basil leaves, cut into a chiffonade

1/2 cup fresh mint leaves, cut into a chiffonade

Coarse, freshly ground black pepper

In a large shallow bowl, combine the melon, tomatoes, goat cheese, cucumber, and onions. Toss with just enough dressing to coat the ingredients lightly and evenly. Shower with the herbs and season generously with pepper. Serve.

WINE SUGGESTION: This purely summer salad calls out for a chilled rosé, a favorite coming from Domaine de la Janasse. Their rosé actually has melon-like tones! A blend of Grenache and Cinsault grapes, it's a fresh and lively wine made to match an equally alert salad.

SPRING SALAD: ASPARAGUS, PEAS, BEANS, AND FENNEL

Come spring, we find asparagus on our table on a daily basis. I never run out of ideas for what to do with these vibrant green spears, often with a mineral flavor from the soil that gave them life. I love to combine them with their bright green cousins, peas and green beans, and their paler white relative, the crispy fennel bulb. My Creamy Lemon-Chive Dressing brings them all together in a delightful salad.

4 SERVINGS

EQUIPMENT: A 5-QUART PASTA POT FITTED WITH A COLANDER; A STEAMER; A MANDOLINE OR A VERY SHARP CHEF'S KNIFE.

16 spears (about 1 pound) fresh green asparagus, trimmed

1 tablespoon coarse sea salt

1 pound slim *haricots verts* (green beans), trimmed at both ends and cut into 3-inch pieces

8 ounces peas, fresh or frozen (no need to thaw)

1 small bulb fennel (about 4 ounces)

Creamy Lemon-Chive Dressing (page 326)

Fine sea salt

Coarse, freshly ground black pepper

1. Prepare 4 large bowls of ice water.

2. Trim the asparagus, discarding the woody ends. Trim the tender tips on the diagonal to about 4 inches. Cut the remaining stalks on the diagonal into 3-inch pieces.

3. Fill the pasta pot with 3 quarts of water and bring it to a rolling boil over high heat. Add the coarse salt and the asparagus stalk pieces. Blanch, uncovered, for 1 minute. Then add the tips (which will cook more quickly) and cook until crisp-tender, about 3 minutes. (Cooking time will vary according to the size and tenderness of the asparagus.) Immediately remove the colander from the water, letting the water drain from the asparagus and reserving the cooking water. Plunge the asparagus into a bowl of ice water so they cool down as quickly as possible and retain their crispness and bright green color. (The asparagus will cool in 1 to 2 minutes. If you leave them longer, they will become soggy and lose crispness and flavor.) Drain the asparagus and wrap them in a thick kitchen towel to dry. (Do not cook them in advance or they will lose their crispness.)

4. Bring the water back to a boil, add the green beans, and blanch, uncovered, until very tender, about 4 minutes. (Cooking time will vary according to the size of the beans.) Immediately drain the beans (again reserving the cooking water) and plunge them into the second bowl of ice water so they cool down as quickly as possible and retain their crispness and bright green color. (The beans will cool in 1 to 2 minutes. After that, they will soften and begin to lose crispness and flavor.) Transfer the beans to a colander, drain, and wrap in a thick towel to dry. (The beans can be cooked up to 2 hours in advance. Keep them wrapped in the towel and hold at room temperature.)

5. Bring 1 quart of water to a simmer in the bottom of a steamer. Place the peas on the steaming rack. Place the rack over the simmering water, cover, and steam just until the peas are cooked al dente, 1 to 2 minutes. Immediately drain the peas and plunge them into another bowl of ice water so they cool down as quickly as possible and retain their crispness and bright green color. (The peas will cool in 1 to 2 minutes. If you leave them longer, they will become soggy and begin to lose crispness and flavor.) Drain the peas.

6. With the mandoline or chef's knife, cut the fennel into very thin slices, dropping them into the last bowl of ice water to crisp them for about 10 minutes.

7. At serving time, drain the fennel, combine all the vegetables in a large bowl and toss with just enough dressing to coat them lightly and evenly. Taste for seasoning. Arrange on 4 large dinner plates. Season with pepper, and serve.

VARIATION: Add about 4 ounces of aged Comté cheese, cut into thin strips.

WINE SUGGESTION: This salad was originally created for my springtime cooking classes in Paris, and we enjoy it with a favorite Loire Valley white, the 100% Sauvignon Blanc Coteaux du Giennois, Domaine de Villargeau.

SUMMER SALAD: GREEN BEANS, TOASTED NUTS, AND CURED OLIVES

This is a regal salad, rich with the flavors of well-aged Parmigiano-Reggiano cheese and fresh garden greens and flavored with local olive oil. Embellished with spicy mixed nuts and home-marinated mixed olives, it sings of our summer garden and the flavors and aromas of Provence.

4 SERVINGS

EQUIPMENT: A **5**-QUART PASTA POT FITTED WITH A COLANDER.

1 tablespoon coarse sea salt

1 pound slim *haricots verts* (green beans), trimmed at both ends

8 cups firmly packed soft salad greens, such as buttercrunch lettuce

1 tablespoon finely minced fresh chives

Lemon and Olive Oil Dressing (page 330)

Fine sea salt

About 20 shavings of Parmigiano-Reggiano cheese

1/2 cup Spicy Basque Mixed Nuts (page 8)

16 olives from Marinated Olive Quartet (page 19)

1. Prepare a large bowl of ice water.

2. Fill the pasta pot with 3 quarts of water and bring it to a rolling boil over high heat. Add the coarse salt and beans and blanch until crisp-tender, about 5 minutes. (Cooking time will vary according to the size and tenderness of the beans.) Immediately remove the colander from the water, letting the water drain from the beans, and plunge the beans into the ice water so they cool down as quickly as possible and retain their crispness and bright green color. (The beans will cool in

1 to 2 minutes. If you leave them longer, they will become soggy and begin to lose flavor.) Drain the beans and wrap them in a thick kitchen towel to dry. (Store the beans in the towel in the refrigerator for up to 4 hours.)

3. Tear the greens into bite-size pieces. In a large salad bowl, combine the greens and chives. Toss with just enough dressing to coat the greens lightly and evenly. Taste for seasoning. Place the beans in another bowl. Toss with just enough dressing to lightly and evenly coat the beans. Taste for seasoning.

4. Mound the greens on each of 4 salad plates. Arrange the green beans on top of the dressed greens. Top with the shavings of cheese. Sprinkle with the nuts and arrange the olives alongside. Serve.

WINE SUGGESTION: With this salad we often enjoy a Picpoul de Pinet (I just love to say the words—*peekpool* duh *peenay*), a white wine from the Languedoc, where the vineyards roll down toward the Mediterranean. A fine offering comes from the *cave coopérative* Cave de Pomérols.

ITALIAN SALAD: CELERY, FENNEL, SPRING ONION, AND RADISH WITH BOCCONCINI, PROSCIUTTO, OLIVES, AND MARINATED ARTICHOKES

Give me celery and radishes any day and I'm a happy camper. I love both the simplicity and the complexity of this salad, one that can be put together in a matter of minutes from the refrigerator and the pantry.

4 SERVINGS

8 tender celery ribs, with leaves, cut crosswise into thin slices

20 radishes, trimmed and cut into thin rounds

6 small spring onions or scallions, white part only, trimmed, peeled, and cut into thin rounds

1 bulb fennel, trimmed and cut lengthwise into very thin slices

Classic Vinaigrette (page 324)

Fine sea salt

18 olives from the Marinated Olive Quartet (page 19)

12 thin prosciutto slices, torn into strips, then rolled

18 bocconcini (small mozzarella balls), drained and halved

12 Baby Artichokes Marinated in Olive Oil (page 24)

Sliced sourdough bread, toasted, for serving

1. Combine the celery, radishes, spring onions, and fennel in a large salad bowl. Toss with just enough dressing to lightly and evenly coat the vegetables. Taste for seasoning.

2. Form mounds of the dressed vegetables in the center of 4 large dinner plates. Arrange the olives, prosciutto, bocconcini, and marinated artichokes around the salad. Serve with the toasted bread.

VARIATIONS: Depending upon the season, add grilled red peppers, braised asparagus, or blanched and refreshed green beans.

WINE SUGGESTION: A light red is nice here—perhaps a favorite Italian, the easy-drinking 100% Sangiovese Tenuta di Capezzana Conti Contini Sangiovese.

WATERCRESS, ENDIVE, AND BEET SALAD

Come winter I crave watercress and weave the gorgeous, pungent green into my menus as frequently as possible. This trio of watercress, Belgian endive, and beets works for me—super-healthy partners that also happen to be quite beautiful together. Be sure to toss the beets separately, for they will quickly bleed their bright red color into the alabaster endive.

4 SERVINGS
EQUIPMENT: A STEAMER.

1 pound beets (without tops), peeled

Creamy Lemon-Mustard Dressing (page 325)

Fine sea salt

Leaves from 2 bunches (about 1 pound) watercress

4 Belgian endive heads, trimmed and sliced lengthwise into fine julienne

1/4 cup minced fresh chives

Coarse, freshly ground black pepper

1. Bring 1 quart of water to a simmer in the bottom of the steamer. Place the beets on the steaming rack. Place the rack over the simmering water, cover, and steam just until the beets are cooked but still firm, about 30 minutes. Remove the beets from the steamer, let them cool, and then cut them into 1/2-inch cubes.

2. Place the beets in a medium bowl. Toss with just enough dressing to coat them lightly and evenly. Taste for seasoning.

3. In a large salad bowl, combine the watercress and endive. Coat with just enough dressing to coat them lightly and evenly. Taste for seasoning. Divide the greens

among 4 large dinner plates. Arrange the dressed beets in the center of the greens. Garnish with the chives and season generously with pepper. Serve.

VARIATIONS: Toss 1 cup cubed firm goat cheese with the beets; add 1 cup Spicy Basque Mixed Nuts (page 8) or Curried Pumpkin Seeds (page 9).

WINE SUGGESTION: Keep it simple here—perhaps a young Pinot Grigio or Chenin Blanc.

BROCCOLI, AVOCADO, AND PISTACHIOS WITH PISTACHIO OIL

There are days when I simply must have broccoli, and on one of those days I created this salad, which has become a favorite in our household and with students in my cooking classes. I love the pairing of the green on green—the broccoli with the avocado—and the texture and sweetness added by the pistachios and pistachio oil.

4 SERVINGS
EQUIPMENT: A SMALL JAR WITH A LID;
A 5-QUART PASTA POT FITTED WITH A COLANDER.

1 tablespoon freshly squeezed lemon juice

1/2 teaspoon fine sea salt

4 tablespoons best-quality pistachio oil (such as Leblanc) or extra-virgin olive oil

3 tablespoons coarse sea salt

8 ounces broccoli florets (about 2 cups)

1 large ripe avocado

1/4 cup salted pistachios, coarsely chopped

Fleur de sel

Coarse, freshly ground black pepper

1. In the jar, combine the lemon juice and fine salt. Cover with the lid and shake to dissolve the salt. Add the oil and shake to blend.

2. Prepare a large bowl of ice water.

3. Fill the pasta pot with 3 quarts of water and bring it to a rolling boil over high heat. Add the coarse salt and the broccoli. Blanch, uncovered, until the broccoli is crisp-tender, 3 to 4 minutes. Immediately remove the colander from the water,

letting the water drain from the broccoli. Plunge the broccoli into the ice water so it cools down as quickly as possible and retains its crispness and bright green color. (The broccoli will cool in 1 to 2 minutes. If you leave it longer, it will soften and begin to lose crispness and flavor.) Drain the broccoli.

4. Halve, pit, and peel the avocado, and cut it lengthwise into very thin slices. Mound the broccoli florets in the center of each plate. Arrange the avocado slices in a circle around the broccoli. Sprinkle with the pistachios. Drizzle with the dressing. Season with *fleur de sel* and pepper. Let marinate for 3 to 4 minutes before serving.

WINE SUGGESTION: This is lovely with a Macon. A favorite is the stony, mildly floral Macon Viré from Andre Bonhomme.

CELERY, GREEN OLIVE, AND ANCHOVY SALAD

In my cooking classes we often have a trattoria day near the end of the week, and this pungent, colorful salad is frequently on the menu, along with Homemade Yogurt Cheese (page 51), Marinated Olive Quartet (page 19), Italian Salt and Sugar–Cured Beef (page 229), and the ever-popular Crispy Flatbread (page 260).

4 SERVINGS

20 green pimiento-stuffed olives, drained

4 cups diced celery (with leaves)

1 cup fresh parsley leaves, minced

1 teaspoon minced fresh oregano leaves

1/4 teaspoon hot red pepper flakes, or to taste

2 tablespoons freshly squeezed lemon juice

4 tablespoons extra-virgin olive oil

16 white anchovy fillets cured in vinegar and oil

1. In a large bowl, combine the olives, celery, parsley, oregano, red pepper flakes, lemon juice, and olive oil. Toss to blend. Cover and refrigerate for at least 2 hours and up to 2 days.

2. At serving time, mound the salad on individual serving plates. Crisscross 4 anchovy fillets on top of each salad. Serve.

CUCUMBER AND YOGURT CHEESE SALAD: *TZATZIKI*

This classic salad is fabulous on its own or as part of a salad buffet that might include a Greek Salad (page 79), Homemade Pita Bread (page 268), Marinated Olive Quartet (page 19), and a small cup of Chilled Evergreen Tomato Velouté (page 32).

2 CUPS

EQUIPMENT: A BOX GRATER, A SIEVE.

1 European or hothouse cucumber (about 1 pound), trimmed

2 tablespoons coarse sea salt

1 cup Homemade Yogurt Cheese (page 51)

2 tablespoons freshly squeezed lemon juice

2 plump, moist garlic cloves, peeled, halved, green germ removed, and minced

1/4 cup finely chopped fresh dill

1. Using the largest holes on the grater, grate the cucumber into the sieve set over a bowl. Toss with the coarse salt. Refrigerate for 3 hours, letting the cucumbers drain.

2. In a large bowl, combine the yogurt cheese, lemon juice, garlic, and most of the dill. Whisk to blend. Squeeze as much liquid as possible from the cucumbers and mix them into the yogurt cheese mixture. Refrigerate for several hours to let the flavors blend. Serve chilled, garnished with the remaining dill. (Store in an airtight container in the refrigerator for up to 1 day.)

ZUCCHINI CARPACCIO WITH AVOCADO, PISTACHIOS, AND PISTACHIO OIL

Neither my students nor I ever tire of this salad. It has all the qualities one looks for in a dish: crunch, smoothness, color, aroma. Serve it with Crispy Flatbread (page 260), Tortilla Chips (page 263), or toasted bread for added crunch. Don't omit the fresh thyme here, for it plays an essential role in the color and aroma.

4 SERVINGS

EQUIPMENT: A SMALL JAR WITH A LID;
A MANDOLINE OR A VERY SHARP CHEF'S KNIFE.

1 tablespoon freshly squeezed lemon juice

1/4 teaspoon Lemon Zest Salt (page 306)

3 tablespoons best-quality pistachio oil (such as Leblanc) or extra-virgin olive oil

4 small, fresh zucchini (about 4 ounces each), rinsed and trimmed at both ends

1 large ripe avocado

1/2 cup salted pistachios

4 fresh lemon thyme sprigs, with flowers if possible

Fleur de sel

1. In the jar, combine the lemon juice and flavored salt. Cover with the lid and shake to blend. Add the oil and shake to blend.

2. With the mandoline or chef's knife, slice the zucchini lengthwise as thin as possible. Arrange the slices on a platter and pour the dressing over them. Tilt the platter back and forth to coat the slices evenly. Cover with plastic wrap and let marinate at room temperature for 30 minutes, so the zucchini absorbs the dressing and does not dry out.

3. Halve, pit, and peel the avocado, and cut it lengthwise into very thin slices. Carefully arrange the slices of marinated zucchini on individual salad plates, alternating with the avocado slices, slightly overlapping them. Sprinkle with the pistachio nuts. Garnish with the thyme sprigs and flowers and *fleur de sel*. Serve.

WINE SUGGESTION: Favorite wine partners for avocado include a young Pinot Grigio, a crisp-style Chardonnay, and a fragrant, well-chilled Sauvignon Blanc.

FISH AND SHELLFISH

I SMILE WHEN I WALK INTO A FISHMONGER'S SHOP, REVELING IN ALL THE SPARKLING FRESH FARE BEFORE ME. I COULD EAT A FISH OR SHELLFISH SALAD EVERY DAY, AND OFTEN DO. HERE AGAIN, AVOCADOS, TOMATOES, CUCUMBERS, ALL MANNER OF HERBS, THE VERSATILE SPRING ONION, FETA CHEESE, AND CITRUS TRANSFORM THE SIMPLE INTO THE SUBLIME.

WARM CLAM SALAD WITH FRESH HERBS AND TOMATOES

When fresh clams appear in the market, they inevitably end up in my shopping basket; I love the simplicity of these tiny shellfish. This salad takes no prisoners, so make it only when the finest heirloom tomatoes are in season and an avalanche of mixed fresh herbs is at your disposal.

4 SERVINGS

1 pound small heirloom tomatoes (each 3 to 4 ounces), preferably a mix of green, yellow, and red

2 pounds small, farmed fresh littleneck or Manila clams, purged (see Note)

1 shallot, trimmed, peeled, and finely minced

2 plump, moist garlic cloves, peeled, halved, green germ removed, and minced

1/4 cup white wine

Several fresh flat-leaf parsley sprigs

1/4 cup mixed minced fresh herbs, including basil, parsley, chives, and cilantro

Lemon and Olive Oil Dressing (page 330)

4 slices sourdough bread, toasted, for serving (see page 270)

1. Core, peel, and chop the tomatoes. Place them in a large, shallow bowl.

2. Place the purged clams, in their shells, in a large skillet. Add the shallot, garlic, wine, and parsley sprigs, and bring to a boil over high heat. Reduce to moderate heat and cook, covered, shaking the skillet occasionally, until all the clams are open, 3 to 4 minutes.

3. Using a large slotted spoon, transfer the clams in their shells to a large bowl. Discard any clams that have not opened. Remove the clams from their shells and place them in the bowl of tomatoes. Strain the cooking liquid from the clams and add it to the

bowl. Add the mixed herbs. Toss with just enough dressing to lightly coat the mixture. Serve with plenty of toasted sourdough bread to absorb the sauce.

NOTE: Purging clams helps to get rid of the sand and grit. First, scrub the shells under cold running water. Discard any clams with broken shells or shells that do not close when tapped. In a large bowl, combine 11/2 quarts cold water and 3 tablespoons fine sea salt. Stir to dissolve the salt. Add the rinsed clams to the saltwater and refrigerate for 3 hours. Then remove the clams from the saltwater with your fingers, leaving the sand and grit behind.

WINE SUGGESTION: A favorite white is the lively, inexpensive, dry Chignin-Bergeron from the Savoie, made from 100% Roussanne grapes. Winemakers André and Michel Quénard make one of the best.

HALIBUT AND *SHISO* TARTARE ON A BED OF HEIRLOOM TOMATOES

If you have a vegetable garden or even a tiny windowsill herb garden, try growing shiso, *the tangy, colorful herb often found in Japanese cuisine. I grow two varieties, one red, one green, and use the herb with abandon throughout the summer. Prepare this with ultra-fresh Pacific halibut or Atlantic bigeye tuna. Toasted sesame oil loves fish tartare, and the addition of tiny cubes of lemon confit contributes just the right touch of acidity and crunch to this ever-favorite fish salad. If shiso leaves are not available, substitute fresh basil leaves.*

4 SERVINGS

EQUIPMENT: **4** CHILLED SALAD PLATES.

1 pound well-chilled, ultra-fresh skinless halibut (or tuna) fillets, cut into 1/4-inch cubes

2 shallots, trimmed, peeled, and finely minced

1 cup fresh *shiso* (or basil) leaves, cut into a chiffonade

1 ripe avocado, halved, pitted, peeled, and cut into small cubes

3 tablespoons best-quality sesame oil (such as Leblanc), or as needed

1/4 cup cubed Quick Lemon Confit (page 297)

Fleur de sel

2 large heirloom tomatoes, peeled and cut into 3/4-inch-thick slices

Best-quality sherry-wine vinegar, for garnish

1. Place the fish in a large bowl. Add the shallots, *shiso,* and avocado and toss gently. Add just enough sesame oil to lightly coat the tartare, tossing gently. Add the lemon confit and season with the *fleur de sel*, and toss once more.

2. Arrange the tomato slices on the plates. Spoon the tartare on top of the tomatoes. Drizzle with a touch of vinegar, and serve immediately.

   WINE SUGGESTION: I love this with a chilled sake.

COD, HERB, AND POTATO SALAD

We had a variation of this dish one summer afternoon at a favorite neighborhood restaurant in Provence. Later, we began playing with the wholesome, comforting combination of ultra-fresh cod, potatoes, garlic, and milk. This is essentially a brandade *made with fresh rather than dried and salted codfish.*

4 SERVINGS

EQUIPMENT: CHEESECLOTH; A FINE-MESH SIEVE.

1 quart whole milk

1 pound skinned fresh cod (or other firm, white fish fillets), cut into 1-inch cubes

5 plump, moist garlic cloves, peeled, halved, and green germ removed

2 fresh or dried bay leaves

2 fresh thyme sprigs

1 teaspoon whole white peppercorns

2 tablespoons coarse sea salt

1 pound firm, yellow-fleshed potatoes (such as Yukon Gold), peeled and cut into 1-inch cubes

1/2 cup minced fresh parsley leaves

3/4 cup minced fresh chives

8 Cornichons, homemade (page 290) or jarred, cut crosswise into thin rounds

1/3 cup Capers in Vinegar (page 289), drained

Fine sea salt

Coarse, freshly ground white pepper

4 thin slices sourdough bread, toasted, for serving (see page 270)

1. In a large saucepan, combine the milk and the cod. Wrap the garlic, bay leaves, thyme sprigs, and peppercorns in a small piece of cheesecloth and tie it in a bundle. Add the herb bundle to the saucepan. Add the coarse salt. Bring the liquid just to a boil over moderate heat. Reduce the heat and simmer just until the fish flakes easily with a fork, 3 to 4 minutes. Using a slotted spoon, transfer the fish to a large bowl. Reserve the cooking liquid and the herb bundle in the saucepan.

2. Place the potatoes in the reserved cooking liquid and simmer, uncovered, over moderate heat, stirring regularly, until a knife inserted into a potato comes away easily, 15 to 20 minutes. Watch carefully, for the liquid can easily boil over. As soon as the potatoes are cooked, pour them into a sieve set over a large bowl. Reserve the potatoes and cooking liquid separately. Discard the herb bundle.

3. Add the potatoes to the cod in the bowl and toss carefully with the parsley, 1/2 cup of the chives, the cornichons, and the capers. If necessary, moisten with a bit of the cooking liquid. Taste for seasoning. Mound on salad plates, shower with the remaining 1/4 cup chives, and season generously with white pepper. Serve with the toasted sourdough bread.

WINE SUGGESTION: A favorite local white wine comes from the Domaine des Escaravailles, a vineyard set high in the hills above the village of Rasteau. Their white La Galopine is a fabulous blend of 45% Roussanne, 45% Marsanne, and 10% Viognier and is aged lightly in wood.

CRAB SALAD WITH LIME AND AVOCADO

I could easily sample this bright, flavorful salad once a week, and often do. It's low in calories and fat and high in protein, just the right fit for someone who loves to exercise, as I do. It goes together in seconds, making it all that much easier to love. This salad as a meal is a good lesson in salad construction: toss each of the ingredients separately with the dressing so that all parts are evenly and lightly dressed. If the limes in your market are not top-rate and don't have enough peel to make a good zest, opt for organic lemons. Serve this with a slice of toasted bread slathered with Guacamole Light (page 23).

4 SERVINGS
EQUIPMENT: **4 CHILLED LARGE DINNER PLATES**

1 pound (2 cups) fresh cooked lump crabmeat

Grated zest of 2 limes or lemons, preferably organic

1/4 cup Creamy Lemon-Chive Dressing (page 326)

Fine sea salt

Coarse, freshly ground black pepper

1 orange or red bell pepper, trimmed, seeds removed, and minced (1 scant cup)

2 celery ribs, finely minced (about 2 cups)

1/4 cup minced fresh cilantro, chervil, or parsley leaves

1/4 teaspoon Red Hot Salt (page 307) or fine sea salt

1 large ripe avocado, halved, pitted, peeled, and cut into very thin half-rounds

4 thin slices sourdough bread, toasted, for serving (see page 270)

1. In a large bowl, combine the crabmeat and citrus zest and toss with just enough dressing to lightly coat the crabmeat. Taste for seasoning.

2. In another bowl, combine the bell pepper, celery, cilantro, and Red Hot Salt and toss with just enough dressing to lightly coat the vegetables. Taste for seasoning. Combine the contents of the two bowls, mixing gently to blend.

3. Mound the salad in the center of the dinner plates. Arrange the avocado slices around the salads. Serve with the toast.

WINE SUGGESTION: The last time I prepared this salad we had it with a mineral-rich Riesling, the Domaine Ostertag Clos Mathis.

CRAB, AVOCADO, AND QUINOA SALAD WITH TECHNICOLOR TOMATOES

Color and texture play such an important role in our enjoyment of food, and the color combination of pink, white, and green is one that I turn to time after time. This crab salad has it all: it's pretty, tangy, and crunchy all at once. I use an especially hardy variety of tarragon from my garden—called Texas or Mexican tarragon—which grows well in dry climates like those of Texas and Provence. I also like to add a touch of Moroccan mint, a very fragrant form of spearmint that is used to make tea. My selection of fresh cherry tomatoes includes the Green Grape, Red Pear, and yellow Mirabelle. This salad as a meal packs a powerful amount of protein and is very low in fat, making it a household favorite. A cup of Chilled Yogurt, Herb, and Jalapeño Soup (page 42) pairs beautifully with this salad.

6 SERVINGS
EQUIPMENT: **6** CHILLED LARGE DINNER PLATES.

3 cups water, Homemade Chicken Stock (page 310), or Homemade Vegetable Stock (page 312)

1/2 teaspoon fine sea salt

1 cup quinoa, well rinsed

2 fresh or dried bay leaves

1 pound (2 cups) fresh cooked lump crabmeat

1/4 cup minced fresh tarragon leaves

1/2 cup minced fresh mint leaves

1 large ripe avocado, halved, pitted, peeled, and cubed

Yogurt and Lemon Dressing (page 331)

2 cups mixed red, yellow, and green cherry or pear tomatoes, halved

1. In a large saucepan, bring the water or stock to a boil over high heat. Add the salt, quinoa, and bay leaves. Bring back to a boil and then reduce the heat to low, cover the pan, and simmer until the quinoa is tender and translucent, about 15 minutes. (When quinoa is perfectly tender, each grain bursts, sporting a tiny white sprout.) Drain any remaining liquid and return the quinoa to the pan. Cover the pan with a clean dish towel, replace the lid, and let it sit, undisturbed, for 10 minutes. Remove and discard the bay leaves. Fluff. Let cool.

2. Place the cooled quinoa in a large, shallow bowl. Add the crabmeat, tarragon, mint, and avocado. Toss with just enough dressing to coat the ingredients lightly and evenly. In another bowl, toss the tomatoes with just enough dressing to coat them lightly and evenly as well.

3. Mound the quinoa salad on the plates. (Alternatively, place a 4-inch mold at one edge of each plate and spoon a portion of the salad into the mold, pressing down lightly. Remove the mold.) Arrange the tomatoes alongside the quinoa salad, and serve.

WINE SUGGESTION: This salad has a fine complexity, an ideal match for one of my favorite whites in the cellar, the Domaine de la Mordorée Lirac Blanc, a mesmerizing blend of Grenache Blanc, Viognier, Roussanne, Marsanne, Picpoul, Clairette, and Bourboulenc. Mesmerizing, yes, but not confusing. Just a great drinking white!

HALIBUT CHEEKS WITH POLENTA AND PARMESAN CRUST AND ASIAN GREENS

Fish cheeks are extremely tender, tasty morsels. They are light and have a fine, firm texture. In fact, many people consider the cheeks the best part of the fish, due to their concentrated sweetness. The flavor is delicate, and so a minimum of embellishment is called for here. If fish cheeks are not available, the same method can be used with any fresh fish fillets cut into 3-inch squares, or with fresh scallops. In our house in Provence, this is a regular after-the-Tuesday-market salad. I like to serve the fish on a bed of Asian greens from our garden, a flavorful, tender mix of tatsoi, mizuna, and red mustard greens.

4 SERVINGS
EQUIPMENT: A MEDIUM-MESH SIEVE; **4** WARMED DINNER PLATES.

2 large eggs

1/4 cup quick-cooking polenta

1/4 cup freshly grated Parmigiano-Reggiano cheese

1/4 teaspoon ground *piment d'Espelette* or other ground mild chile pepper

4 cups mixed spicy salad greens, such as tatsoi, red mustard, and mizuna

Lemon and Olive Oil Dressing (page 330)

Fleur de sel

8 fish cheeks (preferably halibut, about 1 pound total; see Note)

2 tablespoons extra-virgin olive oil

Fresh lemon wedges, for garnish

1. Break the eggs into the sieve set over a shallow bowl. Press the eggs through the sieve. (This will help make an even-textured coating.) Combine the polenta and cheese in another shallow bowl. Season the polenta mixture with the *piment d'Espelette*.

2. Place the salad greens in a large bowl. Dress with just enough dressing to lightly and evenly coat the greens. Taste for seasoning.

3. Dip the fish cheeks in the egg, and then dredge them in the polenta mixture. Place them on a large plate.

4. In a large skillet, heat the oil over moderate heat. When the oil is hot but not smoking, add the coated fish cheeks and cook until they are golden and cooked through, about 2 minutes per side. Season with *fleur de sel*.

5. Mound the salad on the dinner plates. Arrange 2 fish cheeks on top of each salad. Serve immediately, with the lemon wedges for garnish.

NOTE: Alaskan halibut cheeks can be ordered from Great Alaska Seafood at www.great-alaska-seafood.com or by phone at 866-262-8846. They arrive in 1-pound vacuum-sealed packages.

WINE SUGGESTION: A local winemaker, Gilles Ferran at the Domaine des Escaravailles, with their winemaking facility outside the village of Roaix, makes an astonishing assortment of wines. His white Côtes-du-Rhône La Ponce is a blend of Roussanne, Marsanne, Clairette, and Grenache Blanc grapes and makes a fine partner for this welcoming dish.

HALIBUT SALAD WITH AVOCADO-TOMATILLO SALSA

This is a versatile, quick, and easy salsa that can be tossed with almost any fish or shellfish. I have prepared this salad with raw halibut and other ultra-fresh white fish and with cooked crab. Good choices include Pacific Alaskan halibut, farmed or wild-caught striped bass, and farmed bay scallops. I love the sweet crunch of the tomatillo here, along with the rich smoothness of the avocado.

4 SERVINGS
EQUIPMENT: **4** CHILLED LARGE DINNER PLATES.

1 pound well-chilled, ultra-fresh skinless halibut (or other firm, white fish fillets), cut into 1/2-inch cubes, *or* 1 pound (2 cups) fresh cooked lump crabmeat

1 large ripe avocado, halved, pitted, peeled, and cut into 1/2-inch chunks

2 plum tomatoes, cut into 1/2-inch chunks

1 shallot, trimmed, peeled, and cut into thin rings

1 jalapeño pepper, seeded and minced

3 tomatillos, husked, rinsed, and cut into thin wedges (about 1/2 cup)

1 tablespoon extra-virgin olive oil

1/2 cup minced fresh cilantro

2 tablespoons freshly squeezed lime juice

1/2 teaspoon Lemon Zest Salt (page 306)

In a large bowl, combine all the ingredients, tossing gently to blend. Taste for seasoning. Arrange on the dinner plates and serve.

WINE SUGGESTION: Denis Alary in the village of Cairanne makes outstanding wines: a favorite is his 100% Roussanne, called La Grange Daniel, with a perfect balance of fruit and acid.

LOBSTER SALAD WITH GREEN BEANS, APPLE, AND AVOCADO

I first sampled a version of this light and lively salad as a meal at chef Yves Camdeborde's Le Comptoir in Paris's 6th arrondissement. Yves and I participated in the New York marathon in 2006, and I am sure that the strength gained from this protein-rich salad helped me make it to the finish line! This dish has it all: color (the red bits are lobster roe), crunch, and a light touch imparted by a dressing of yogurt and mustard.

4 SERVINGS

EQUIPMENT: A 5-QUART PASTA POT FITTED WITH A COLANDER;
4 CHILLED LARGE DINNER PLATES.

3 tablespoons coarse sea salt

10 ounces slim *haricots verts* (green beans), trimmed at both ends and cut into 1/2-inch pieces
    (2 cups)

1 cup Greek-style yogurt

1 tablespoon imported French mustard

1/4 teaspoon fine sea salt

1/4 cup minced fresh chives

1 Granny Smith apple, cored, and cut into 1/4-inch cubes (do not peel)

1 large ripe avocado, halved, pitted, peeled, and cut into 1/4-inch cubes

1 pound (2 cups) cooked lobster meat, cut into bite-sized pieces

1. Prepare a large bowl of ice water.

2. Fill the pasta pot with 3 quarts of water and bring it to a rolling boil over high heat. Add the coarse salt and the beans, and blanch until crisp-tender, 3 to 4 minutes. (Cooking time will vary according to the size and tenderness of the beans.)

Immediately remove the colander from the water, letting the water drain from the beans. Plunge the beans into the ice water so they cool down as quickly as possible. (The beans will cool in 1 to 2 minutes. If you leave them longer, they will become soggy and begin to lose flavor.) Drain the beans and wrap them in a thick kitchen towel to dry. (Store the cooked beans in the refrigerator for up to 4 hours.)

3. In a large, shallow bowl, combine the yogurt, mustard, and fine salt and whisk to blend. Taste for seasoning. Add the green beans, chives, apple, avocado, and lobster. Toss to coat. Arrange on the plates and serve.

WINE SUGGESTION: A fine Chardonnay is in order here, such as a dependable Burgundy, like the well-priced and well-made Viré Clessé from the Cave de Viré, particularly their Cuvée Les Acacias, with its hints of fresh apples and honey.

HOME-SMOKED MACKEREL

Mackerel gets a bad rap: some people find it too strong, many don't want to deal with the bones, and most have little idea what to do with this eco-friendly fish, which is cheap, nutritious, and delicious when prepared with care and attention. I love to smoke fresh mackerel in a little stovetop smoker, a process that is quick and easy. Serve this with a homemade potato salad alongside.

4 SERVINGS

EQUIPMENT: A SCISSORS; **1** TABLESPOON ALDER WOOD CHIPS; A STOVETOP SMOKER.

4 very fresh whole king or Spanish mackerel (each about 10 ounces)

Several tablespoons imported French mustard (either coarse-grain or flavored with peppers, spices, herbs, or lemon)

Coarse, freshly ground black pepper

1 recipe Potato Salad with Capers, Spring Onions, and Mint (recipe follows)

1. Clean the mackerel: Rinse them under cold running water, rubbing gently to remove any scales. Gently twist the head off each fish, pulling the guts with it, and discard. With scissors, gently cut the fish open from the back side, head to tail, and press it open like a book. With your fingertips, gently pull up the central bone from head to tail, being careful not to tear the flesh. With the scissors, gently detach the bone from the flesh, leaving the tail intact. Discard the bone. Open the fish flat but do not cut it into fillets.

2. Place the fish, skin side down, on a platter, keeping them open like a book. Slather the flesh with the mustard. Season with pepper. Close the fish fillets to enclose the mustard. Cover with plastic wrap and refrigerate to marinate for up to 4 hours.

3. Place the wood chips in a small pile in the center of the smoker base. Place the drip tray on top of the wood chips inside the smoker base. Arrange the wire rack on top of the drip tray. Place the whole fish, side by side, on top of the wire rack. Slide the lid closed.

4. Set the entire unit on a burner over moderate heat. Counting from the time you place the smoker on the burner, smoke for 15 minutes. Remove the unit from the heat and open the lid. The fish should flake when touched with a fork.

5. Serve warm or at room temperature, within an hour or two of cooking, accompanied by the potato salad.

NOTE: Camerons smokers and alder wood chips are available from my Amazon Store at PatriciaWells.com.

WINE SUGGESTION: Smoked mackerel destroys wine; instead, try a good lager, chilled vodka, or a Manzanilla sherry.

POTATO SALAD WITH CAPERS, SPRING ONIONS, AND MINT

A decades-old caper bush is my pride and joy in our Provençal garden. If you live in a Mediterranean climate, by all means try growing one. They are the devil to get started, but once they begin producing, they'll keep on giving for months on end. On a very good day, I can collect enough capers for a tiny jarful, and it makes me feel like the wealthiest woman in the world! This favorite family salad appears on our table with great frequency, since it's versatile and seems at home with all sorts of fare, especially smoked foods.

4 SERVINGS
EQUIPMENT: A STEAMER.

1 pound firm, yellow-fleshed potatoes (such as Yukon Gold)

1 quart water

1/4 cup extra-virgin olive oil

2 tablespoons freshly squeezed lemon juice

1 tablespoon imported French mustard

6 small spring onions or scallions, white part only, trimmed, peeled, and thinly sliced

1/4 cup Capers in Vinegar (page 289), drained

Fine sea salt

1/4 cup fresh mint leaves, cut into a chiffonade

1. Scrub the potatoes but do not peel them. Bring the water to a simmer in the bottom of a steamer. Place the potatoes on the steaming rack. Place the rack over the simmering water, cover, and steam just until the potatoes are fully cooked, about 25 minutes.

2. Meanwhile, prepare the dressing: In a large salad bowl, combine the oil, lemon juice, and mustard and whisk to blend. Add the spring onions and capers, and toss to blend. Taste for seasoning.

3. Once the potatoes are cooked, cut them crosswise into thin slices. Add the potatoes directly to the dressing while they are still warm (so they will absorb the dressing). Toss to thoroughly coat the potatoes with the dressing. Add the mint chiffonade and toss again. Taste for seasoning. Serve warm.

Uncured capers, fresh from the caper bush

MACKEREL MARINATED IN WHITE WINE

I love anything with a touch of vinegar and fresh herbs, and these marinated mackerel find their way to our table often.

6 SERVINGS

EQUIPMENT: A **9** X **13**-INCH GLASS OR
CERAMIC BAKING DISH.

6 very fresh whole king or Spanish mackerel (each about 10 ounces), heads removed, gutted, boned, and filleted (see page 134, step 1)

Marinade

2 teaspoons fine sea salt

1 bottle (750 ml) dry white wine

1/2 cup white-wine vinegar

4 shallots, trimmed, peeled, and cut into thin rounds

2 carrots, trimmed, peeled, and thinly sliced

2 celery ribs, cut crosswise into thin slices

4 fresh or dried bay leaves

3 whole cloves

10 whole black peppercorns

2 fresh thyme sprigs

Fresh oregano leaves, for garnish

1 recipe Potato Salad with Capers, Spring Onions, and Mint (page 136)

1. Arrange the mackerel fillets side by side, skin side down, in the baking dish.

2. Prepare the marinade: In a large saucepan, combine all the marinade ingredients and bring to a boil over high heat. Reduce the heat to low and simmer just until the vegetables are tender, about 20 minutes. Immediately pour the hot marinade over the mackerel, spreading the vegetables in an even layer. Cover tightly with plastic wrap and let cool to room temperature. Refrigerate overnight. (Store the marinated mackerel in an airtight container in the refrigerator for up to 2 days.)

3. Transfer the mackerel fillets to plates, skin side up. Top with some of the vegetables and a drizzle of the marinade. Garnish with the oregano leaves. Serve with the potato salad.

WINE SUGGESTION: Here sample a touch of gin or aquavit, or a nice cold beer.

MUSSEL *TARTINES* WITH CHORIZO, TOMATOES, AND BASIL

My friend Todd Murray, the jazz singer, e-mailed me one day in July and asked for a mussel salad recipe. His timing was perfect, for in France the mussel season opens around the first of July. My first thought was to create a mussel bread salad, along the lines of the Italian specialty. That didn't work, but this version—an open-faced sandwich, or tartine—hit the target. All the flavors of summer are here, including tomatoes and fresh basil, and all are enhanced by a generous hit of spicy salt and the rich and pleasing chorizo sausage. The blend stands up beautifully to the deep golden-orange mussels.

4 SERVINGS
EQUIPMENT: A LARGE, FINE-MESH SIEVE;
DAMPENED CHEESECLOTH.

2 pounds fresh mussels

1 tablespoon extra-virgin olive oil

2 onions, peeled, halved crosswise, and thinly sliced crosswise

1/2 teaspoon fine sea salt

1/2 cup dry white wine

Freshly ground black pepper

3 cups cubed heirloom tomatoes

1 cup fresh basil leaves, chopped if large

1/2 teaspoon Red Hot Salt (page 307)

6 ounces smoked chorizo, skin removed, cut in half lengthwise and then into 1/2-inch-thick half-moons

4 thin slices sourdough bread, toasted (see page 270)

1. Thoroughly scrub the mussels and rinse them with several changes of water. If an open mussel closes when you press on it, it is good; if it stays open, the mussel should be discarded. Beard the mussels. (Do not beard the mussels more than a few minutes in advance or they will die and spoil. Note that in some markets mussels are pre-prepared, in that the small black beard that hangs from the mussel has been clipped off but not entirely removed. These mussels do not need further attention.)

2. In a large saucepan, combine the oil, onions, and fine sea salt and stir to blend. Sweat—cook, covered, over low heat until soft and translucent—for about 3 minutes. Add the wine. Bring to a boil and cook, uncovered, for 5 minutes. Add the mussels, cover, and cook just until they open, about 5 minutes. Do not overcook. Discard any mussels that do not open. Place the sieve over a bowl and line it with several layers of the dampened cheesecloth. Transfer the mussels and liquid to the cheesecloth-lined sieve to strain the liquid. Reserve the mussels and liquid separately.

3. Carefully shell the mussels, placing them in a large bowl and discarding the shells. To the mussels in the bowl, add plenty of freshly ground black pepper, the tomatoes, basil, seasoned salt, and chorizo. Coat with just enough of the reserved strained liquid to moisten all the ingredients. Toss to blend. Taste for seasoning.

4. Mound the mixture on the toast, and serve.

WINE SUGGESTION: Mussels call out for a fine, well-chilled Muscadet-sur-Lie, the crisp white made near the city of Nantes on France's Atlantic coast. Try a young Château de Cleary, Réserve Haute Culture, made from the Melon de Bourgogne grape, a wine from flinty and clay-rich soils that offers a touch of salinity. It's a great match for mussels.

SALMON AND AVOCADO TARTARE WITH CUCUMBER RIBBONS

I could eat raw or quickly marinated fish several times a week, and do! This is the sort of salad as a meal we enjoy at lunch as well as dinner, for it is light and comes together quickly with a minimum of fuss and just a few ingredients.

4 SERVINGS
EQUIPMENT: A VEGETABLE PEELER OR A MANDOLINE;
4 CHILLED LARGE DINNER PLATES.

1 large European or hothouse cucumber (about 1 pound), peeled

Lemon and Olive Oil Dressing (page 330)

1 pound well-chilled, ultra-fresh skinless salmon fillets, cut into 1/2-inch cubes

1 large ripe avocado, halved, pitted, peeled, and cut into 1/2-inch cubes

Grated zest of 1 lime, preferable organic

Fleur de sel

Coarse, freshly ground black pepper

4 thin slices sourdough bread, toasted, for serving (see page 270)

1. With the vegetable peeler or mandoline, slice the cucumber lengthwise into thin ribbons. Arrange them in a bowl and coat with the dressing, reserving some dressing for the salmon and avocado.

2. In a large bowl, combine the salmon, avocado, and lime zest. Toss with enough dressing to lightly coat the ingredients. Season with *fleur de sel* and pepper.

3. Mound the cucumber ribbons on the plates. Arrange the salmon and avocado mixture on top. Serve with the toast.

   WINE SUGGESTION: A lively Chardonnay, such as a Chablis from Jean-Claude Bessin, loves the company of salmon and avocado.

SALMON AND HALIBUT TARTARE
WITH FENNEL, CHIVES, AVOCADO,
AND PISTACHIO OIL

One sunny weekday in September, I accompanied students from our Provence cooking school to a wine tasting in Fabrice Langlois and Michel Granier-Poncet's wonderful wine bistro, Vinoe & Co, in Avignon. They offered this stunning first course, a variation on the usual tartare. The chef set the colorful salmon and halibut mix on a bed of braised fennel, offering a pleasant crunch and an appealing variety of textures. If you can, use the pistachio oil here, for it marries beautifully with the richness of avocado.

4 SERVINGS
EQUIPMENT: **4** CHILLED LARGE DINNER PLATES;
A **4**-INCH-RING MOLD (OPTIONAL).

1 large bulb fennel, trimmed and cut into thin slices

2 tablespoons extra-virgin olive oil

1/2 teaspoon fine sea salt

8 ounces well-chilled, ultra-fresh skinless Pacific halibut fillet, cut into 1/4-inch cubes

8 ounces well-chilled, ultra-fresh skinless salmon fillet, cut into 1/4-inch cubes

2 scallions or 1 small spring onion, white part only, trimmed, peeled, and cut into thin rings

1/2 cup finely minced fresh chives

1/2 cup fresh basil leaves, cut into a chiffonnade

1 large ripe avocado, halved, pitted, peeled, and cut into 1/4-inch cubes

About 1 tablespoon best-quality pistachio oil (such as Leblanc) or extra-virgin olive oil

Fleur de sel

1. In a small skillet, combine the fennel, olive oil, and the salt. Sweat—cook, covered, over low heat until soft and translucent—for about 8 minutes. Drain, and divide among the plates.

2. Place the halibut and salmon in a large bowl. Add the scallions, chives, basil, and avocado. Add just enough pistachio oil to lightly coat the tartare, tossing gently. Season with *fleur de sel* and toss once more. Mound the tartare on top of the braised fennel. (Or place a mold over the fennel and spoon a portion of the tartare into the center of the mold, pressing down lightly. Remove the mold.) Serve.

WINE SUGGESTION: That day, Fabrice and Michel served the almost creamy-textured Sancerre from François Cotat, with enough minerality and fruit to marry beautifully with the fish duo, herbs, and vegetables here.

RAINBOW TROUT SALAD WITH STURGEON ROE

American rainbow trout is farm-raised, most of it in Idaho and generally in an ecologically responsible way. It is underutilized and a delicious source of high-quality protein, so weave it into your repertoire whenever you can. Domestic sturgeon farming has also grown steadily in the past few years, and sturgeon roe is a ready substitute for the partially banned imported sturgeon roe, or caviar.

4 SERVINGS
EQUIPMENT: **4** CHILLED SALAD PLATES.

1 pound well-chilled, ultra-fresh American-farmed rainbow trout fillets, cut into 1/4-inch cubes

3 tablespoons freshly squeezed lime juice

Fine sea salt

1 shallot, trimmed, peeled, and minced

2 ounces sturgeon roe

Grated zest of 2 limes, preferably organic

6 fresh chervil or flat-leaf parsley sprigs, minced

4 thin slices sourdough bread, toasted, for serving (see page 270)

1. Spread the cubed trout on a large plate. Drizzle with the lime juice and season with fine sea salt. Add the shallot and toss gently to blend. Cover with plastic wrap and refrigerate for 1 hour.

2. Mound the trout salad on the salad plates. Carefully spoon the sturgeon roe on top of the trout. Garnish with the lime zest and chervil. Serve with the toast.

WINE SUGGESTION: A chilled, crisp Sauvignon Blanc would be my choice here.

BRAISED SALMON WITH CUCUMBER RIBBONS, HERB SALAD, AND GINGER DRESSING

Salmon, cucumbers, and ginger make a perfect triumvirate, combining color, crunch, and a good hint of spice. This is a salad we often turn into a light, refreshing meal, enjoying a crisp white wine and some freshly toasted country bread on the side.

4 SERVINGS
EQUIPMENT: A SMALL JAR WITH A LID; TWEEZERS;
A VEGETABLE PEELER OR A MANDOLINE.

Ginger dressing

1 lemongrass stalk

1/4 cup extra-virgin olive oil

2 tablespoons Japanese brown rice vinegar

1 teaspoon sugar

1 tablespoon finely grated fresh ginger

1 tablespoon tamari or other Japanese soy sauce, or to taste

Cucumber ribbons

1 large European or hothouse cucumber (about 1 pound)

Herb salad

1/2 cup fresh mint leaves

1/2 cup fresh cilantro leaves

1/2 cup fresh basil leaves

Salmon

1 pound salmon fillet, skin intact

2 cups dry white wine or water

Several rosemary sprigs, fennel fronds, or lemongrass stalks

1. Prepare the dressing: Trim the ends of the lemongrass, remove and discard the outer layers, and mince the pale heart. Place the minced lemongrass in the small jar, and add the oil, vinegar, sugar, ginger, and tamari. Cover and shake to blend. Taste for seasoning.

2. Prepare the cucumber ribbons: Peel the cucumber, and use the vegetable peeler or mandoline to slice it lengthwise into thin ribbons. Place the ribbons in a small bowl and drizzle generously with the ginger dressing, reserving some dressing for the herb salad. Toss to evenly coat the cucumbers with dressing.

3. Prepare the herb salad: In a small bowl, combine the herbs and toss with the remaining dressing. Taste for seasoning.

4. Prepare the salmon: Run your fingers over the top of the salmon fillet to detect any tiny bones that remain. Use tweezers to remove the bones. Cut the salmon into equal 4-ounce portions.

5. In a large skillet, bring the wine to a boil over high heat and cook until reduced by half. Reduce the heat to a simmer, and add the rosemary, fennel, or lemongrass. Place the fish on top of the herbs, cover, and braise gently until the fish is cooked through, about 6 minutes. Remove the skillet from the heat and let rest while assembling the salad.

6. Divide the cucumber ribbons among large dinner plates. Gently flake the salmon into large pieces and arrange on top of the cucumbers. Top with the herb salad, and serve.

WINE SUGGESTION: This simple salad pairs nicely with a light white from the Loire Valley, such as the 100% Sauvignon Blanc Menetou-Salon from the Domaine Philippe Gilbert.

SALMON GRAVLAX WITH POTATO AND PARMESAN GALETTES

This simple and delicious cured salmon is actually halfway between sushi and a traditional salt and sugar–cured gravlax. If you prefer your salmon on the sushi side, you can dine on this within 3 or 4 hours of preparation. For a firmer, gravlax-like texture and flavor, give it a 24-hour cure. We enjoy this dish with crispy, golden Potato and Parmesan Galettes, and it also comes in handy as a quick and easy appetizer: arrange thin slices of the gravlax on Tortilla Chips (page 263). I love the hit of white pepper here, a distinctive flavor with the right level of pungency.

4 SERVINGS
EQUIPMENT: TWEEZERS; A SHARP, FLEXIBLE KNIFE.

Two 12-ounce salmon fillets, skin intact

1/4 cup finely chopped fresh dill leaves

3 tablespoons coarse sea salt

1 tablespoon sugar

1 tablespoon coarse, freshly ground white pepper

1 recipe Potato and Parmesan Galettes (recipe follows)

1. Run your fingers over the top of the salmon fillets to detect any tiny bones that remain. Use tweezers to remove the bones.

2. In a small bowl, combine the dill, salt, sugar, and pepper. Sprinkle this over the salmon fillets. Place the fillets flesh to flesh and wrap securely in several layers of plastic wrap. Place on a platter. Cover with a brick or heavy cutting board and refrigerate for at least 3 hours and up to 2 days, turning every 12 hours and discarding any excess liquid.

3. Remove the salmon from the marinade, and with the sharp, flexible knife, cut into paper-thin slices. Serve with the galettes.

WINE SUGGESTION: This gravlax is delicious with a tiny, ice-cold glass of aquavit.

Salmon Gravlax, Potato and Parmesan Galettes, and a simple cucumber salad

POTATO AND PARMESAN GALETTES

Many an evening we prepare these golden, tasty potato galettes for dinner, ready to accompany a lush green salad and a few slices of home-cured gravlax or smoked salmon. The touch of Parmesan adds richness and color as well as texture.

4 SERVINGS
EQUIPMENT: A BOX GRATER;
A 12-INCH CREPE PAN OR A LARGE SKILLET;
A LARGE SPATULA.

1 pound yellow-fleshed potatoes (such as Yukon Gold), peeled

2 large eggs

3 tablespoons whole wheat flour

2 tablespoons minced fresh chives

2 tablespoons freshly grated Parmigiano-Reggiano cheese

Fine sea salt

1 tablespoon extra-virgin olive oil

Freshly ground black pepper

Capers in Vinegar (page 289), drained, for garnish

Fresh dill sprigs, for garnish

1. Using the largest holes of the box grater, coarsely grate the potatoes. Wrap the potatoes in a thick kitchen towel, pressing hard to extract all the liquid and to completely dry them.

2. Break the eggs into a large bowl and beat lightly. Add the flour, chives, cheese, and 1 teaspoon salt. Whisk to blend. Add the potatoes and stir to coat them evenly with the egg mixture.

3. Warm the crepe pan for a few seconds over high heat. Then add the oil and heat until it is hot but not smoking. Reduce to moderate heat. Drop one-fourth of the potato mixture into the pan and flatten it with the spatula to form an even galette, about 4 inches in diameter. Cook on one side until crisp and golden, 2 to 3 minutes. Flip the galette and cook on the other side until crisp and golden, 2 to 3 minutes. Season with salt and pepper. Serve warm, garnished with capers and fresh dill.

HOME-SMOKED TROUT, TARRAGON, AND CUCUMBER SALAD WITH HORSERADISH CREAM

I find a small stovetop home smoker to be essential in my kitchen and on average smoke fish, shellfish, or poultry once a week for a very quick, carefree salad meal. I make this dish with the traditional dill as well as tarragon. A particular variety of tarragon known as Mexican tarragon grows well in dry climates and has a fine, smooth, peppery taste.

4 SERVINGS

EQUIPMENT: A STOVE-TOP SMOKER; **1** TABLESPOON ALDER WOOD CHIPS; A SMALL JAR WITH A LID; **4** CHILLED LARGE DINNER PLATES.

4 whole American farm-raised rainbow trout, cleaned and gutted

5 tablespoons finely minced fresh tarragon (or dill)

Fine sea salt

Freshly ground black pepper

1/2 cup light cream

2 tablespoons freshly squeezed lemon juice

1 tablespoon prepared horseradish

1 European or hothouse cucumber, trimmed and cut into thin rounds

4 scallions or small spring onions, white part only, trimmed, peeled, and cut into thin rings

Zest of 1 lemon, preferably organic

1. Arrange the wood chips in a small pile in the center of the smoker base. Place the drip tray on top of the wood chips inside the smoker base. Arrange the wire rack on top of the drip tray. Stuff the cavity of each trout with 1/2 tablespoon of the

tarragon, and season with salt and pepper. Place the trout side by side on top of the wire rack. Slide the lid closed.

2. Set the entire unit on the burner over moderate heat. Counting from the time you place the smoker on the burner, smoke for 15 minutes. Remove from the heat and open the lid. The fish should flake when touched with a fork. Fillet the trout and break it into small flaked pieces.

3. Meanwhile, prepare the dressing: In the small jar, combine the cream, lemon juice, 1/2 teaspoon salt, the horseradish, and 2 tablespoons of the remaining tarragon. Cover and shake to blend.

4. Place the cucumbers and scallions in a large, shallow bowl. Toss with half of the dressing. Toss the flaked trout with the remaining 1 tablespoon tarragon and the remaining dressing. Arrange the cucumbers on the plates. Place the dressed trout alongside. Garnish with the lemon zest. Serve.

NOTE: Camerons smokers and alder wood chips are available from my Amazon Store on PatriciaWells.com.

VARIATION: In the summer, add slices of slightly under-ripe Evergreen or Green Zebra tomatoes.

WINE SUGGESTION: Home-smoked trout has a very delicately smoky flavor, one that marries well with a young, light white. My choice is a Burgundian Aligoté, particularly one from Aubert de Villaine. His is considered the greatest example of wine made from the Aligoté grape and offers a fine balance of acid and fruit, perfect for this light fish salad.

SARDINE *TARTINES* WITH HERB SPREAD, TOMATOES, AND MIXED GREENS

This bright-flavored tartine, *or open-faced sandwich, can be prepared with either fresh or canned sardines with equal enjoyment. The blast of sharp herb spread is an instant wake-up call, and the saltiness of the fish and crunch of the toast make for a delightful salad as a meal. Just add a glass of white wine and, if available, a glistening sunset!*

8 SERVINGS

EQUIPMENT: A FOOD PROCESSOR OR A BLENDER.

A handful of mixed fresh sharp herb leaves, such as coriander, fennel, basil, and tarragon

2 tablespoons oil drained from canned sardines (or extra-virgin olive oil)

2 shallots, trimmed, peeled, halved, and minced

3 tablespoons extra-virgin olive oil

Fine sea salt

Freshly ground black pepper

8 whole sardines, filleted (see Note), or 2 tins top-quality sardine fillets packed in olive oil

8 slices Multigrain Sourdough Bread (page 270), toasted

16 thin slices ripe heirloom tomatoes

Fresh fennel fronds or parsley leaves, for garnish

About 4 cups mixed salad greens

Classic Vinaigrette (page 324) or dressing of choice

1. Prepare the herb spread: In the food processor or blender, combine the herbs and the sardine oil. Puree. Transfer to a small bowl.

2. In a small bowl, combine the shallots, olive oil, 1 teaspoon coarse salt, and pepper to taste. Toss to blend. Place the sardine fillets, skin side down, on a flat, shallow dish.

Scatter with the shallot mixture. (Store the sardines, covered, in the refrigerator for up to 8 hours.)

3. Spread the toasts with the herb spread. Arrange the tomato slices on top, and season with salt and pepper. Place 2 sardine fillets, skin side up, on top of the tomatoes. Garnish with the fennel fronds or parsley. In a large bowl, toss the mixed greens with just enough dressing to coat the ingredients lightly and evenly. Arrange the dressed mixed greens alongside, and serve.

NOTE: To clean fresh sardines, first rinse them under cold running water, rubbing the scales off. Twist the heads off, pulling the guts with them, and discard. With your fingertips, press down on the belly side, pressing each sardine open like a book. Gently pull up the central bone from head to tail, being careful not to tear the flesh. With scissors, detach the bone from the flesh. Discard the bone. Open the sardine flat. Cut each one into 2 fillets.

WINE SUGGESTION: A nice white loves sardines. Try a crispy Muscadet-sur-Lie, from the Melon de Bourgogne grape.

SCALLOP CARPACCIO WITH LIME AND VANILLA DRESSING AND ASIAN GREENS

I am the sort of person who craves raw food. Even during the bitterest winter season, I find that I could live on raw fish and shellfish almost exclusively. This brightly flavored dish is enlivened by the mysterious flavors of lime, vanilla, and olive oil. It's a dream, particularly when paired with forward-flavored greens such as mizuna, tatsoi, and red mustard. As an alternative to the scallops, one could use fresh red snapper, sea bass, or cod.

4 SERVINGS
EQUIPMENT: 4 CHILLED LARGE DINNER PLATES;
A SHARP, FLEXIBLE KNIFE.

Lime and Vanilla Dressing (page 329)

Fine sea salt

1 pound well-chilled, ultra-fresh sea scallops (or skinless, firm white fish fillets)

4 cups mixed Asian salad greens, such as mizuna, tatsoi, and red mustard

1. Drizzle each plate with a thin layer of dressing. Sprinkle very lightly with fine sea salt.

2. Gently rinse the scallops and pat dry with paper towels. Remove and discard the little muscle on the side of each scallop. With a very sharp knife (a flexible fish boning knife is ideal here), cut the scallops horizontally into 1/8-inch-thick slices. (The diameter of the pieces is not so important, but the thinness is.) Arrange the scallop slices, overlapping slightly, in a circle around the edge of each plate. Drizzle once more with the dressing. Season very lightly with salt.

3. In a large bowl, toss the greens with just enough dressing to lightly and evenly coat them. Mound the dressed greens in the center of the plates, and serve.

WINE SUGGESTION: With this delicate touch of vanilla, I enjoy a chilled dry Chenin Blanc, such as a young Vouvray Sec from Champalou, with overtones of quince, orange, and lime.

SCALLOP CEVICHE WITH SMOKED TROUT, TROUT EGGS, AND TANGY LIME CREAM

When ultra-fresh scallops can be found in the market, go for them and create this tangy and light salad as a meal: Scallops are simply halved horizontally and quickly marinated in a creamy lime-chive dressing. The scallops are then arranged on top of slices of top-quality smoked trout or salmon and garnished with colorful trout or salmon eggs. Be sure to toast plenty of rye bread to go with it!

4 SERVINGS
EQUIPMENT: A SMALL JAR WITH A LID;
A DEMITASSE SPOON; **4** CHILLED DINNER PLATES.

1 tablespoon freshly squeezed lime juice

1/4 teaspoon fine sea salt

1/2 cup light cream

2 tablespoons finely minced fresh chives

12 large, well-chilled, ultra-fresh sea scallops (1 1/2 to 2 inches)

8 slices (about 12 ounces) smoked trout or smoked salmon

2 tablespoons trout or salmon eggs

Grated zest of 1 lime, preferably organic

4 slices rye bread, toasted, for serving

1. In the jar, combine the lime juice and salt. Shake to dissolve the salt. Add the cream and chives. Tighten the lid and shake to blend. Taste for seasoning. (Store in the jar in the refrigerator for up to 3 days. Reblend at serving time.)

2. Gently and lightly rinse the scallops and pat them dry with paper towels. Remove and discard the little muscle on the side of each scallop. Cut each scallop in half

horizontally. Place in a shallow bowl and coat lightly with the lime-chive dressing, tossing gently. (Store the scallops, covered, in the refrigerator for up to 30 minutes.)

3. On each dinner plate, arrange 2 slices of smoked trout. Arrange the dressed scallops on top of the fish. Garnish with the fish eggs and lime zest. Serve immediately, with toast.

WINE SUGGESTION: I think that the elegance of scallops deserves a wine of the same stature, so I enjoy a young white Burgundy with these delicate shellfish. A favorite is the Macon Milly-Lamartine, Clos du Four, made by Domaine des Héritiers du Comte Lafon. The wine is clean, neat, elegant, and mineral-rich with just a light touch of oak.

MARINATED SHRIMP SALAD

This is one of our favorite and most beautiful seafood salads; it can be prepared in a matter of minutes. The cooked shrimp is added to the flavorful marinade while still warm, allowing it to absorb the maximum amount of flavor.

4 SERVINGS

EQUIPMENT: A **5**-QUART PASTA POT FITTED WITH A COLANDER.

3 small spring onions or scallions, white part only, trimmed, peeled, and cut into thin rings

3 tablespoons Capers in Vinegar (page 289), drained

2 plump, moist garlic cloves, peeled, halved, green germ removed, and minced

1/4 cup freshly squeezed lemon juice

1/2 cup extra-virgin olive oil

3 tablespoons coarse sea salt

2 pounds (30 to 40) raw large shrimp, peeled and deveined

1 teaspoon Lemon Zest Salt (page 306)

4 thin slices Multigrain Sourdough Bread (page 270), toasted, for serving

1. In a large, shallow bowl, combine the spring onions, capers, garlic, lemon juice, and olive oil.

2. Fill the pasta pot with 3 quarts of water and bring it to a rolling boil over high heat. Add the coarse salt and the shrimp, and cook just until the shrimp are pink, about 30 seconds. Drain and immediately transfer to the marinade.

3. Arrange the shrimp and the marinade on dinner plates. Season with the Lemon Zest Salt. Serve with the toasted bread.

VARIATIONS: Each time I make this salad, I change it a bit. One can add cubed celery, chopped parsley, fennel seeds, or cubes of Quick Lemon Confit (page 297) to the cooked shrimp. For an all-lemon salad of marinated shrimp, add lemon zest, Lemon Zest Salt, lemon confit, and chopped fresh lemon verbena and/or finely minced lemongrass.

WINE SUGGESTION: I am a big fan of Chablis and feel its elegance and distinctive, flinty character are a good match for this salad with the same qualities. A favorite comes from the vineyards of Christian Moreau, who makes a generic AOC that is well priced and offers the proper Chablis flintiness.

RAOUL'S SHRIMP SALAD

Think of this as a modern shrimp cocktail, enlivened by a touch of fresh chives or cilantro. Protein-rich and a snap to prepare, this recipe comes from Raoul Reichrath, chef and owner of one of our favorite haunts in Provence, his Michelin-starred Le Grand Pré, in Roaix.

4 SERVINGS
EQUIPMENT: **4** CHILLED LARGE DINNER PLATES.

1/2 cup tomato juice

1 tablespoon freshly squeezed lemon juice

2 teaspoons Worcestershire sauce

Several drops Tabasco sauce

Fine sea salt

1 to 2 red bell peppers, trimmed, seeds removed, cut into 1/4-inch cubes (about 1 1/2 cups)

2 celery ribs, cut into crosswise slices (about 1 1/2 cups)

1 1/2 pounds (25 to 30) cooked large shrimp, peeled and deveined

1/2 cup minced fresh chives or cilantro

1. In a large bowl, whisk together the tomato juice, lemon juice, Worcestershire sauce, Tabasco, and salt. Taste for seasoning. Add the red peppers and celery. Stir to blend. Cover and refrigerate for at least 1 hour to let the flavors develop.

2. Toss the shrimp with just enough sauce to lightly and evenly coat the ingredients. Add the chives and toss to blend. Taste for seasoning. Mound the shrimp salad on plates, and serve.

WINE SUGGESTION: Raoul's wife, Flora, is the hostess and sommelier at Le Grand Pré. She introduced us to one of our favorite local white wines—Domaine Chaume-Arnaud's La Cadène Vinsobres Blanc, an atypical blend of 50% Viognier and 50% Marsanne. This white wine has the vivacity and complexity to stand up to the pungent flavors in this dish.

WARM ASIAN SHRIMP SALAD WITH KAFFIR LIME DUST

This warm Asian salad uses three favored items from my garden in Provence: kaffir lime leaves, jalapeño peppers, and limes. Now I just need a coconut tree and a fish pond for growing shrimp! This is a quick, easy, no-fuss salad that is put together quickly and offers big-time flavor rewards. A best choice is U.S. shrimp farmed in a closed system or inland ponds. A good alternative is wild-caught shrimp from the south Atlantic; these are usually marketed as white shrimp, brown shrimp, pink shrimp, or rock shrimp.

2 SERVINGS

2 teaspoons vegetable oil

2 plump, moist garlic cloves, peeled, halved, green germ removed, and minced

2 tablespoons grated fresh ginger

1 pound (15 to 20) raw large shrimp, peeled and deveined

1/2 teaspoon freshly ground toasted cumin seeds

1 fresh red bird's-eye chile, finely chopped

6 fresh kaffir lime leaves, chopped and ground to a powder in a spice mill (1 teaspoon)

1 tablespoon Vietnamese fish sauce, preferably Phu Quoc brand

1/3 cup unsweetened coconut milk

2 tablespoons freshly squeezed lime juice

1/3 cup fresh cilantro leaves, finely minced

Lime wedges, for garnish

1. In a large skillet, heat the oil over high heat until it just begins to smoke. Reduce the heat to medium-high and stir in the garlic and ginger. Add the shrimp and cumin, and sauté until the shrimp turns pink around the edges, about 2 minutes. Stir in the chile and the lime dust. Stir in the fish sauce and coconut milk. Bring the mixture to a boil over medium-high heat; then reduce the heat and simmer for 1 minute. Stir in the lime juice, and taste for seasoning.

2. Transfer to small plates, shower with the cilantro, and serve with the lime wedges.

WINE SUGGESTION: Asian restaurants all over France keep a fine stock of Tavel rosé in their cellars, and for a good reason: it has enough fruit and acid to stand up to the more forward-flavored Asian dishes. My favorite vineyard there is Domaine de la Mordorée, and their Tavel, to my mind, is the best in the world.

DEEP-FRIED FLATFISH: *GOUJONNETTES* WITH PARSLEY SALAD

These delicate little strips of breaded and fried fish have been called highbrow fish sticks, and I guess they are. Goujons *are actually tiny river fish that were once abundant in the Seine and Marne rivers outside of Paris. The little fried fish were a popular dish served at outdoor waterside restaurants known as* guinguettes. *Today the term* goujonnettes *is generally applied to fillets of any small, firm flatfish that are breaded and deep-fried. We love to make a meal out of these, accompanied by lemon wedges, homemade Sauce Rémoulade, and a nicely dressed parsley salad.*

4 SERVINGS

EQUIPMENT: A SHARP, FLEXIBLE KNIFE; AN ELECTRIC DEEP-FAT FRYER; A WIRE SKIMMER; A TRAY; A MEDIUM-MESH SIEVE.

1 pound whole sole (or any firm, white-fleshed fish, such as flounder, trout, or perch)

Vegetable oil for deep frying

1/4 cup superfine flour (such as Wondra)

3 large eggs

1 cup (4 ounces) dry breadcrumbs

2 tablespoons finely grated Parmigiano-Reggiano cheese

1/2 teaspoon cayenne pepper

Parsley salad

1 cup fresh flat-leaf parsley leaves

Classic Vinaigrette (page 324)

Fleur de sel

Lemon wedges, for garnish

1 recipe Sauce Rémoulade (page 335)

1. To fillet the fish, cut around the back of the head, down to the backbone. With the sharp, thin-bladed, flexible knife, make a cut down the belly of the fish, from head to tail.

2. Starting at the head, slide the knife under one fillet and carefully cut it away from the bones, keeping the blade as flat and as close to the bones as possible. Turn the fish over and repeat to remove the second fillet.

3. Lay a fillet skin side down, with the narrower end facing you. Hold the tip of the skin with your fingers, and angling the blade of the knife down toward the skin and working it away from you, start to cut between the flesh and the skin. Firmly take hold of the skin and continue to work away from you, sawing the knife from side to side and keeping the blade close against the skin, until the fillet is released.

4. Trim the frills (or tiny fins) away from the edge of the skinless fillets to give them a neat finish.

5. Slice the fillets diagonally into *goujonnettes* about the width of your little finger.

6. Pour the oil into the deep-fat fryer. The oil should be at least 2 inches deep. Place a wire skimmer into the oil, so that when you lift the fish from the oil, it will not stick to the skimmer. Heat the oil to 375°F. Line the tray with paper towels.

7. Prepare 3 shallow bowls: Place the flour in the first bowl. Crack the eggs into the sieve set over a second bowl. Press the eggs through the sieve. (This will help make an even-textured coating.) In the third bowl, combine the breadcrumbs, cheese, and cayenne pepper, and toss to blend.

8. Dip a slice of fish into the flour, turning to coat it evenly and shaking off any excess. Then dip the fish into the eggs, turning to coat evenly and shaking off the excess. Finally, dip the fish into the breadcrumb mixture, turning to coat evenly and

shaking off the excess. Repeat, breading all the remaining *goujonnettes*. Place them on a large plate.

9. Fry the fish in batches, about 6 slices at a time, until deep golden, 1 to 2 minutes per batch. Lift the slices out with the strainer, and transfer them to the paper-lined tray to drain. Cover with another layer of paper towels to further absorb any excess oil. Repeat with the remaining fish, making sure that the oil has come back to 375°F before continuing.

10. Prepare the parsley salad: Place the parsley leaves in a large salad bowl. Add just enough vinaigrette to coat the greens lightly. Toss gently. Season with *fleur de sel*. Arrange the salad on large dinner plates.

11. Place a delicate mound of fish next to the salad on each plate. Garnish with the lemon wedges and Sauce Rémoulade.

WINE SUGGESTION: I love to serve this with a Muscadet, a white wine that at its best is loaded with minerality, a hint of saltiness, and a touch of iodine. Made from the Melon de Bourgogne grape, Muscadet developed a bad reputation, for much of the wine was of average quality. That has changed with a crop of new, young winemakers taking over. A good offering comes from André-Michel Brégeon, with vineyards near the town of Nantes.

WARM PARMESAN-CRUSTED SOLE SALAD WITH POTATOES AND LAMB'S LETTUCE

My tasting notes for this dish read yummy *in all capital letters. This is a great cold-weather salad, fragrant with the aromas of potatoes braised with bay leaves and garlic, a whiff of Parmigiano-Reggiano cheese, and a touch of walnut oil.*

4 SERVINGS
EQUIPMENT: A MEDIUM-MESH SIEVE; A POTATO MASHER.

1 pound firm, yellow-fleshed potatoes (such as Yukon Gold), scrubbed (do not peel)

5 fresh or dried bay leaves

1 teaspoon coarse sea salt

2 tablespoons plus 1 teaspoon extra-virgin olive oil

4 plump, fresh, moist garlic cloves (do not peel)

2 large eggs

1/4 cup quick-cooking polenta

1/4 cup freshly grated Parmigiano-Reggiano cheese

1 tablespoon superfine flour (such as Wondra)

1/4 teaspoon ground *piment d'Espelette* or other ground mild chile pepper

1 pound sole fillets (or any firm, white-fleshed fish, such as flounder, trout, or perch)

Fleur de sel

4 cups lamb's lettuce or spinach

Classic Vinaigrette (page 324)

About 1 tablespoon best-quality walnut or hazelnut oil (such as Leblanc)

2 tablespoons Capers in Vinegar (page 289), drained

8 Cornichons (page 290), cut into thin rounds

Lemon wedges, for garnish

1. Place the potatoes in a large pot. Add the bay leaves, salt, 1 teaspoon olive oil, garlic, and several tablespoons of cold water. Cover and braise over the lowest possible heat, turning the potatoes from time to time, until they are tender when pierced with a fork and browned in patches, about 25 minutes. (Cooking time will vary according to the size and freshness of the potatoes.) Keep warm.

2. Crack the eggs into the sieve set over a bowl. Press the eggs through the sieve. (This will help make an even-textured coating.) In another bowl, combine the polenta, cheese, flour, and *piment d'Espelette*.

3. Dredge the fish fillets in the egg, then in the polenta mixture. Place on a large plate.

4. In a large, shallow skillet, heat the 2 tablespoons olive oil over moderate heat. When the oil is hot but not smoking, add the coated fish and cook until golden and cooked through, about 2 minutes per side. Transfer to a double thickness of paper towels to absorb any excess oil. Season with *fleur de sel*.

5. Place the lamb's lettuce in a large salad bowl. Add just enough vinaigrette to lightly coat the greens. Toss gently. Season with *fleur de sel*. Taste for seasoning. Arrange the salad on large dinner plates.

6. With a potato masher or a large fork, crush the potatoes. They should remain fairly coarse. Mound the warm, crushed potatoes on top of the salad. Drizzle with the walnut oil, and shower with the capers and cornichons. Arrange the fish on top of the potatoes. Garnish with the lemon wedges, and serve immediately.

WINE SUGGESTION: This salad calls out for a crisp, flinty white. Why not a Chablis, with its hint of citrus and deep minerality? My favorites come from Domaine François and Jean-Marie Raveneau and Domaine Jean Dauvissat.

SPICY ASIAN SQUID SALAD

An assertive sauce of chile paste, sesame oil, Asian fish sauce, lime juice, ginger, and shallots makes a perfect marinade for the delicate flavor of fresh baby squid. I like to round out the salad with ripe cherry tomatoes, garnishing all with lime zest and herbs.

4 SERVINGS

EQUIPMENT: A SMALL JAR WITH A LID;

A **5**-QUART PASTA POT FITTED WITH A COLANDER.

Grated zest of 2 limes, preferably organic

1/3 cup minced fresh cilantro leaves

1/3 cup minced fresh basil or mint leaves

Sauce

1 to 2 teaspoons chile paste

2 tablespoons best-quality sesame oil (such as LeBlanc)

2 tablespoons Vietnamese fish sauce, preferably Phu Quoc brand

2 teaspoons raw sugar

2 tablespoons freshly squeezed lime juice

2 shallots, trimmed, peeled, and cut into thin rings

1 tablespoon finely minced fresh ginger

1 1/2 pounds ripe cherry tomatoes

3 tablespoons coarse sea salt

1 1/2 pounds small squid, gutted, cleaned, and rinsed (or have your fishmonger do this for you),
    tentacles reserved and tubes cut into 1/3-inch rings

Fleur de sel

1. In a large, shallow bowl, combine the lime zest, cilantro, and basil. Toss to blend, and set aside.

2. Prepare the sauce: In the small jar, combine the chile paste, sesame oil, fish sauce, sugar, lime juice, shallots, and ginger. Tighten the lid and shake to blend. Taste for seasoning. Pour the sauce into the large bowl.

3. Core the tomatoes, halve them crosswise, and cut them into thin strips about 1/8 inch wide.

4. Fill the pasta pot with 3 quarts of water and bring it to a rolling boil over high heat. Add the salt and the squid tubes and tentacles, and cook for about 20 seconds from the time the squid enter the water. Drain immediately. Transfer the hot squid to the large bowl and toss gently with the sauce. (The squid will better absorb the sauce while warm.) Add the tomatoes and toss again. Taste for seasoning.

5. Serve warm or at room temperature, seasoned lightly with *fleur de sel*.

WINE SUGGESTION: This spicy salad pairs well with a favorite chilled beer.

CRUNCHY OCTOBER GARDEN SALAD WITH TUNA

One Friday in October, Walter and I sat in our kitchen, marveling at the freshness of this colorful fall salad. The vegetable garden was still prospering, and that morning I had gathered crunchy green peppers, tiny zucchini, baby cucumbers, and plenty of our salad burnet, a green with parsley-like leaves and the flavor of cucumber. I drained a jar of French tuna in olive oil, prepared the vegetables, made a dressing with the tuna oil, and voilà! *Note: I'm holding the finished dish on the front cover.*

4 SERVINGS
EQUIPMENT: A SMALL JAR WITH A LID.

One 10-ounce jar best-quality tuna in extra-virgin olive oil, drained, oil reserved

1 tablespoon freshly squeezed lemon juice

Grated zest of 1 lemon, preferably organic

1 cup fresh salad burnet leaves or fresh parsley leaves

4 ripe green heirloom tomatoes such as Evergreen (about 1 pound total), cored and quartered

1 green bell pepper, trimmed, seeds removed, and cut into thin strips

2 scallions or 1 spring onion, white part only, trimmed, peeled, and cut into thin rings

1 small zucchini, rinsed, trimmed, and cut into thin rounds

1 small cucumber, trimmed and cut into thin rounds

20 cherry tomatoes, halved

1 tablespoon Capers in Vinegar (page 289), drained

10 Cornichons (page 290), cut into thin rounds

Fine sea salt

1. To make the dressing, in the small jar, combine 3 tablespoons of the reserved tuna oil and the lemon juice. Cover and shake to blend.

2. Place the tuna in a large, shallow bowl, and with a fork, break it up into small pieces. Add all the remaining ingredients and the dressing, tossing to evenly coat the ingredients. Taste for seasoning. Serve at room temperature.

WINE SUGGESTION: In late spring I always note the date we sample our first rosé of the season, for it suggests that summer and festive outdoor meals are not far behind. In the fall, I also note our last rosé of the season, suggesting that winter and some heartier wines, such as the red Châteauneuf-du-Pape, will soon be decanted. So an end-of-the-season salad calls for an end-of-the-season rosé, and my all-time favorite is Domaine de la Mordorée's complex and satisfying Tavel.

TUNA TARTARE WITH SHAVED FENNEL, SHALLOTS, AND CHIVES

This is a Technicolor salad as a meal, with the mahogany of the fresh, glistening tuna set against the alabaster of the fresh fennel, tinged with flecks of green chives. The fennel, shallots, chives, and sesame seeds add that essential crunch, the sesame oil tunes in with an exotic, almost smoky touch, and the chilled tuna is the star, with its rich, meaty flavor.

4 SERVINGS

EQUIPMENT: A MANDOLINE OR A VERY SHARP KNIFE; 4 CHILLED LARGE DINNER PLATES; A 4-INCH RING MOLD, 2 INCHES HIGH (OPTIONAL).

3 tablespoons freshly squeezed lemon juice

4 small bulbs fennel, trimmed, with any fennel fronds reserved

2 shallots, trimmed, peeled, and cut into thin rounds

1/4 cup finely minced fresh chives

2 teaspoons toasted sesame seeds

3 to 4 tablespoons best-quality sesame oil (such as Leblanc)

Fine sea salt

1 pound well-chilled, ultra-fresh sashimi-quality tuna (bigeye or ahi), cut into 1/4-inch cubes

Several slices Crispy Flatbread (page 260)

1. Fill a container with 1 quart cold water and add the lemon juice. Cut the fennel lengthwise into very thin slices, dropping the slices into the lemon water. Cover the container and refrigerate. (Store the fennel in the lemon water in the refrigerator for up to 4 hours. The fennel will crisp up and the lemon juice will deter it from darkening.)

2. Drain the fennel. In a bowl, toss the fennel with half of the shallots, chives, and sesame seeds, and just enough sesame oil to coat the fennel. Season with salt. In another bowl, combine the tuna with the remaining shallots, chives, and sesame seeds, tossing to blend. Drizzle with just enough sesame oil to lightly coat the tuna. Season with salt.

3. With your fingertips, drop a mound of the dressed fennel on one side of each plate. Set a mold next to the fennel salad on one plate. Lightly pack the tuna mixture into the mold. Remove the mold. (Or simply mound the tuna on the plate next to the fennel salad.) Repeat for the remaining salads. Serve.

WINE SUGGESTION: I love this salad with a crisp, well-chilled Sauvignon Blanc. A favorite comes from the Sancerre vineyards of Alphonse Mellot, whose wine offers a fine minerality and often a touch of salinity, a good match for the fresh tuna.

POULTRY

WHAT COULD BE MORE VERSATILE THAN A ROTISSERIE CHICKEN? EVERY TUES-
DAY, OUR MARKET DAY IN PROVENCE, I BUY A FARM CHICKEN FROM A LAOTIAN
MERCHANT WHO ALSO OFFERS SUBLIME ASIAN SPRING ROLLS AND TINY CRISPY
NEMS. ONCE HOME FROM THE MARKET, I GATHER HERBS AND CITRUS FROM
THE GARDEN AND CORNICHONS FROM THE PANTRY, BLANCH SOME SEASONAL
VEGETABLES, AND SOON WE HAVE A SUPERB MEAL ON THE TABLE.

CHICKEN SALAD WITH PEAS, FETA, AND MINT

Peas, feta, and mint are a remarkable combination, a perfect play of color, texture, and distinctive flavors. The lactic tang of the cheese, the garden freshness of the mint, and the sweet crunch of the peas make for an ideal spring salad. Radishes, baby romaine lettuce, avocado, chives, and cherry tomatoes turn it into a real bonanza, all punctuated by the protein-rich addition of moist shredded chicken or turkey.

4 SERVINGS
EQUIPMENT: A 5-QUART PASTA POT FITTED WITH A COLANDER;
4 CHILLED LARGE DINNER PLATES.

3 tablespoons coarse sea salt

1 cup shelled fresh or frozen peas (no need to thaw)

3 small spring onions or scallions, white part only, trimmed, peeled, and cut into thin rounds

4 ounces Greek feta cheese, crumbled (1 cup)

1/4 cup fresh mint leaves, cut into a chiffonade

3 cups shredded cooked chicken or turkey (see page 197)

8 ounces cherry tomatoes, halved

1 large ripe avocado, halved, pitted, peeled, and thinly sliced

2 heads baby romaine (sucrine or Little Gem), coarsely shredded

4 radishes, rinsed, trimmed, halved, and thinly sliced

1/4 cup minced fresh chives

Creamy Lemon-Chive Dressing (page 326)

Fine sea salt

1. Prepare a large bowl of ice water.

2. Fill the pasta pot with 3 quarts of water and bring it to a rolling boil over high heat. Add the coarse salt and the peas and blanch until crisp-tender, about 2 minutes. Immediately remove the colander from the water, letting the water drain from the peas. Plunge the peas into the ice water so they cool down as quickly as possible. Drain the peas and return them to the colander. (Store the peas in an airtight container in the refrigerator for up to 4 hours.)

3. In a large, shallow bowl, combine all the ingredients except the dressing and fine salt. Toss with just enough dressing to coat the ingredients lightly and evenly. Taste for seasoning. Arrange the salad on dinner plates, and serve.

WINE SUGGESTION: Keep it simple here with a light and crisp white, such as a non-oaky Chardonnay, Sauvignon Blanc, or Chenin Blanc.

CHICKEN SALAD WITH GREEN BEANS, TAHINI-LEMON-YOGURT DRESSING, AND CILANTRO

This colorful and tangy salad is packed with flavor, texture, and character. We eat green beans several times a week when they are in season, and never get enough of their great crunch, brilliant green color, and healthful, refreshing flavors.

4 SERVINGS
EQUIPMENT: A **5**-QUART PASTA POT FITTED
WITH A COLANDER.

3 tablespoons coarse sea salt

8 ounces green beans, trimmed at both ends and cut into 1-inch pieces

3 1/2 cups (about 1 pound) cubed cooked chicken (see page 197)

1 1/2 cups sliced celery (1/4-inch slices)

Tahini-Lemon-Yogurt Dressing and Dipping Sauce (page 332)

1/2 cup finely minced fresh cilantro or parsley leaves

Coarse, freshly ground black pepper

1. Prepare a large bowl of ice water.

2. Fill the pasta pot with 3 quarts of water and bring it to a rolling boil over high heat. Add the salt and the beans and blanch until crisp-tender, about 5 minutes. (Cooking time will vary according to the size and tenderness of the beans.) Immediately remove the colander from the water, letting the water drain from the beans. Plunge the beans into the ice water so they cool down as quickly as possible. (The beans will cool in 1 to 2 minutes. If you leave them longer, they will become soggy and begin to lose flavor.) Drain the beans and wrap them in a thick kitchen towel to dry. (Store the beans in the towel in the refrigerator for up to 4 hours.)

3. In a large bowl, combine the beans, chicken, and celery. Toss to blend. Add just enough dressing to coat the ingredients lightly and evenly. Add the cilantro and toss again. Taste for seasoning. At serving time, season with pepper.

WINE SUGGESTION: This salad calls for a slightly exotic wine. I never tire of the unique, spicy flavors and aromas of Austria's flagship white wine, Grüner Veltliner.

AUSTRALIAN CORONATION CHICKEN SALAD

I love recipes with a story, especially if the end results are delicious. Australian Coronation Chicken Salad was created in 1953 for a luncheon served to heads of the British Commonwealth to honor the coronation of Queen Elizabeth. The original recipe included both curry and apples, ingredients that added a touch of spice and a welcome crunch. This is a favorite summer lunch salad in our home, and one that can be put together in minutes, especially when prepared with a roasted chicken from the market.

4 SERVINGS

1 cup nonfat Greek-style yogurt

1 teaspoon Homemade Curry Powder (page 292), or more to taste

Grated zest of 1 lemon, preferably organic

1 tablespoon freshly squeezed lemon juice

1/2 teaspoon fine sea salt

1 1/2 cups diced celery

1/2 cup finely minced fresh cilantro or parsley leaves

3 1/2 cups (about 1 pound) cubed cooked chicken (see page 197)

1 Granny Smith apple, cored, peeled, and cubed

Coarse, freshly ground black pepper

In a large bowl, combine the yogurt, curry powder, lemon zest, lemon juice, and salt. Whisk to blend. Taste for seasoning. Add the celery, cilantro, chicken, and apple. Toss to coat the ingredients lightly and evenly. Taste for seasoning. (Store in an airtight container in the refrigerator for up to 1 day.) At serving time, season with pepper.

WINE SUGGESTION: Curry loves a wine with a touch of spice of its own, such as an Alsatian Pinot Blanc.

ASIAN CHICKEN SALAD WITH ASPARAGUS AND SESAME

*Come spring, we dine on asparagus at lunch and dinner, and that's when this simple but satisfying salad appears on our table. I grow a mix of tasty, piquant Asian greens—*mizuna, tatsoi, komatsuna, mibuna, *and* amsoi—*colorful baby greens that are perfect for this dressing and this salad. In place of chicken, turkey is also delicious.*

4 SERVINGS

EQUIPMENT: A **5**-QUART PASTA POT FITTED WITH A COLANDER;
A SMALL JAR WITH A LID.

3 tablespoons coarse sea salt

12 thin spears green asparagus, trimmed

2 tablespoons rice vinegar

2 tablespoons tamari or other Japanese soy sauce

1 tablespoon best-quality sesame oil (such as Leblanc)

4 small spring onions or scallions, white part only, trimmed, peeled, and very thinly sliced

2 cups (about 3 ounces) Asian salad leaves (or mixed baby salad leaves)

3 1/2 cups (about 1 pound) shredded cooked chicken (or turkey) breast (see page 197)

1 tablespoon toasted sesame seeds, for garnish

1. Prepare a large bowl of ice water.

2. Fill the pasta pot with 3 quarts of water and bring it to a rolling boil over high heat. Add the salt and the asparagus and blanch until crisp-tender, 2 to 3 minutes. (Cooking time will vary according to the size and tenderness of the asparagus.) Immediately remove the colander from the water, letting the water drain from the asparagus. Plunge the asparagus into the ice water so they cool down as quickly as

possible. (The asparagus will cool in 1 to 2 minutes. If you leave them longer, they will become soggy and begin to lose flavor.) Drain the asparagus and wrap them in a thick kitchen towel to dry. (Do not cook the asparagus in advance, for they will lose their crispness.)

3. In the small jar, combine the vinegar, tamari, sesame oil, and spring onions. Shake to blend.

4. Place the asparagus in a bowl and toss with just enough dressing to coat lightly and evenly. Taste for seasoning. Place the Asian salad greens in another bowl, and toss with just enough dressing to coat them lightly and evenly. Taste for seasoning. Place the shredded chicken in another bowl, and toss with just enough dressing to coat the poultry lightly and evenly.

5. Place the dressed greens on large plates. Arrange the dressed asparagus on the greens, and the chicken on top of the asparagus. Garnish with the sesame seeds.

WINE SUGGESTION: For this dish I enjoy a wine that's plentiful in my cellar, Domaine de la Janasse's easy-drinking white Côtes-du-Rhône. It's an excellent blend of Grenache Blanc, Bourboulenc, Viognier, and Roussanne, a complex wine that is far from simple yet so uncomplicated.

CHICKEN AND SOBA NOODLES WITH GINGER-PEANUT SAUCE

This is a favorite weeknight dinner in our house, a vibrant combination of soba noodles bathed in a rich sauce of soy, sesame, peanut butter, and vinegar, with a hint of garlic and ginger. The sliced scallions add the essential element of crunch, and the smoothness of the chicken is punctuated by a garnish of toasted sesame seeds, peanuts, and cilantro.

4 SERVINGS

EQUIPMENT: A **5**-QUART PASTA POT FITTED WITH A COLANDER.

6 tablespoons tamari or other Japanese soy sauce

2 tablespoons best-quality sesame oil (such as Leblanc)

1 tablespoon unsweetened smooth peanut butter, preferably organic

4 tablespoons Japanese rice vinegar or Chinese black rice vinegar

1 tablespoon grated fresh ginger

2 plump, moist garlic cloves, peeled, halved, green germ removed, and minced

3 tablespoons coarse sea salt

10 ounces soba noodles

2 cups shredded cooked chicken (see page 197)

5 scallions, both green and white parts, trimmed, peeled, and very thinly sliced

1/4 cup toasted sesame seeds

1/4 cup chopped salted peanuts

1/4 cup fresh cilantro leaves

1. In a large, shallow bowl, whisk together the tamari, sesame oil, peanut butter, vinegar, 2 tablespoons of water, the ginger, and the garlic.

2. Fill the pasta pot with 3 quarts of water and bring it to a rolling boil over high heat. Add the coarse salt and the noodles, stirring to prevent the pasta from sticking. Cook until tender, about 5 minutes. Drain thoroughly in a colander and run hot water over the colander full of noodles until the water runs clear. (This is important, for if the noodles are not properly washed, they will be starchy and sticky.) Drain thoroughly again.

3. Add the noodles directly to the bowl containing the sauce. Toss to coat the noodles evenly and thoroughly. Add the chicken and scallions, and toss again. Garnish with the sesame seeds, peanuts, and cilantro.

WINE SUGGESTION: A good chilled sake is perfect with this Asian salad.

GINGER AND SESAME CHICKEN SALAD WITH GLASS NOODLES

I look forward to this salad when it's on "the menu" at home. It packs a lot of flavor for very little effort: the smooth texture and glistening color of the glass noodles always appeal, and moist chicken meat is always ready to absorb the bright-flavored Asian sauce.

4 SERVINGS
EQUIPMENT: A SMALL JAR WITH A LID.

2 tablespoons tamari or other Japanese soy sauce

4 tablespoons toasted sesame seeds

2 tablespoons best-quality sesame oil (such as Leblanc)

2 tablespoons Chinese black rice vinegar

2 plump, moist garlic cloves, peeled, halved, green germ removed, and minced

1 tablespoon grated fresh ginger

3 1/2 cups (about 1 pound) cubed cooked chicken (see page 197)

3 scallions, both white and green parts, trimmed, peeled, and sliced on the diagonal

7 ounces glass (cellophane) noodles

Fresh *shiso* leaves, cut into a chiffonade (or fresh cilantro leaves), for garnish

1. In the small jar, combine the tamari, sesame seeds, sesame oil, vinegar, garlic, and ginger. Cover and shake to blend. Taste for seasoning.

2. Place the chicken and half the scallions in a large bowl and toss with about half of the dressing, or just enough to moisten the ingredients evenly. Taste for seasoning.

3. In a large saucepan, bring 2 quarts of water to a boil. Do not salt the water. Add the glass noodles, swirl them in the water, and cook just until soft, about 1 minute. Drain, and rinse thoroughly under cold running water. Drain again.

4. In a bowl, toss the noodles with the remaining dressing. Place the seasoned noodles on large plates. Scatter the cubed chicken over the noodles. Garnish with the *shiso* or cilantro and the remaining scallions.

WINE SUGGESTION: This is another salad that is just *great* with cold sake!

SMOKED CHICKEN BREAST SALAD WITH SORREL CHIFFONADE AND PARMESAN CROUTONS

I first sampled a version of this salad at Le Pain Quotidien, a wonderful restaurant that offers light, varied fare. I enjoy making this with tangy, bright-colored greens such as sorrel or spinach, cut into a fine chiffonade.

4 SERVINGS

4 cups sorrel greens (or spinach), cut into a chiffonade

Lemon and Olive Oil Dressing (page 330)

1 cup cherry tomatoes, halved

4 small spring onions or scallions, white part only, trimmed, peeled, and very thinly sliced

1 small bulb fennel, trimmed and very thinly sliced

1 large ripe avocado, halved, pitted, peeled, and cut lengthwise into thin slices

2 smoked chicken breasts (see page 213)

About 2 1/2 ounces Parmigiano-Reggiano cheese, cut into thin strips (about 1/2 cup)

1 cup Parmesan Croutons (page 281)

Place the greens in a large bowl and toss with just enough dressing to coat them lightly and evenly. In separate small bowls, toss the tomatoes, onions, the fennel, and the avocado with the dressing. Mound the greens on 4 large dinner plates. Scatter with the tomatoes, onions, and fennel. Slice each chicken breast lengthwise into 8 even slices. Arrange the chicken slices like the spokes of a wheel on top of the greens. Place the avocado around the edge of the salad. Top the chicken with the cheese. Scatter the croutons at the edge of the plate. Serve.

WINE SUGGESTION: I enjoy a lively young red here, a slightly chilled Beaujolais-Villages Chiroubles (love saying that word out loud!) from Daniel Bouland. You might say it's a red wine masquerading as a white, it is so lithe and light.

POACHED CHICKEN BREASTS

Here's a simple, infallible way to preserve the sweet, dense flavor of chicken breasts. You will have extremely tender meat and a highly fragrant stock when you are done. Once poached, the breasts can be used in any salad calling for cooked chicken.

2 CHICKEN BREASTS

1 quart Homemade Chicken Stock (page 310)

1 onion, quartered (do not peel)

Several fresh tarragon leaves

Several fresh thyme sprigs

1 celery rib or several celery leaves, chopped

2 fresh or dried bay leaves

6 whole black peppercorns

4 plump, moist garlic cloves, peeled and halved

6 fresh parsley sprigs

2 boneless, skinless chicken breasts (each about 8 ounces)

1. In a medium saucepan, combine all the ingredients except the chicken. Cover, bring to a simmer, and simmer, uncovered, for 5 minutes.

2. Carefully slip the chicken breasts into the stock, making sure they are fully covered by the liquid. Cover and simmer for 7 minutes. Remove the pan from the heat (keeping it covered), and let the chicken cool in the stock for 1 hour.

3. The chicken can be used immediately or refrigerated, covered in the stock. The stock can be strained and used to prepare chicken soup or reduced to use for a sauce. (Store the chicken in an airtight container in the stock in the refrigerator for up to 3 days.)

VIETNAMESE CHICKEN AND GREEN PAPAYA SALAD

A ten-day trip to Vietnam inspired this classic Asian salad as a meal. It offers that perfect, satisfying bit of crunch with a fine burst of herbal flavors that I love. I prepare this salad with chicken, but it can also be made with cooked pork or beef. And I generally make it with green papaya, but one could substitute water chestnuts, jicama, or fresh banana flowers.

4 SERVINGS

EQUIPMENT: A **5**-QUART PASTA POT FITTED WITH A COLANDER.

1/2 cup salted peanuts, chopped

1/4 cup toasted sesame seeds

1 to 2 fresh red bird's-eye chiles, seeded and chopped

5 cups fresh bean sprouts

8 ounces green papaya, peeled and julienned (3 cups)

2 cups shredded cooked chicken breast (see page 197)

1 cup fresh cilantro leaves, chopped

1 cup Vietnamese Dipping Sauce (page 336)

1. In a small bowl, combine the peanuts, sesame seeds, and chiles. Set aside.

2. Prepare a large bowl of ice water.

3. Fill the pasta pot with 3 quarts of water and bring it to a rolling boil over high heat. Do not add salt. Add the bean sprouts and blanch for 1 minute. Immediately remove the colander from the water, allowing the water to drain from the sprouts. Plunge the sprouts into the ice water for just 30 seconds so they cool down as quickly as possible. Drain in a colander.

4. In a large bowl, combine the bean sprouts, papaya, chicken, and 3/4 cup of the cilantro. Toss with just enough dipping sauce to coat the ingredients lightly and evenly. Arrange on dinner plates. Garnish with the remaining 1/4 cup cilantro and about half of the chile mixture. Serve, passing the remaining chile mixture as an additional garnish, along with the dipping sauce.

WINE SUGGESTION: It should be an unassuming daily drinking white but one with enough backbone to stand up to the fire and saltiness of the salad. I love a Chardonnay here, my favorite being a light Macon from the house of Domaine des Héritiers du Comte Lafon.

FRANCK'S JELLIED CHICKEN SALAD

Before our Provençal butcher Franck Peyraud moved on, I was probably his most frequent customer for the shop's jellied chicken salad: it met my needs for lean protein at lunch, required no work whatsoever, and was simply the most convenient and delicious fast food to keep on hand. Franck is gone and so is his chicken salad, so now I prepare it myself, with plump, moist poached chicken breasts and fresh herbs and lemons from the garden. This salad lends itself to endless variation: give it an Asian flair with slices of ginger and lemongrass, try cilantro in place of the tarragon, or add a Mediterranean touch with sliced green or black olives.

4 SERVINGS
EQUIPMENT: A **2** 1/2-CUP RECTANGULAR TERRINE
(7 1/2 × **5** INCHES); BAKING PARCHMENT.

Grated zest of 1 lemon, preferably organic

1/4 lemon, preferably organic, cut crosswise into paper-thin slices

1/4 cup minced fresh tarragon leaves

1 tablespoon Capers in Vinegar (page 289), drained

6 Cornichons (page 290), cut into thin rounds, plus extra whole Cornichons for serving

2 Poached Chicken Breasts (page 197)

Fine sea salt

Gelatin

2 teaspoons (1 package) gelatin

3 tablespoons freshly squeezed lemon juice

Imported French mustard or Homemade Mayonnaise (page 333), for serving

1. In a small bowl, combine the lemon zest, sliced lemon, tarragon, capers, and sliced cornichons, and toss to blend.

2. Line the terrine with baking parchment, letting several inches hang over each end. (This will make it easier to remove the salad in one piece once it is jelled.) Spoon about one-third of the lemon mixture into the terrine. Cut each chicken breast lengthwise into 5 or 6 slices, about 1/4-inch thick. Arrange one-third of the chicken in a layer on top of the lemon mixture. Season the chicken lightly with salt. Repeat two more times, seasoning the chicken each time and spooning one-third of the lemon mixture over the seasoned chicken. The top layer will be chicken.

3. Prepare the gelatin: In a small bowl, combine the gelatin and lemon juice and stir to blend. Pour 1 cup of boiling water over the mixture. Pour the hot gelatin mixture over the chicken in the terrine. Cover and refrigerate until the mixture is jelled, about 3 hours.

4. To serve, turn the jellied salad out onto a rectangular serving plate. Remove the parchment. Cut it into thin slices, as with a terrine or bread. (The salad may break up a bit.) Serve with mustard or mayonnaise and additional cornichons.

WINE SUGGESTION: A dish that has local origins calls out for a local wine. My choice would be the white from the nearby Château Pesquié. Their exotic and highly aromatic Côtes-du-Ventoux Quintessence is a fabulous blend of my favorite white grape, Roussanne, with a touch of the classic Clairette. I think I'll have a second glass . . .

CHICKEN LIVER TERRINE
WITH BLACK PEPPERCORNS

Here the silken richness of chicken livers teams up with a spicy hit of black peppercorns in a country-style terrine that is perfect for cool days. I make this often in the winter, when we sample a thin slice with a green salad and a pungent garnish of capers, cornichons, and mustard.

2 SERVINGS

EQUIPMENT: A FOOD PROCESSOR; A **2**-CUP TERRINE; BAKING PARCHMENT;
A ROASTING PAN.

12 ounces chicken livers, trimmed

1 tablespoon Cognac

2 teaspoons fresh thyme leaves

2 plump, moist garlic cloves, peeled, halved, green germ removed, and minced

1/2 teaspoon freshly grated nutmeg

1 teaspoon fine sea salt

1/2 cup light cream

1 large egg

1 cup finely diced carrots

1 cup finely diced celery or Swiss chard ribs

1/2 cup coarsely chopped hazelnuts

2 teaspoons crushed or coarsely ground black pepper

Several handfuls of salad greens, tossed with dressing of choice, for serving

Cornichons (page 290), for garnish

Imported French mustard, for garnish

Capers in Vinegar (page 289), for garnish

1. Preheat the oven to 350°F.

2. In the food processor, combine the chicken livers, Cognac, thyme, garlic, nutmeg, salt, cream, and egg. Puree.

3. With a rubber spatula, scrape the chicken liver mixture into a large bowl. Fold in the carrots, celery, and hazelnuts.

4. Line the terrine with baking parchment, letting several inches hang over each end. (This will make it easier to remove the terrine in one piece once cooked.) Spoon the chicken liver mixture into the prepared terrine, smoothing the top with a spatula. Sprinkle with the pepper.

5. Fill a roasting pan with several inches of hot water and place the terrine in the water bath. Place the roasting pan in the oven and cook until a skewer inserted into the center of the terrine is hot to the touch when removed, about 1 1/2 hours. The water should just simmer gently; check it halfway through the cooking time and if necessary, add some boiling water.

6. Remove the terrine from the water bath and let it cool on a wire rack for 2 hours. Then cover and refrigerate for 12 hours before eating. (Store in the refrigerator for up to 3 days.)

7. To serve, pull up on the parchment to remove the terrine. Cut into thin slices. Serve at room temperature, with a green salad, cornichons, mustard, and capers.

WINE SUGGESTION: Those black peppercorns deserve a peppery wine, so I'll go for the always dependable Minervois from Château d'Oupia, a rich and elegant wine made from 100-year-old Carignan grapes, with a touch of Syrah and Grenache.

CHIBERTA'S 1980S DUCK SALAD

When I began reviewing restaurants for the International Herald Tribune *in 1980, Chiberta was the place to go in Paris, and chef Jean-Michel Bédier wowed us with his take on nouvelle cuisine. I still dream of this duck salad: paper-thin slices of raw* magret de canard *atop a bed of spinach, showered with shallots, chives, and lemon juice.*

4 SERVINGS

EQUIPMENT: AN ELECTRIC MEAT SLICER OR
A VERY SHARP CHEF'S KNIFE; **4** CHILLED SALAD PLATES.

1 duck breast (about 1 pound), trimmed of fat

4 cups baby spinach leaves

Lemon and Olive Oil Dressing (page 330)

Sliced whole-grain bread, toasted, for serving

Garnish and seasoning

2 shallots, trimmed, peeled, halved, and finely minced

Finely minced fresh chives

Extra-virgin olive oil

Lemon wedges

Coarse, freshly ground black pepper

Fleur de sel

1. Wrap the duck breast in plastic wrap and chill it in the freezer for 15 minutes, to make it easier to slice.

2. With a meat slicer or a very sharp chef's knife, cut the chilled duck breast lengthwise into 16 paper-thin slices. Transfer the slices to a plate, cover with plastic wrap, and let thaw for at least 10 minutes before serving.

3. Place the spinach leaves in a large bowl and toss with just enough dressing to coat the greens lightly and evenly. Taste for seasoning. Mound the salad on the dinner plates. Drape the slices of duck breast on top of the greens. Serve with the toast, and let your guests choose from among the garnishes.

NOTE: *Magret de canard* can be found in some specialty markets and can be ordered online from D'Artagnan at www.dartagnan.com. Ask for moulard duck magret, which weigh 1 pound each.

WINE SUGGESTION: I like to walk into my wine cellar and grab a bottle of the fresh and fruity Côtes-du-Rhône Villages Vinsobres "Les Cornuds," from the house of Perrin & Fils, one of the Perrin family's finest daily drinking reds. This versatile wine finds its way to our table often, for it manages to please all palates.

POACHED TURKEY BREAST SALAD WITH LEMON, CAPERS, CORNICHONS, AND MINT

My good friend Carol Allen so raved about this cold marinated turkey breast, I had to ask for the recipe! I have adapted it a bit and find that the simplicity and ease of poaching a whole turkey breast makes it ideal for salads for a crowd. And if you are not *a crowd, a portion of the poached turkey can be sliced thinly and dressed while the rest can be cubed and used in any recipe calling for poached or roasted chicken. Serve this with a simple tossed green salad.*

12 SERVINGS

EQUIPMENT: A **6**-QUART STOCKPOT; AN ELECTRIC MEAT SLICER OR A VERY SHARP CHEF'S KNIFE.

1 boneless turkey breast (about 4 pounds)

1 large onion, halved (do not peel) and stuck with 2 cloves

3 carrots, chopped

2 fresh or dried bay leaves

2 tablespoons coarse sea salt

1 teaspoon whole black peppercorns

A 1-inch knob of fresh ginger, peeled

4 plump, moist garlic cloves, peeled, halved, and green germ removed

6 tablespoons distilled white vinegar

Marinade

Grated zest of 2 lemons, preferably organic

1/2 cup freshly squeezed lemon juice

1 cup extra-virgin olive oil

1 tablespoon imported French mustard

6 small spring onions or scallions, white part only, trimmed, peeled, and cut into very thin slices

12 Cornichons (page 290), thinly sliced

1/2 cup Capers in Vinegar (page 289), drained

1/4 cup fresh mint leaves, cut into a chiffonade, for garnish

1. Place the turkey breast in the stockpot and add enough cold water to cover by 1 inch. Remove the turkey to a platter. Add the onion, carrots, bay leaves, salt, peppercorns, ginger, garlic, and vinegar to the pot. Bring to a boil over high heat. Carefully lower the turkey into the pot, reduce the heat to a bare simmer, and poach, covered, for 1 1/4 hours.

2. Remove the pot from the heat and let the turkey cool in the liquid, uncovered, for 30 minutes.

3. Drain the turkey and discard the poaching liquid and solids.

4. Prepare the marinade: In a bowl, whisk together the lemon zest, juice, oil, and mustard. Stir in the spring onions, cornichons, and capers.

5. Place the turkey in a sturdy resealable plastic bag and pour the marinade into the bag. Seal the bag and turn it back and forth to coat the turkey. Refrigerate for at least 4 hours and up to 24 hours.

6. At serving time, remove the turkey from the bag, reserving the marinade, and place it on a cutting board. With a meat slicer or a very sharp chef's knife, cut the turkey into paper-thin slices. Arrange the turkey slices on a platter. Moisten the turkey with the marinade. Garnish with the mint, and serve.

WINE SUGGESTION: I enjoy a lively Chenin Blanc here, such as the Vouvray from Domaine Huet.

LEMON AND HAZELNUT OIL DRESSING

Once you sample the rich, elegant hazelnut oil from the Leblanc family mill in southern Burgundy, you will never turn back. Blend it with a touch of Lemon Zest Salt and lemon juice for a memorable dressing.

ABOUT 1/4 CUP DRESSING
EQUIPMENT: A SMALL JAR WITH A LID.

1/4 teaspoon Lemon Zest Salt (page 306) or fine sea salt

1 tablespoon freshly squeezed lemon juice

1/4 cup best-quality hazelnut oil (such as Leblanc)

Place the salt and lemon juice in the jar and shake to blend. Add the oil and shake once more. Taste for seasoning. The dressing can be used immediately or stored, covered and refrigerated, for up to 3 days. Shake again at serving time to create a thick emulsion.

SMOKED DUCK BREAST WITH MUSHROOMS, MIXED NUTS, CRACKLINGS, AND CHESTNUTS

A stormy night, a roaring fire, a sip of top-quality Gigondas, and this colorful, cold-weather salad as a meal. It's a festive dish: smoked duck breasts coddled in a warm hazelnut dressing and studded with chestnuts, mushrooms, and delicious, slightly spicy mixed nuts. Everything can be prepared ahead of time, with a quick, last-minute assembly.

4 SERVINGS
EQUIPMENT: **4** WARMED LARGE DINNER PLATES.

2 smoked duck breasts (recipe follows)

16 cooked chestnuts, halved

1 pound mixed wild mushrooms, trimmed, cleaned, and sliced

Lemon and Hazelnut Oil Dressing (page 209)

Spicy Basque Mixed Nuts (page 8)

Rendered Duck Fat and Cracklings (page 303), drained, salted, and peppered

1. Slice the smoked duck breasts crosswise into very thin slices. In a large skillet, combine them with the chestnuts and mushrooms. Moisten with just enough dressing to coat the ingredients lightly and evenly. Warm over low heat for a minute or two, letting all the flavors meld.

2. Evenly divide the mixture among the dinner plates. Sprinkle with the nuts and cracklings, and serve.

WINE SUGGESTION: This calls for a grand Gigondas, such as our winemaker Yves Gras's top wine, his Domaine Santa Duc cuvée Prestige des Hautes Garrigues, a rich, lively wine with a great length, one that guarantees surefire satisfaction.

HOME-SMOKED DUCK OR CHICKEN BREAST

Smoking chicken or duck breasts is a great way to retain their moisture, add a slightly exotic touch, and keep the protein lean and full-flavored. I consider a small stovetop smoker an essential piece of equipment for any kitchen. One is not limited to smoking poultry; scallops, scallop roe, sardines, trout, and mackerel are all favorite smoked foods in our house. A home smoker does not give food an overtly smoky flavor—just a gentle hint—and does not smoke up the kitchen!

4 SERVINGS

EQUIPMENT: A STOVE-TOP SMOKER; 1 TABLESPOON WOOD CHIPS.

2 skinless duck breasts or 2 boneless, skinless chicken breasts

Coarse sea salt

Coarse, freshly ground black pepper

1. Place the wood chips in a small pile in the center of the smoker base. Arrange the drip tray on top of the wood chips inside the smoker base. Place the metal rack on top of the drip tray. Arrange the poultry on top of the metal rack. Slide the lid closed.

2. Place the entire unit on the burner set to moderate heat. Counting from the time you place the smoker on the burner, smoke for 15 minutes. Remove the unit from the heat and open the lid. Transfer the poultry to a warmed plate. Season generously with salt and pepper. Cover with foil and let rest for at least 10 minutes, to let the juices retreat into the meat. Then cut lengthwise into very thin slices. (Store in an airtight container in the refrigerator for up to 3 days.)

> **NOTE:** Camerons smokers and wood chips are available from my Amazon Store at PatriciaWells.com. This is the brand that I have used for years. It is an inexpensive, all-purpose smoker and can easily be cleaned in a dishwasher.

MEAT

RARE-ROASTED BEEF, WHETHER HOME-COOKED OR PURCHASED FROM THE BUTCHER, LEFTOVER ROASTED LAMB, HOMEMADE OR PURCHASED LAMB OR PORK SAUSAGES, FILET OF VEAL, AND PORK TENDERLOIN OFTEN TAKE CENTER STAGE IN MY REPERTOIRE OF SALADS AS A MEAL. NO MATTER THE SEASON, THERE'S A VEGETABLE, A GREEN, OR A CHEESE THAT WILL PAIR NICELY WITH THE MEAT, ADDING VIBRANCY AS WELL AS SUBSTANCE.

WALTER'S LIME AND LEMONGRASS— CURED BEEF SALAD

We named this dish after my husband, Walter, since he was the first one to prepare and perfect this refreshing warm-weather salad. Ever since serving it at our cooking class in Vietnam, it has been up there on the charts of Best Taste of the Week.

4 SERVINGS

1/3 cup freshly squeezed lime juice

1/4 cup Vietnamese fish sauce, preferably Phu Quoc brand

2 tablespoons sugar

1 plump, moist garlic clove, peeled, halved, green germ removed, and minced

2 lemongrass stalks, trimmed, outer leaves removed, and sliced paper-thin

1 to 2 fresh red bird's-eye chiles, sliced on the diagonal

3 tablespoons extra-virgin olive oil

1 pound beef top round or filet mignon, trimmed of fat

Fine sea salt

Coarse, freshly ground black pepper

20 large fresh holy basil leaves (*bai kaprao*), or a combination of basil and mint leaves, julienned

20 large fresh mint leaves, julienned

1. In a small bowl, whisk together the lime juice, fish sauce, and sugar, stirring to dissolve the sugar. Add the garlic, lemongrass, and chile and set aside at room temperature for 20 minutes for the flavors to blend.

2. Heat the oil in a nonstick skillet over high heat until it is hot but not smoking. Sear the meat for 3 to 4 minutes on each side. Transfer the meat to a cutting board and season generously with salt and pepper. Tent lightly with foil and let rest for 10 minutes.

3. Transfer the beef to a bowl and pour the marinade over it, turning to coat it evenly. Set aside to marinate for 30 minutes. (The meat and the marinade can be prepared separately several hours in advance. Do not marinate for more than 30 minutes or the flavors and colors will begin to dull.)

4. At serving time, remove the meat from the marinade and place it on a cutting board. Strain the marinade, reserving the garlic, lemongrass, and chile. Cut the meat into very thin slices. Toss the slices with two-thirds of the holy basil and mint julienne, including the reserved garlic, lemongrass, and chile. Arrange on a serving plate. Garnish with the remaining basil and mint.

VARIATION: For a raw beef salad, cut the beef into 2-inch-wide blocks, wrap in plastic wrap, and freeze for 1 hour to facilitate slicing. Slice paper-thin and proceed with steps 1, 3, and 4.

SUGGESTION: A nice chilled beer of choice.

RARE-ROASTED BEEF WITH ROSEMARY, MINT, AND TARRAGON

One sunny Tuesday in August we were invited to lunch on the terrace at the historic Provençal restaurant Baumanière, in Les Baux. That day we feasted on abalone and bright red mullet, spiny lobster, and a version of this delicious beef preparation. Chef Sylvestre Wahid presented us with a plate adorned with rare-roasted beef showered with fresh herbs. Here is my take on his creation, with a final drizzle of colorful, fragrant basil oil. This beef can be served with a salad of heirloom tomatoes tossed in the dressing of choice or with a simple green salad, or it can be part of a larger salad buffet.

5 SERVINGS
EQUIPMENT: A MEDIUM SKILLET WITH OVENPROOF HANDLE.

1/2 cup mix of finely minced fresh herbs, including rosemary, mint, and tarragon

1 pound beef for roasting (use a beef fillet, tri-tip roast, or any thick steak cut from the top round or sirloin), trimmed of fat and sinew and wiped dry with paper towels

Fine sea salt

Coarse, freshly ground black pepper

2 tablespoons extra-virgin olive oil

Basil Oil (page 320), for garnish

1. Position a rack in the center of the oven. Preheat the oven to 475°F.

2. Place half of the herbs on a large plate. Roll the meat in the herbs to coat it evenly. Season the meat generously on all sides with salt and pepper. In the skillet, heat the olive oil over moderately high heat until it is hot but not smoking. Add the meat and brown on all sides for 3 minutes total. Drain and discard the fat. Return the meat to the skillet.

3. Place the skillet in the oven and roast until the meat has a slight springiness when pressed and an instant-read thermometer plunged into the center of the meat reads 120°F, about 15 minutes for rosy rare (or cook to desired doneness). Season the meat generously on all sides with salt and pepper. Transfer to a cutting board, cover loosely with foil, and let rest for at least 10 minutes.

4. Cut the meat against the grain into thin slices. Arrange on a platter and sprinkle with the remaining herbs and a drizzle of the basil oil.

WINE SUGGESTION: That sunny afternoon we sampled a red from one of our favorite winemakers, Laurent Charvin, who makes one of the best and least heralded of wines from Châteauneuf-du-Pape. That day we savored his totally amazing and unpretentious Côtes-du-Rhône, a mouth-filling, satisfying blend of old-vine Grenache with a touch of Carignan and Syrah.

HAND-CUT BEEF TARTARE
WITH FRENCH FRIES

In our house, Walter is the one who keeps all the knives as sharp as they can be, and it's often a Saturday morning chore. That means I'll be the one to go to the village and pick up the pre-ordered special cut of beef from our butcher, Gilles Diglé. In France, the prized cut of beef is called a surprise, *while in the United States it is known as a flatiron steak, the cut that comes from the tender top blade roast cut from the shoulder. When we savor our steak tartare we always accompany it with homemade French fries, an essential part of our weekend salad as a meal. No salad greens, you say? Sometimes a touch of raw meat is salad enough.*

4 SERVINGS
EQUIPMENT: A VERY SHARP CHEF'S KNIFE; 4 CHILLED SALAD PLATES.

1 pound lean flatiron steak, top round beef, trimmed filet mignon, or trimmed very lean sirloin,
 chilled

Accompaniments, set in small, individual bowls:

Imported French mustard

Finely minced shallots

Finely minced fresh celery leaves

Finely minced fresh parsley leaves

Capers in Vinegar (page 289), drained

Extra-virgin olive oil

Fresh lemon wedges

Fleur de sel

Coarse, freshly ground black pepper

Hot pepper sauce

Worcestershire sauce

Sliced whole-grain bread, toasted, for serving

Using a very sharp chef's knife, chop the beef by hand into 1/4-inch cubes. Mound the beef onto the chilled plates and let the guests choose from among the garnishes. Serve with the toasted bread.

WINE SUGGESTION: Throughout the year we conduct wine tastings with various experts, my two favorites being Juan Sanchez in Paris and Fabrice Langlois in Provence. Every now and then we sample wines that amaze us with their explicit, intense flavors of fresh blood or raw meat. One that would go beautifully is the Saint Chinian from Mas Champart, their *cuvée* Clos de la Simonette. For sure it's the fact that this wine is made with 70% Mourvèdre, a grape that often offers overtones of blood, meat, barnyard, and wet horse!

FRENCH FRIES

Nothing can compare to fresh, homemade fries prepared with top-quality potatoes. These are the classic accompaniment to a well-seasoned steak tartare as well as a nice grilled steak.

4 SERVINGS
EQUIPMENT: AN ELECTRIC DEEP-FAT FRYER FITTED WITH A BASKET; A WIRE SKIMMER.

2 pounds large yellow-fleshed Bintje or Russet potatoes (about 8 ounces each)

Vegetable oil for deep-frying

Fleur de sel

1. Scrub and peel the potatoes. Cut each potato lengthwise into 1/4-inch-thick slices. Stack several slices and cut them into 1/4-inch-wide strips (or use a French fry cutter). Wash the potatoes in warm water, drain, and pat dry. Arrange the potatoes in a single layer on a large dish towel. Cover with another towel to thoroughly dry them.

2. Pour the oil into a deep-fat fryer. The oil should be at least 2 inches deep. Heat the oil to 325°F. Place about one-fourth of the potato strips in the frying basket and lower it into the hot oil, gently shaking it to prevent the potatoes from clinging to one another. Cook the potatoes until they are stiff and are beginning to color lightly, about 5 minutes. Do not let them brown. With the wire skimmer, transfer the potatoes to another wire basket or sieve to drain over a large bowl. Repeat with all the remaining potatoes. (This first frying can be done several hours in advance.)

3. At serving time, add 1 cup of fresh oil to the oil in the fryer. Heat the oil to 375°F and fry the potatoes, in batches, until deep golden brown, about 1 minute per batch. Be sure to let the oil heat to 375°F before continuing with additional batches. As they are browned, transfer the potatoes to drain as before.

4. Place the fries on a serving platter, sprinkle with *fleur de sel*, and serve immediately.

BAR DE LA CROIX ROUGE *ASSIETTE SAINT-GERMAIN*

When we are in Paris, Walter and I can often be found lunching at one of our favorite haunts, the Bar de la Croix Rouge, just a few blocks from our Left Bank apartment. The café's most famous tartine—*or open-faced sandwich*—*is their* Assiette Saint-Germain, *which consists of several slices of fresh, perfectly toasted Poilâne bread lightly spread with mayonnaise and butter, then topped with ultra-thin slices of the most delicious roast beef. The garnish is pretty much of an afterthought: a few forgettable slices of tomato, a touch of dressed greens, and some puckery cornichons. There is always a jar of pungent mustard on the table, as well as a small glass or two of a fruity, crisp Beaujolais. It is always hard to stop at just one sandwich, but somehow I do, knowing the moist, rewarding* tartine *will still be there tomorrow.*

4 SERVINGS

4 thin slices Multigrain Sourdough Bread (page 270), toasted

1 tablespoon salted butter

1 tablespoon Homemade Mayonnaise (page 333)

24 ultra-thin slices rare roast beef (see page 219)

2 handfuls of soft salad greens

Creamy Lemon-Mustard Dressing (page 325)

4 ripe red tomatoes, cored and sliced crosswise

16 Cornichons (page 290), cut into thin slices, for garnish

Imported French mustard, for garnish

1. Spread the warm toast with the butter and mayonnaise. Top with the slices of beef. Cut each slice of toast crosswise into 6 slices. Arrange on each of 4 large dinner plates.

2. In a large bowl, combine the greens and the dressing, coating with just enough dressing to coat the greens lightly and evenly. Arrange the salad alongside the *tartines.* Arrange the tomatoes alongside, and drizzle with a bit of dressing. Garnish with the cornichons and serve with a jar of imported French mustard.

WINE SUGGESTION: We usually drink a fruity Beaujolais-Villages Morgon with these *tartines;* we love the offering from Jean Cabot, a thirst-quenching wine with a touch of smoke and fine minerality.

BEEF CARPACCIO WITH ARTICHOKES, CAPERS, ARUGULA, AND PARMESAN

At lunchtime especially, I love this refreshing and filling salad as a meal: paper-thin slices of top-quality beef topped with many of my favorite ingredients, including marinated artichokes, strips of moist Parmigiano-Reggiano cheese, home-cured capers, and peppery arugula. Freezing the beef for about 15 minutes makes for easy slicing. Season each plate before arranging the beef to create a well-flavored carpaccio. If in doubt about which cut of beef to use here, simply ask your butcher for the best cut of beef for carpaccio.

4 SERVINGS
EQUIPMENT: AN ELECTRIC MEAT SLICER
OR A VERY SHARP CHEF'S KNIFE.

4 lemons, preferably organic

Several teaspoons extra-virgin olive oil

Fine sea salt

Coarse, freshly ground black pepper

1 pound beef filet, or choice bottom or top round, trimmed of fat and sinew

8 Baby Artichokes Marinated in Olive Oil (page 24), drained and quartered

2 tablespoons Capers in Vinegar (page 289), drained

About 20 shavings of Parmigiano-Reggiano cheese

Several handfuls of arugula

Freshly squeezed lemon juice

Crispy Flatbread (page 260), for serving

1. Remove the zest from the lemons in fine strips, and arrange the strips over 4 large salad plates. Drizzle with olive oil. Season generously with salt and pepper. Wrap each plate in plastic wrap, and place in the freezer for 15 minutes.

2. About 15 minutes before slicing the beef, wrap it in foil and place it in the freezer.

3. With the meat slicer or a very sharp chef's knife, slice the very cold meat paper-thin. Arrange the slices in several layers on each chilled plate. Garnish with the artichokes, capers, cheese, and arugula. Drizzle with olive oil and a touch of lemon juice. Serve with the flatbread.

WINE SUGGESTION: Each summer for more than a decade, my wine buddy Andrew Axilrod and I have spent at least a week searching out both new discoveries and old favorites in our neighborhood in Provence. Inevitably, we spend several days in Châteauneuf-du-Pape, always making an appointment for a visit with Laurent Charvin at the Charvins' modest 20-acre vineyard. His silken and seductive red Châteauneuf-du-Pape has just a hint of blood and rare red meat, the ideal accompaniment to this classic salad as a meal.

ITALIAN SALT AND SUGAR—CURED BEEF: *CARNE SALADA*

During a weeklong visit to Verona, Italy, I was fortunate enough to sample two versions of this quick, easy, delicious cured beef. Sugar, salt, black peppercorns, and an abundance of fresh rosemary help to create a mahogany-toned home-cured meat that serves as a perfect appetizer and/or part of an antipasto plate. A relative of the air-cured bresaola—*a specialty of Valtellina, an Alpine valley in Lombardy, where it is cured for 2 1/2 to 3 months—this home version is ready to eat in just 2 to 3 days. Traditionally, the beef is sliced paper-thin and served with a drizzle of olive oil, lemon juice, and freshly ground black pepper. Other accompaniments might include caper berries, Marinated Olive Quartet (page 19), Homemade Yogurt Cheese (page 51), and Celery, Green Olive, and Anchovy Salad (page 112).*

6 SERVINGS
EQUIPMENT: AN ELECTRIC MEAT SLICER OR A VERY SHARP CHEF'S KNIFE.

1/2 cup coarse sea salt

1/3 cup sugar

1/4 cup coarse, freshly ground black pepper

1/2 cup coarsely chopped fresh rosemary leaves

2 fresh or dried bay leaves

1 pound beef fillet, or choice bottom or top round, trimmed of fat and sinew

Garnish

Olive oil

Freshly squeezed lemon juice

Capers in Vinegar (page 289)

Freshly ground black pepper

1. In a glass or stainless steel bowl, combine the salt, sugar, pepper, and herbs and toss to blend. Add the beef, rolling it in the mixture to coat. Slide the beef into a sturdy resealable plastic bag. Place the bag in a clean bowl and refrigerate for 2 to 3 days, turning the beef several times daily. The mixture will give off quite a bit of liquid. The beef can be eaten within 2 days but is traditionally cured for 15 days.

2. Several hours before serving, place the cured beef, still in the bag, in the freezer.

3. Remove the beef from the bag, discarding the brine. With the meat slicer or very sharp knife, slice the meat paper-thin. Serve immediately, drizzled with the olive oil and lemon juice. Sprinkle with the capers and season with plenty of freshly ground black pepper.

WINE SUGGESTION: The first time I sampled this beef was with our good friend Rolando Beramendi, who took us to the cozy Enoteca della Valpolicella outside of Verona. That day at lunch we sampled a myriad of wonderful dishes and wines, and with this dish Rolando ordered Giuseppe Quintarelli's concentrated Valpolicella Classico, a wine that has a leathery edge, perfect for pairing with this cured beef.

POT-AU-FEU BEEF SALAD

The cold-weather French classic of beef short ribs and beef shank simmered with winter vegetables can easily be transformed into a bright-flavored salad, one hearty enough to warm the body and light enough to lift one's spirits. The meat is best cooked a day in advance, so at serving time the salad is put together in a matter of minutes.

4 SERVINGS
EQUIPMENT: A **6**-QUART STOCKPOT;
A MESH SKIMMER; A FINE-MESH SIEVE;
DAMPENED CHEESECLOTH.

1 pound beef short ribs

1 pound beef shank

1 leek, white part only, washed and coarsely chopped

2 medium carrots, scrubbed and cut into 1/4-inch-thick rounds

1 celery rib, coarsely chopped

3 medium onions, peeled and halved

1 bouquet garni: fresh bay leaves, parsley sprigs, and thyme sprigs encased in a wire-mesh tea
   infuser or bound in a piece of cheesecloth

1 tablespoon coarse sea salt

2 shallots, trimmed, peeled, and finely minced

8 Cornichons (page 290), cut into thin rounds

12 ounces baby spinach

Classic Vinaigrette (page 324)

Fine sea salt

Coarse, freshly ground black pepper

1. In the stockpot, combine the short ribs and 3 quarts of water. Bring to a boil over high heat. With the skimmer, skim off and discard any foam that rises to the top. Reduce the heat to a simmer. Add the beef shank, leek, carrots, celery, onions, bouquet garni, and coarse salt. Simmer, uncovered, for 2 hours.

2. Remove the meat and onions from the broth and let cool. Line the sieve with dampened cheesecloth, set it over a bowl, and strain the broth through it. Let the broth cool. Discard the other vegetables and the bouquet garni. Refrigerate the meat, onions, and broth, separately, overnight.

3. Shred the meat, discarding the bones and any fatty parts. Mince the reserved onions and combine them with the shredded meat. Moisten the mixture with just enough of the reserved broth to give it a soft, smooth consistency. Add the shallots and cornichons, and refrigerate for 1 hour.

4. In a large salad bowl, toss the spinach with the vinaigrette. Mound the leaves on plates. Taste the pot-au-feu mixture for seasoning. Using 2 large spoons, shape the mixture into sausage-like *quenelles*, each about 2 inches long and 1 inch wide, and arrange them around the spinach salad.

WINE SUGGESTION: This salad requires a beefy red wine, such as the sublime Gigondas vinified at the Domaine de la Bouïssière. Their Gigondas is dense, concentrated, and full of charm.

WINTER OXTAIL SALAD WITH CORNICHONS AND CAPERS

One of the many welcoming dinners at my childhood home in the Middle West was my mother's oxtail stew, a delicately simmered mixture of oxtail and winter vegetables. I don't think I had oxtail salad until much later in life, and I think of it now as a special Saturday lunch, enjoyed in front of a roaring fire, accompanied by a tart and tangy garnish of cornichons (homemade if you can do it!), pickled onions, and hearty doses of horseradish. A few sips of lightly chilled Saint-Amour would help the mood immensely!

12 TO 16 SERVINGS
EQUIPMENT: A WIRE SKIMMER; A FINE-MESH SIEVE;
DAMPENED CHEESECLOTH.

3 pounds oxtail, cut into 4-inch pieces

1 tablespoon coarse sea salt

4 carrots, scrubbed, trimmed, and cut into 1/4-inch-thick rounds

2 leeks, white part only, washed and coarsely chopped

2 celery ribs, coarsely chopped

1 onion, halved (do not peel)

4 plump, moist garlic cloves, peeled, halved, and green germ removed

1 bouquet garni: fresh parsley stems, black peppercorns, fresh thyme sprigs, and a bay leaf, encased in a wire-mesh tea infuser or bound in a piece of cheesecloth

1 teaspoon imported French mustard

Fine sea salt

Freshly ground black pepper

2 tablespoons Capers in Vinegar (page 289), drained

12 Cornichons (page 290), cut into thin rounds, plus extra whole cornichons for garnish

Several tablespoons finely chopped fresh chives

Pickled onions, for garnish

Prepared horseradish, for garnish

1. One or 2 days before you plan to serve the salad, tie the oxtail pieces in a large bundle with string. Place the bundle in a large pot and add cold water to cover. Bring just to a simmer over moderate heat. Simmer, uncovered, skimming regularly to remove all impurities, for about 40 minutes.

2. Add the coarse sea salt to the cooking liquid. Add the vegetables, garlic, and bouquet garni. Return to a simmer, skim again, and simmer, partially covered and undisturbed, until the meat is falling off the bone, 3 to 4 hours. Let the meat cool in the cooking liquid.

3. Remove the meat from the bones and shred it, placing it in a large bowl. You should have about 4 cups of shredded meat. Discard the bones. Remove and discard the bouquet garni and the vegetables from the pot. Line the sieve with the dampened cheesecloth and strain the cooking liquid into a bowl. Mix 2/3 cup of the strained liquid with the mustard. Add this to the shredded meat and toss to blend. Season generously with fine salt and pepper. Add the capers and sliced cornichons, and toss to blend.

4. To serve, mound the oxtail salad on small salad plates. Sprinkle with the chives. Serve, passing the whole cornichons, pickled onions, and horseradish separately.

WINE SUGGESTION: Try a *cru* Beaujolais, such as a light and fruity chilled Saint-Amour.

SPRING BEEF SALAD WITH SPINACH, CHERRY TOMATOES, AND ASPARAGUS

Normally, when I am planning a meal, I have half a dozen ideas when I head for the market, and I end up choosing whatever is freshest that day. That's certainly what happened one early spring morning in Provence, when there were slim pickings around our little village. Half the items on my list were just not available, so I simply bought everything that looked good. As I often do when stumped, I said, "You're Patricia Wells. You should know what to cook!" I returned home with a basket of goodies and had a good head start with items already in the refrigerator. The light and tangy dressing unites all the colorful, full-flavored vegetables, topped with thin slices of rare-roasted beef. Here, I like to steam both the broccoli and the asparagus, simplifying the salad and making for an easy cleanup.

4 SERVINGS

EQUIPMENT: A STEAMER WITH **2** STEAMING BASKETS.

3 cups broccoli florets and stems

16 thin green asparagus spears (about 1 pound), trimmed

8 ounces baby spinach

4 small spring onions or scallions, white part only, trimmed, peeled, and cut into thin slices

Creamy Lemon-Mustard Dressing (page 325)

Fine sea salt

Coarse, freshly ground black pepper

24 cherry tomatoes, halved

8 ounces very thin slices Rare-Roasted Beef (page 219)

1. Prepare a large bowl of ice water.

2. Bring 1 quart of water to a simmer in the bottom of a steamer. Place the broccoli in one steamer basket and the asparagus in another. Stack the baskets over the simmering water, cover, and steam just until the vegetables are lightly cooked but still firm, 5 to 10 minutes.

3. Remove the steamer baskets and let the water drain from the vegetables. Plunge the vegetables into the ice water so they cool down as quickly as possible. The vegetables will cool in 1 to 2 minutes, any longer and they will become soggy. Drain, and wrap in a thick kitchen towel to dry.

4. In a large bowl, combine the spinach, broccoli, and spring onions. Toss with just enough dressing to lightly and evenly coat the ingredients. Taste for seasoning. Mound the salad on large salad plates. Artfully arrange the cherry tomatoes and the asparagus around the edges of the salads. Drape the slices of roast beef over the center of the salads. Season with salt and pepper, and serve.

WINE SUGGESTION: More often than not, our choice will be our own peppery red wine, Clos Chanteduc, a Côtes-du-Rhône that is a fine blend of old Grenache vines, teamed up with touches of Syrah and Mourvèdre.

THAI BEEF SALAD

All manner of Asian food finds its way into salad-as-a-meal menus, and this is a regular favorite on our lunch or dinner table. Marinate your rare-roasted beef with a touch of citrus, sesame oil, soy sauce, and fresh ginger. Try to do this at least 2 hours in advance, to let the Thai flavors blend into the meat. At mealtime, add the avalanche of delicious vegetables, herbs, and nuts that will turn that marinated beef into a tasty, tempting meal.

4 SERVINGS

EQUIPMENT: A SMALL JAR WITH A LID.

3 tablespoons freshly squeezed lime or lemon juice

2 tablespoons Vietnamese fish sauce, preferably Phu Quoc brand

1 tablespoon best-quality sesame oil (such as Leblanc)

2 teaspoons tamari or other Japanese soy sauce

1 tablespoon finely grated fresh ginger

2 plump, moist garlic cloves, peeled, halved, green germ removed, and minced

1 pound Rare-Roasted Beef (page 219), cut across the grain into paper-thin slices, then into thin strips (See Note)

8 ounces cherry tomatoes, halved

1 large cucumber, halved lengthwise and thinly sliced on the diagonal (do not peel)

1 red onion, peeled, halved crosswise, and cut into thin rings

2 fresh red bird's-eye chiles, halved lengthwise, seeded, and thinly sliced lengthwise

1 cup fresh mint, leaves only, large leaves torn

1 bunch fresh cilantro, leaves only

1 bunch fresh basil, leaves only, large leaves torn

1/3 cup toasted peanuts, coarsely chopped

4 fresh kaffir lime leaves, center veins removed, cut into julienne

1. In the small jar, whisk together the citrus juice, fish sauce, sesame oil, tamari, ginger, and garlic. Cover and shake to blend. Taste for seasoning.

2. Layer the beef in a glass or ceramic dish. Pour half the dressing over the beef. Cover and refrigerate for 2 hours, turning the meat from time to time, to infuse the meat with the dressing.

3. At serving time, combine the tomatoes, cucumber, onion, and chiles in a large, shallow bowl. Toss with the remaining dressing. Add the beef and toss to coat. Serve, garnished with the herbs, peanuts, and kaffir lime leaves.

NOTE: Cutting the beef across the grain will make the slices as tender as possible.

WINE SUGGESTION: A good chilled beer is perfect here. Choose your favorite brand.

SPICY LAMB SAUSAGES FROM BORDEAUX

Almost everyone loves sausages, and this traditional French pairing of spicy lamb sausages and oysters lives on for good reason: the hot, well-seasoned meat pairs beautifully with the bright, cool tang of the oysters. The combination is often served at roadside shacks along the water near Bordeaux and makes a fine late-morning snack or quick lunchtime meal. The sausage patties can be prepared in a flash, even the day before. Have your fishmonger open the oysters and you have a meal on the table before you know it.

4 SERVINGS

EQUIPMENT: A SPICE GRINDER OR A COFFEE MILL.

1 tablespoon cumin seeds

1 1/2 pounds ground lamb

1 tablespoon ground cinnamon

1/8 teaspoon hot red pepper flakes

1 tablespoon fresh or dried thyme leaves

1 teaspoon fine sea salt

3 lemons, each cut into 4 wedges

12 oysters on the half shell

1. Place the cumin seeds in a small, dry skillet over moderate heat. Shake the skillet regularly until the seeds are fragrant and evenly toasted, about 2 minutes. Watch carefully! They can burn quickly. Transfer the cumin to a large plate to cool. Grind to a fine powder in a spice grinder.

2. In a large, shallow bowl, combine all the ingredients except the lemon and oysters. With your hands, mix to blend the spices into the lamb. The sausage is best if the mixture is made at least 1 hour and up to 24 hours in advance, to let the spices permeate the meat. Store in an airtight container in the refrigerator.

3. For each sausage, shape 1/4 cup of the mixture into a patty that is 1/2 inch thick and about 2 1/2 inches in diameter, to make about 12 patties in all. Heat a large skillet over moderately high heat until hot. Add as many sausage patties as will fit without crowding. Cook the patties for 4 minutes, turning them over halfway through cooking. Reduce the heat to moderately low and continue cooking until the patties are no longer pink in the center, several minutes more, turning halfway through cooking. Repeat with remaining sausage patties.

4. Place several sausage patties and a lemon wedge on one side of each of 4 dinner plates. Serve with the oysters on the half shell, and pass the remaining lemon wedges separately.

WINE SUGGESTION: I'd go for a white that can stand up to the spicy lamb but that will also pair with the briny oysters: Try a white Bordeaux Graves. I especially love the offerings from Château Villa Bel-Air.

LAMB SALAD WITH POTATOES, PEPPERS, TARRAGON, AND CHERRY TOMATOES

One evening after a week's worth of work organizing a special cooking class in Provence, we sat down with friends Jeffrey and Katherine Bergman to enjoy this quickly made Sunday night salad as a meal. Use any leftover meat or poultry here. The tarragon adds a nice bite.

4 SERVINGS
EQUIPMENT: A STEAMER.

8 ounces firm, yellow-fleshed potatoes (such as Yukon Gold)

Lemon and Olive Oil Dressing (page 330)

1 pound roasted leg of lamb (see page 244), trimmed of fat and cut into 1/2-inch cubes

6 Cornichons (page 290), cut into 1/4-inch-thick rounds

1 tablespoon Capers in Vinegar (page 289), rinsed

1 or 2 Pickled Peppers (page 301), finely chopped

1/2 cup minced fresh tarragon leaves

1 shallot, trimmed, peeled, and cut into thin rings

1 cup mixed red and yellow cherry tomatoes, halved

1. Scrub the potatoes but do not peel them. Bring 1 quart of water to a simmer in the bottom of the steamer. Place the potatoes on the steaming rack. Place the rack over simmering water, cover, and steam just until the potatoes are fully cooked, about 25 minutes.

2. Place several tablespoons of the dressing in a large bowl. While the potatoes are still warm, cut them crosswise into thin slices and add them directly to the dressing.

Toss to thoroughly coat them. Add the lamb, cornichons, capers, jalapeño, tarragon, shallot, and tomatoes. Toss to coat all the ingredients. Serve.

WINE SUGGESTION: In my wine cellar in Provence, I arrange all the daily drinking reds right inside the door, so any guest can just step in and reach out and a welcome bottle is at the ready. A steady favorite is the red Côtes-du-Rhône Villages Cairanne from Perrin & Fils, a wine that won hands down in a Cairanne tasting in our wine class several years ago. The wine, a classic blend of Grenache, Syrah, and Mourvèdre, has a long finish, a great balance of fruit and acidity.

THYME-MARINATED ROAST LEG OF LAMB

During our cooking classes in Provence, we often open with a Sunday night dinner that includes this fragrant, moist local lamb cooked in our wood oven, fired with the previous year's grapevine clippings and various oak logs from the property. It has become a perennial favorite and one of which we never tire. I always hope for plenty of leftovers so the next day I can turn it into a salad.

16 SERVINGS
EQUIPMENT: A ROASTING PAN WITH A RACK;
AN INSTANT-READ THERMOMETER; A FINE-MESH SIEVE.

1 butterflied leg of lamb (2 to 3 pounds), trimmed to a thickness of 2 to 2 1/2 inches

2 fresh thyme sprigs

6 fresh or dried bay leaves

2 fresh oregano sprigs

2 fresh rosemary sprigs

2 fresh mint sprigs

12 plump, moist garlic cloves, peeled, halved, and green germ removed

12 whole black peppercorns

1/2 cup extra-virgin olive oil

Fine sea salt

1/2 teaspoon ground *piment d'Espelette* or other ground mild chile pepper

Freshly ground black pepper

1. Place the lamb in a sturdy resealable plastic bag. Arrange the herbs on both sides of the lamb. Add the garlic and peppercorns. In a small bowl, combine the oil, 2 teaspoons salt, and the Espelette pepper. Stir to dissolve the salt. Pour the oil mixture into the bag and seal. Massage the meat to distribute the seasoning. Refrigerate for at least 24 and up to 72 hours.

2. Remove the lamb from the refrigerator about 3 hours before roasting.

3. Preheat the oven to 450°F. Place a rack in the center of the oven.

4. Remove the lamb from the bag and place it on a platter. Pour the marinade ingredients into the roasting pan. Place the lamb on the rack in the roasting pan. Place the roasting pan in the oven and roast, turning the lamb once, until an instant-read thermometer inserted into the thickest part of the meat reads 130° to 135°F, 30 to 45 minutes (or cook to desired doneness).

5. Remove the lamb from the oven and season both sides of the meat generously with salt and pepper. Transfer the lamb to a platter and tent it loosely with foil, reserving the sauce in the pan. Let the lamb rest for at least 10 minutes. (It will continue to cook as it rests.)

6. Meanwhile, prepare the sauce: Remove and discard the herbs, peppercorns, and garlic. Place the pan over medium heat and use a metal spatula to scrape up any bits that cling to the bottom. Cook for 2 to 3 minutes, scraping and stirring. Do not let the liquid burn. Spoon off and discard any excess fat. Add several tablespoons cold water to deglaze (hot water will cloud the sauce). Bring to a boil. Reduce the heat to low and simmer until thickened, about 5 minutes.

7. While the sauce is cooking, carve the lamb into thick slices and place them on a warmed platter.

8. Strain the sauce through the fine-mesh sieve and pour it into a sauceboat. Serve immediately, with the lamb.

SCRUBBED BREAD *TARTINES* WITH CHORIZO, MANCHEGO, AND TOMATOES

Chorizo is certainly having its moment in the sun, showing up on tables small and tables grand, in magazines and cookbooks. And it's no wonder: the best chorizo packs a flavor punch, with a sit-up-and-take-notice spicy personality. Paired with the equally assertive Manchego sheep's milk cheese, this makes for a forward-flavored salad. I like to grill my bread, then "scrub" it with fresh tomatoes so the warm bread instantly absorbs the delicious juices. The toast is then topped with tomato slices. I scatter the cubed cheese and sausage around the tartines, *and fill out the meal with a simple tossed green salad.*

4 SERVINGS

4 thin slices Multigrain Sourdough Bread (page 270), toasted

4 ripe heirloom tomatoes, cut into thin slices

Fleur de sel

8 ounces Manchego cheese (or other sheep's milk cheese), cut into small cubes

8 ounces thinly sliced or cubed smoked chorizo sausage

24 large Spanish olives or green Picholine olives

6 cups mixed salad greens tossed with dressing of choice

Scrub a toasted bread slice with the bottom slice of tomato, until all that is left of the tomato is the skin. Sprinkle with a little *fleur de sel*. Top with a quarter of the tomato slices. Place the bread on a plate. Scatter some of the cheese, sausage, and olives around the bread. Arrange a mound of dressed salad alongside. Repeat for the remaining *tartines* and salads.

WINE SUGGESTION: Spanish, of course. Our good friends Marivi Pulido and her husband, Gordon Brown, are always spoiling us with fantastic wines from Spain. Their latest treasure came from the Hacienda Monasterio Ribera del Duero, an elegant and smoky red wine that honors this simple but sublime salad.

PORK AND SPINACH TERRINE WITH MUSTARD SORBET

Terrines can be complicated and laborious or quick and easy, and this one falls into the latter category. It is also beautiful. One simply mixes a nice dose of cloves, garlic, and black pepper into already seasoned bulk pork sausage, then adds a healthy, colorful layer of wilted spinach. The result is moist, pretty, and full-flavored. I serve this with mustard sorbet, a most unusual idea but one that always pleases as well as surprises.

8 SERVINGS

EQUIPMENT: A SPICE GRINDER OR A COFFEE MILL; A **10**-QUART PASTA POT FITTED WITH A COLANDER; A FOOD PROCESSOR OR A BLENDER; A **2**-CUP TERRINE OR LOAF PAN WITH A LID; BAKING PARCHMENT; A ROASTING PAN.

1/2 teaspoon whole cloves

2 tablespoons coarse sea salt

12 ounces fresh spinach or Swiss chard leaves

1/2 teaspoon freshly ground nutmeg

12 ounces seasoned bulk pork sausage

4 plump, moist garlic cloves, peeled, halved, green germ removed, and minced

3/4 teaspoon fine sea salt

2 teaspoons coarsely ground black pepper

Garnish

Cornichons (page 290)

Imported French mustard

Prepared horseradish

Pickled onions

Mustard Sorbet (recipe follows), for serving

1. Preheat the oven to 350°F. In the spice grinder, grind the cloves to a fine powder.

2. Fill the pasta pot with 8 quarts of water and bring it to a rolling boil over high heat. Add the salt and spinach and blanch, uncovered, just until the spinach is wilted, 1 to 2 minutes. Immediately remove the colander from the water and drain. Run cold water over the spinach so that it cools down as quickly as possible. This will help the spinach retain its bright green color. Drain. With your hands, press the spinach several times to remove excess water. Wrap in an absorbent kitchen towel.

3. In the food processor or the blender, puree the spinach with the nutmeg.

4. Place the pork sausage meat in a large bowl and sprinkle with the ground cloves, garlic, fine salt, and pepper. With your hands, work the seasoning into the pork. Fry up a spoonful of the mixture and taste it for seasoning.

5. Line the terrine with baking parchment, letting several inches hang over each end. (This will make it easier to remove the terrine in one piece once cooked.) Spoon half of the seasoned meat into the terrine. Press down to even out the meat. Spoon all of the spinach puree over the meat, pressing down to even out the spinach. Spoon the remaining meat on top of the spinach, pressing down to even out the meat. Fold the parchment over the top of the meat. Place the lid of the terrine on top of the parchment, or cover loosely with foil.

6. Fill a roasting pan with several inches of hot water and place the terrine in the water bath. Place the roasting pan in the oven and cook until the terrine is firm but not browned, 45 minutes to 1 hour. The water should just simmer gently; check it halfway through the cooking time and if necessary, add some boiling water.

7. Remove the terrine from the water bath and let it cool on a wire rack for 2 hours. Then cover and refrigerate for 12 hours before serving. (Store in the refrigerator for up to 3 days.)

8. To serve, pull up on the parchment to remove the terrine. Cut in thin slices. The terrine can be served warm as a main course or cold as a first course. Serve with a

garnish of cornichons, mustard, horseradish, and pickled onions, and a scoop of Mustard Sorbet. (Store the terrine, without the garnishes, in the covered container in the refrigerator for up to 3 days.)

WINE SUGGESTION: I am a white-wine lover, and feel that the pork, paired with the acidity of the mustard sorbet, cornichons, horseradish, and pickled onions, deserves a very simple, daily-drinking white. An easy choice is Lavieille Ferme from Perrin & Fils.

MUSTARD SORBET

I first sampled this tangy, spectacular sorbet at the fine, modern Paris bistro Itinéraires in the 5th arrondissement. It was served with a meaty terrine, so I created my Pork and Spinach Terrine to team up with this savory sorbet.

8 SERVINGS

EQUIPMENT: AN ELECTRIC MIXER FITTED WITH A WHISK; AN ICE-CREAM MAKER.

2 large egg whites

2 cups fresh, soft cheese (such as *fromage blanc* or yogurt cheese)

6 tablespoons imported French mustard from a freshly opened jar

1. With the mixer, whisk the egg whites at low speed until frothy. Gradually increase the speed to high. Continue whisking at high speed until stiff but not dry.

2. In a large bowl, whisk together the cheese and mustard until smooth. With a spatula, gradually fold the cheese mixture into the egg whites. Transfer to the ice-cream maker and freeze according to the manufacturer's instructions.

GRILLED SAUSAGE SALAD WITH QUICK APPLE COMPOTE AND WATERCRESS

This cold-weather salad was inspired by a visit to Afaria, a lively bistro in Paris's 15th arrondissement specializing in fare from France's southwest. While dining there one evening, I sampled a delicious salad of boudin noir *(blood sausage) with a grilled mustard topping. I set my mind to work and came up with this version, a classic French combination of blood sausage and apples. I have made it with a variety of sausages:* boudin noir *of course, but also fresh chorizo,* boudin blanc *(a fine veal sausage), and fresh kielbasa-style pork sausage. For apple varieties, I favor Cox's Orange Pippen, Boskoop, or Reine de Reinettes. You can also try McIntosh, Cortland, or Gravenstein. Serve the sausage with a bright-flavored watercress salad dressed with a nutty touch of sesame oil.*

4 SERVINGS

4 cooking apples, cored and cut into eighths (do not peel)

1/2 cup water

1 teaspoon ground cinnamon

1 teaspoon ground ginger

3 tablespoons lavender honey

1 pound sausage links of choice, cut crosswise into 1 1/2-inch pieces

2 tablespoons imported French coarse-grain mustard, plus extra for serving

Several handfuls of fresh watercress, stemmed

1 to 2 tablespoons best-quality sesame oil (such as Leblanc)

Fine sea salt

Coarse, freshly ground black pepper

1. Preheat the broiler.

2. In a medium saucepan, combine the apples with the water and the cinnamon, ginger, and honey. Cook, covered, over low heat until the apples fall apart and create a loose compote, about 8 minutes. Keep warm.

3. Place the sausage slices side by side, cut-side up, on a baking sheet. Broil for 1 to 2 minutes. Turn the sausages over and coat the tops with the mustard. Return to the broiler and broil for 1 to 2 minutes more.

4. In a large salad bowl, toss the watercress with just enough sesame oil to lightly and evenly coat the greens. Season with salt and pepper.

5. Mound the watercress on large dinner plates. Arrange the apple compote alongside. Arrange the sausages on top of the watercress. Serve with additional mustard for the sausages.

WINE SUGGESTION: A fruity wine from France's southwest is ideal here. I love the all-organic Irouléguy, and favor the offering from Domaine Arretxea, a blend of three grapes—Tannat, Cabernet Franc, and Cabernet Sauvignon. It pairs beautifully with this salad.

SEARED PORK TENDERLOIN SALAD WITH TURNIP GREENS AND STEAMED TURNIPS

Pork tenderloin seems to be everyone's favorite meat for searing and grilling, and the light, moist, flavorful cut finds its way into this delightful cool-weather salad. In the fall we always plant turnips in our winter garden and look forward to unearthing tiny specimens. We also covet the tender greens, which are a pure, delicious, tangy delight. The red wine sauce can be prepared well in advance, but if there is no time for the sauce, serve this with homemade fig chutney or a store-bought fruit chutney.

4 SERVINGS
EQUIPMENT: A FINE-MESH SIEVE;
A MANDOLINE OR A VERY SHARP KNIFE; A STEAMER.

Marinade

1/2 teaspoon ground cinnamon

1/4 cup extra-virgin olive oil

2 tablespoons honey

3 whole cloves

Coarse, freshly ground black pepper

1 large pork tenderloin (about 1 1/4 pounds), trimmed of fat and silverskin

Sweet spiced red wine sauce

Grated zest of 2 lemons, preferably organic

1 cup reduced Homemade Chicken Stock (page 310)

1 cup ruby port wine

1/2 cup best-quality sherry-wine vinegar

2 cinnamon sticks

2 segments star anise

4 pitted prunes, coarsely chopped

Fine sea salt

Freshly ground black pepper

2 teaspoons unsalted butter

1 tablespoon extra-virgin olive oil

Fleur de sel

Coarse, freshly ground black pepper

1 pound small, firm turnips

About 4 cups fresh young turnip greens or baby spinach, washed and dried

About 1 tablespoon Classic Vinaigrette (page 324)

Fig Chutney (page 296) or Figs in Vinegar (page 294), for serving

1. Prepare the marinade: In a medium bowl, combine all the marinade ingredients and whisk to blend.

2. Cut the tenderloin in half, cutting crosswise through the meat. Cut each half lengthwise into 4 even slices. Add the pork to the marinade and toss to coat. Cover and refrigerate for at least 3 hours and up to 6 hours.

3. Meanwhile, prepare the sauce: Place the lemon zest in a medium saucepan. Add the stock, port, vinegar, cinnamon sticks, star anise, and prunes to the pan and bring to a boil. Reduce the heat and simmer for 30 minutes. Strain the sauce through a fine-mesh sieve into a clean saucepan, and simmer until reduced to 2/3 cup, 10 to 15 minutes. Season with salt and pepper to taste.

4. At least 1 hour before cooking the pork, remove it from the refrigerator.

5. In a skillet that is large enough to hold the pork, heat the 1 tablespoon olive oil over moderately high heat. Drain the meat and sear it, turning the pieces regularly with a pair of tongs, until richly browned, 3 to 4 minutes. Remove from the heat and season with *fleur de sel* and pepper. Let rest for 10 minutes before serving.

6. Rewarm the sauce as necessary, and whisk in the butter. Transfer the sauce to small individual bowls to use as a dipping sauce. (The sauce can be served slightly warm or at room temperature.) Store in an airtight container in the freezer for up to 3 months; then thaw and rewarm at serving time.

7. Just before serving the salad, steam the turnips: Peel the turnips, and using the mandoline or very sharp knife, cut them crosswise into very thin slices. Bring 1 quart of water to a simmer in the bottom of the steamer. Place the turnips on the steaming rack. Place the rack over simmering water, cover, and steam just until the turnips are cooked through, 1 to 2 minutes.

8. Place the turnip greens in a large bowl, and toss with just enough vinaigrette to coat them lightly and evenly. Mound the salad on large dinner plates. Top with the steamed turnips. Arrange the pork on top of the turnips. Place a small bowl of the wine sauce at the edge of each plate. Serve warm, with a bowl of Fig Chutney or Figs in Vinegar.

WINE SUGGESTION: I love a bright white with this salad, such as a Riesling from Ostertag or Zind-Humbrecht, or a light red Pinot Noir such as a Savigny from the house of Tollot-Beaut.

QUICK-SEARED VEAL LOIN WITH CAPERS AND RADICCHIO-ARUGULA SALAD

The afternoon I set out to prepare this quick-seared veal fillet, I stopped in at butcher Gilles's shop to order the meat. Never one to stint on freshness, he took an entire calf out of his cooler and prepared my loin of veal! Now that's service.

4 SERVINGS

1 pound boneless veal (or pork) loin, trimmed of fat

Fine sea salt

Coarse, freshly ground black pepper

Several tablespoons extra-virgin olive oil

Several handfuls fresh arugula

1 head radicchio, outer leaves discarded, leaves separated and coarsely shredded

About 20 shavings of Parmigiano-Reggiano cheese

1/4 cup Capers in Vinegar (page 289), drained

1. Season the veal all over with salt and pepper. In a large skillet, heat 1 tablespoon of the oil over moderate heat until it is hot but not smoking. Sear the veal until cooked to your liking, about 3 minutes per side for medium-rare (or cook to desired doneness). Remove from the heat, transfer to a cutting board, season once more, and let rest, loosely covered with foil, for 10 minutes.

2. In a large bowl, combine the arugula, radicchio, and cheese. Toss with just enough olive oil to lightly and evenly coat the ingredients. Season with salt and pepper.

3. Slice the meat into very thin slices and layer on the side of 4 large dinner plates. Arrange the salad alongside, add the capers, and serve.

   WINE SUGGESTION: A fine Vouvray Chenin Blanc from the house of Huet or a crisp Pinot Gris from the Alsatian winemaker André Ostertag.

VEAL AND POTATO SALAD WITH OLIVES, SPRING ONIONS, CAPERS, AND PARSLEY

Leftover meats, poultry, or firm fish can be the backbone of a perfect salad as a meal. One evening in Provence we had some leftover veal roast and I gathered these ingredients to make a delightful, flavorful, light dinner. Other possibilities here are roast pork, beef, or poultry or cooked firm fish, such as tuna.

4 SERVINGS

EQUIPMENT: A STEAMER.

1/4 cup extra-virgin olive oil

Grated zest of 2 lemons, preferably organic

2 tablespoons freshly squeezed lemon juice

1 tablespoon imported French mustard

6 small spring onions or scallions, white part only, trimmed, peeled, and cut into very thin slices

1/4 cup Capers in Vinegar (page 289), drained

1 tablespoon Quick Lemon Confit (page 297), chopped

12 green Picholine olives, pitted

1 red or orange bell pepper, trimmed, seeds removed, and cubed

8 ounces roasted veal, cut into 1/2-inch cubes

1 pound firm, yellow-fleshed potatoes (such as Yukon Gold)

Dressing for the potatoes

1/4 cup extra-virgin olive oil

2 tablespoons freshly squeezed lemon juice

1 tablespoon imported French mustard

Fine sea salt

Coarse, freshly ground black pepper

1/2 cup fresh parsley leaves, coarsely chopped

1. In a salad bowl, combine the olive oil, lemon zest, lemon juice, mustard, spring onions, capers, lemon confit, olives, and bell pepper. Toss to blend. Taste for seasoning. Add the veal, and toss to coat.

2. Scrub the potatoes but do not peel them. Bring 1 quart of water to a simmer in the bottom of the steamer. Place the potatoes on the steaming rack. Place the rack over simmering water, cover, and steam just until the potatoes are fully cooked, about 25 minutes.

3. Meanwhile, prepare the dressing for the potatoes: In a shallow bowl, combine the oil, lemon juice, and mustard. Season with salt and pepper.

4. Once the potatoes are cooked, quarter them (without peeling) and add them directly to the dressing. Do this while the potatoes are still warm so they absorb the dressing. Toss to thoroughly coat the potatoes with the dressing. Add the parsley and toss again. Taste for seasoning. Combine the potato mixture and the veal mixture and toss gently to evenly distribute all the ingredients. Serve warm.

WINE SUGGESTION: Veal takes a crisp white. Try a Sancerre from the houses of Alphonse Mellot or François Cotat.

BREAD

I AM SURE THAT I WAS A BAKER IN A FORMER LIFE, FOR I CANNOT IMAGINE A SALAD MEAL WITHOUT A PERFECT BREAD ACCOMPANIMENT. MY HOMEMADE SOURDOUGH IS MY BREAD OF CHOICE, BUT FOR VARIETY, I ALSO ENJOY A THICK SLICE OF HAM AND CHEESE BREAD, A ROUND OF CRISPY FLATBREAD, WARM CHICKPEA FLOUR CREPES, OR THIN BREAD CRISPS. EVEN MORE SUB-STANTIAL SIDEKICKS INCLUDE A SIZZLING-FROM-THE-OVEN TOMATO AND MUSTARD TART AND A FRAGRANT ALSATIAN ONION TART. EVERY SALAD LOVES THAT EXTRA TOUCH OF CRUNCH, AND THAT'S WHERE SPICY TORTILLA CHIPS OR PARMESAN CROUTONS ARE IDEAL EMBELLISHMENTS.

CRISPY FLATBREAD

An intense feeling of satisfaction comes over me as I knead, as the triumvirate of flour, water, and salt transforms into all manner of golden, fragrant breads, thick and thin, hearty and delicate. This is a variation on the Sardinian Parchment Bread, or Carta da Musica, from my Trattoria *cookbook. While the former is rolled by hand into thin rounds, this version is rolled with a pasta machine. If you have an electric machine, the entire batch can be made in about 15 minutes!*

10 FLATBREADS
EQUIPMENT: A FOOD PROCESSOR; A PASTA MAKER;
2 NONSTICK BAKING SHEETS.

1 cup whole wheat pastry flour, plus extra if needed and for dusting

1/2 cup fine semolina flour

1 teaspoon fine sea salt

1/2 cup lukewarm water

1. Preheat the oven to 500°F.

2. In the food processor, combine the 1 cup whole wheat pastry flour with the semolina flour and salt. With the motor running, slowly add the water through the feed tube. Stop just as the dough forms a ball. Transfer the dough to a clean, floured work surface. Knead gently just until smooth, working more flour into the dough if necessary. The dough should be firm and pliable, and not sticky.

3. Divide the dough into 4 even balls. Set the adjustment knob on a pasta roller to No. 1. Roll the first ball through the machine 3 to 4 times. The dough will be ragged at first and will become more firm and supple each time it is rolled through the machine. Roll the dough into thin sheets through settings No. 2 and 3. Once the dough has been rolled through No. 3, cut the dough in half crosswise. Roll each

of those pieces of dough through rollers No. 4, 5, 6, and 7. Each piece of dough should measure roughly 4 by 10 inches.

4. Place the 2 pieces of dough on the baking sheets and bake until golden and crisp, 5 to 7 minutes. Watch carefully; ovens vary and the flatbreads may cook more quickly in some than in others. Remove to a basket to cool.

5. Repeat the procedure with the remaining rounds of dough. Consume the bread the day it is baked.

VARIATION: Knead 1 tablespoon finely minced fresh rosemary leaves into the dough.

TORTILLA CHIPS

These small and crispy chips fulfill one's need for a good crunch. I love to have these on hand as a snack, to serve as a base for all manner of appetizers, or just to break up and add to salads. Try the chips topped with a paper-thin slice of gravlax (see page 150), garnished with a bit of horseradish.

64 CHIPS

EQUIPMENT: **3** BAKING SHEETS.

Eight 8-inch yellow corn tortillas, preferably without preservatives

Olive oil or olive oil spray for brushing the tortillas

Flavorings: Red Hot Salt (page 307), Lemon Zest Salt (page 306), Fennel and Saffron Salt (page 305), sesame seeds, red pepper flakes, fennel seeds, coarsely ground black pepper, ground toasted cumin seeds

1. Arrange 3 racks in the oven. (If you do not have 3 racks, bake the chips in two batches.) Preheat the oven to 425°F.

2. Stack the tortillas and cut them into 8 even wedges. Arrange the wedges in a single layer on the baking sheets. Brush or spray the chips with the olive oil. Sprinkle with your choice of flavoring. Place the baking sheets in the oven and bake until deep golden, 8 to 10 minutes. Remove from the oven and let sit for 2 to 3 minutes to cool and to crisp up. (Store in an airtight container at room temperature for up to 1 week.)

FIG AND HAZELNUT BREAD

This wholesome quick bread, loaded with dried figs and whole hazelnuts, helps to make up an ideal salad as a meal when served with a crisp green salad and a cheese platter.

1 LOAF, **24** THIN SLICES

EQUIPMENT: A NONSTICK **1**-QUART RECTANGULAR BREAD PAN.

1 teaspoon best-quality hazelnut oil (such as Leblanc)

2 cups (8 ounces) dried figs, diced

1 cup whole hazelnuts, toasted

1/2 teaspoon baking soda

1/2 teaspoon fine sea salt

1/2 cup honey

2 large eggs, lightly beaten

1 teaspoon vanilla extract

1 1/2 cups whole wheat flour

1. Center a rack in the oven. Preheat the oven to 375°F. Coat the pan with the oil, and set it aside.

2. In a large bowl, combine the figs, hazelnuts, baking soda, salt, and honey. Add 3/4 cup hottest possible tap water and stir to blend. Add the eggs and vanilla extract, and stir to blend thoroughly and evenly. Slowly add the flour, stirring to blend thoroughly. The batter will be fairly thick.

3. Pour the batter into the prepared bread pan, evening out the top with the back of a spatula. Bake until a toothpick inserted into the center of the bread comes out clean, 40 to 50 minutes.

4. Remove the pan from the oven. Let it sit for at least 10 minutes before carefully running a blunt knife along the sides of the pan to release the bread. Carefully turn it out onto a wire rack to cool. Do not slice the bread for at least 1 hour, for it will continue to bake as it cools. (The bread can be stored at room temperature for up to 3 days, tightly wrapped in plastic.) Serve in very thin slices.

HAM AND CHEESE BREAD

My Provençal cheese merchant, Josiane Deal, always has a stack of recipe cards arranged near the entrance of her fragrant shop, and as often as not I slip a card or two into my purse as I exit. One Christmas a recipe for this ham and cheese bread caught my eye. I instantly re-created it, making it a bit more Provençal by using olive oil instead of butter and cutting back a tad on the cheese and ham. The addition of yogurt here makes for a very tender, moist bread. It's been a family favorite ever since and finds its way to the table often, worthy as an accompaniment to any salad one might serve. Try it toasted— delicious!

1 LOAF

EQUIPMENT: A NONSTICK 1-QUART RECTANGULAR BREAD PAN.

5 tablespoons extra-virgin olive oil, plus extra for oiling the pan

1 1/4 cups unbleached, all-purpose flour

2 teaspoons baking powder

1/2 teaspoon fine sea salt

3 large eggs, lightly beaten

1/3 cup plain yogurt

5 ounces aged French Comté cheese, cut into 1/4-inch cubes

5 ounces best-quality cooked ham, cut into 1/4-inch cubes

1/3 cup best-quality black olives, pitted and halved

1. Center a rack in the oven. Preheat the oven to 400°F. Lightly oil the pan.

2. In a large bowl, combine the flour, baking powder, salt, eggs, olive oil, and yogurt. Stir to blend. Add the cheese, ham, and olives, and stir just to combine the ingredients.

3. Pour the batter into the prepared pan. Place the pan in the oven and bake until the bread is firm and golden, 25 to 30 minutes. Remove the pan from the oven and place it on a wire rack to cool. Once cooled, unmold and serve the bread at room temperature. (Store at room temperature wrapped in foil for up to 3 days.)

HOMEMADE PITA BREAD

I admit that the first time I made this bread and the lovely rounds ballooned into flying saucers right before my eyes, I nearly jumped for joy. Little things do sometimes offer us exceptional satisfaction! These breads bear no resemblance to gummy store-bought pita breads. Rather, they are ultra-crispy flatbreads that are a perfect match for all the Middle Eastern salads one can conjure up, including the Smoky Eggplant Dip (page 13) and the Chickpea and Sesame Dip (page 10). Make these with a mix of whole wheat flour and unbleached white flour and you will be rewarded with a truly wholesome flavor as well as a deep golden color. The first time I made these, the baked breads lacked salt, so the next time I sprinkled a touch of fleur de sel *on the dough as it went into the oven. Loved it, and have continued to do so ever since.*

16 BREADS, ABOUT **7** INCHES IN DIAMETER
EQUIPMENT: A HEAVY-DUTY MIXER FITTED WITH A DOUGH HOOK; A BAKING STONE;
A WOODEN PIZZA PEEL; A METAL PIZZA PEEL OR A LARGE METAL SPATULA.

2 teaspoons active dry yeast

1 tablespoon sugar

3 cups whole wheat flour

1 tablespoon coarse sea salt

1 tablespoon extra-virgin olive oil

2 cups unbleached, all-purpose flour, plus extra if needed and for dusting

Polenta, for dusting the pizza peel

Fleur de sel

1. In the bowl of the heavy-duty mixer, combine the yeast, sugar, and 2 1/2 cups lukewarm water and stir to dissolve the yeast. Add the whole wheat flour, a cup at a time, stirring to create a loose sponge. Cover and let the sponge rest for at least 10 minutes and up to 2 hours.

2. Add the coarse salt and the olive oil to the sponge, and mix. Add the 2 cups all-purpose flour, mixing at medium speed until most of the flour has been absorbed and the dough forms a ball. Continue to mix until the dough is soft and satiny but still firm, 2 to 3 minutes, adding flour as necessary to keep the dough from sticking. Transfer the ball of dough to a clean work surface and knead by hand for 1 minute. The dough should be smooth and should spring back when you indent it with your fingertip.

3. Place the dough in a large bowl and cover it tightly with plastic wrap. Let the dough rise at room temperature until doubled in bulk, about 1 1/2 hours. (The dough can be kept for up to 7 days in the refrigerator. Simply punch down the dough as it doubles or triples. Over time, the dough develops an almost tangy, sourdough flavor and the final bread will be crispier.)

4. At baking time, place the baking stone in the center of the oven and preheat the oven to 500°F.

5. Divide the dough into 16 even portions. Roll each into a ball. On a generously floured work surface, roll each ball of dough into a 7-inch round. The dough should be very thin.

6. Sprinkle the wooden pizza peel with polenta and place a round of dough on the peel. Sprinkle with *fleur de sel*. Slide the dough off the peel and onto the baking stone. Bake until the dough is puffed, crisp, and golden, about 5 minutes. With the metal pizza peel or large spatula, remove the bread from the baking stone and let it cool on a wire rack or in a large basket.

7. Repeat with the rest of the dough. The bread is best consumed the day it is baked.

NOTE: If you don't have a pizza stone and a wooden peel, simply sprinkle the polenta on a baking sheet, place a round of dough on top, and bake on the baking sheet.

MULTIGRAIN SOURDOUGH BREAD:
PAIN AU LEVAIN

I believe that sourdough bread baking is not cooking, or baking—it's religion. There is something almost mystical in succeeding at a perfect sourdough loaf, a venerable pain au levain. *I like to joke that two of the best moments of my day are when I finish a run and when I take my sourdough bread out of the oven and lean down to get as close to the loaf as possible and inhale deeply. I know few greater personal satisfactions. That said, sourdough bread will test your will and your patience, but once you succeed, you'll not regret the trials along the way. I have been making sourdough bread on and off for 30 years, and to my mind, the secret is a sturdy starter* (levain) *that is fully half the weight of the flour that is added to it. I am happy to say that I have shared my starter with friends all over the world, and it pleases me to know that they are succeeding with their esteemed loaves.*

Be sure to keep your starter pure—nothing but water and flour. If the dough is not rising as you want, it is okay to add 1 teaspoon or less of active dry yeast when adding water to the levain *until your starter is lively and bubbly.*

Before you begin, measure everything. Be sure to dust your bowl or your linen-lined basket (banneton) *with plenty of flour, measure out all the flours, have a clean container for your* levain, *and so on. Your hands will get sticky, and the more you do in advance while your hands are clean, the better!*

Your first several loaves may not rise very much. You can adjust the rising time, from 6 hours to 24 hours, depending upon your schedule and the vitality of the starter. If you bake every few days, the starter will get more and more active and the bread will rise more quickly and will of course be lighter.

ONE **3**-POUND LOAF
EQUIPMENT: A LARGE BOWL OR A LINEN-LINED BASKET (*BANNETON*); A CLOTH;
A SHAKER FILLED WITH FLOUR FOR DUSTING; A LARGE BOWL;
A HEAVY-DUTY MIXER FITTED WITH A PADDLE; A SCALE; A BAKING STONE;
RAZOR BLADE; INSTANT-READ THERMOMETER.

Sourdough starter (levain)

2 cups white bread flour

Bread

3 cups white bread flour

1 cup light whole wheat bread flour

1 cup rye flour

1 cup spelt or *épeautre* flour

1 pound sourdough starter (*levain*)

2 tablespoons malt flakes or malt powder (available at health food stores)

1 tablespoon coarse sea salt

1 cup mixed seeds: equal parts sesame, flax, and sunflower seeds

1. Prepare the starter: In a small bowl, combine 1/4 cup of water and 1/2 cup of the flour and stir until the water absorbs all the flour and forms a soft dough. Transfer to an airtight container and set aside at room temperature for 24 hours. The mixture should rise slightly and take on a faintly acidic aroma. Repeat this for 3 more days, each day adding 1/4 cup water and 1/2 cup flour to the dough. Each day the starter should rise slightly and should become more acidic in aroma. By day 5 you should have 1 pound of lively starter. If you are in doubt, add up to 1 teaspoon active dry yeast when combining the starter and water.

2. On baking day, line the bowl or basket with a cloth and dust the cloth heavily with flour.

3. In a large bowl, combine all the flours and mix to blend. In the bowl of the heavy-duty mixer fitted with the paddle (not the bread attachment), combine the starter and 3 cups room temperature water and mix at low speed to dissolve the starter. Add the flour cup by cup, mixing just until the dough is hydrated. This should take 1 to 2 minutes. Do not overmix: let the flour and water do all the work.

4. Remove 1 pound of the dough and transfer it to an airtight container to reserve as a starter for the next baking. (Store the starter, refrigerated in an airtight container, for up to 3 days. It can also be frozen almost indefinitely. Thaw at room temperature for 24 hours before the next baking.)

5. Add the malt flakes, salt, and seeds to the remaining dough, mixing at low speed just until all the ingredients are well incorporated, 1 to 2 minutes. The dough will be sticky. Place the dough in the flour-dusted basket. Cover and let rise for 6 hours, or until the dough has risen slightly. (To gauge how the dough is rising, leave your starter, in its airtight container, on the counter. If the starter is rising nicely—with big air bubbles throughout—you can be assured that your bread dough is rising as well.)

6. About 20 minutes before baking the bread, place a baking stone in the oven and preheat the oven to 500°F.

7. Remove the baking stone from the oven. Turn the dough out onto the baking stone. Score the loaf with a razor blade. Return the baking stone to the oven and bake for about 25 minutes, or until the loaf is evenly browned. Reduce the heat to 425°F and bake until the bread reaches an interior temperature of 200°F, another 20 minutes. Watch carefully, since ovens vary: if the bread seems to be browning too quickly, reduce the heat.

8. Transfer the bread to a wire rack to cool. The bread continues to bake as it cools, so resist the temptation to cut the loaf before it is thoroughly cooled, at least 4 hours. (Though I do cheat from time to time.) Store the bread at room temperature in a cloth towel or cloth bag, slicing off only as much as you need at a time. The bread will stay fresh for 1 week.

THIN BREAD CRISPS

Breadmaking is a passion for me. And as much as I love a fresh, thin slice of my homemade bread, I adore the crunch of these ultra-thin slices of bread, sprayed with olive oil and, if desired, a touch of one of my salt mixtures, and baked. Their crispiness has no equal. The bread can be cut into many attractive forms—formal rounds or squares or free-form rectangles—or left as a whole slice.

48 CRISPS

EQUIPMENT: AN ULTRA-SHARP KNIFE OR AN ELECTRIC SLICER; A BAKING SHEET.

1 loaf Multigrain Sourdough Bread (page 270)

Olive oil spray

Fine sea salt or seasoned salt of your choice (see pages 304–307; optional)

1. Preheat the oven to 375°F.

2. With the sharp knife, cut 12 ultra-thin slices from the loaf of bread. Cut each slice crosswise into 4 thin slices. Arrange the slices in a single layer on the baking sheet (as many as will fit), and spray them with olive oil spray. Sprinkle with the salt if desired.

3. Place the baking sheet in the oven and bake until the breads are crisp and golden, about 10 minutes. Transfer them to a wire rack to cool, and repeat with the remaining slices. (Stored in a sealed plastic bag at room temperature, the crisps will stay fresh for up to 3 days.)

CHICKPEA FLOUR CREPES: *SOCCA*

These golden brown chickpea flour crepes—known as socca *in Nice and* farinata *in Liguria—are a delightful accompaniment to salad, with a glass of wine any time of year. The batter can be made several hours ahead, with the crepes baked at the very last moment. They are served still warm from the oven, seasoned generously with coarsely ground black pepper, then torn into ragged shards and eaten out of hand. But this is also the sort of seemingly simple preparation that can be outrageously frustrating to get "just right." The batter should contain oil, but the end result should not be oily. Once baked, the crepe should be just thick enough to fold into moist, torn portions, not dry handkerchiefs. The oven should be hot, but not so hot that the* socca *cooks and browns unevenly. I bake mine in a specially designed tin-lined copper* socca *pan, much like a flat paella pan, but any large, round, flat pan that fits in the oven is fine. I find that heating the pan for 5 minutes with just the oil helps the bottom to brown and the crepe to cook more evenly.*

ONE **14**-INCH CREPE, ABOUT **8** SERVINGS
EQUIPMENT: A **14**-INCH-ROUND OVENPROOF *SOCCA* PAN OR PAELLA PAN.

1 cup chickpea (garbanzo bean) flour

1 teaspoon fine sea salt

4 tablespoons extra-virgin olive oil

Coarse, freshly ground black pepper

1. Center a rack in the oven. Preheat the oven to 450°F.

2. In a bowl, whisk together the flour, 1 1/3 cups water, salt, and 2 tablespoons of the oil. The batter should be thin and crepelike.

3. Pour the remaining 2 tablespoons of oil into the pan and brush to evenly distribute the oil. Place the oiled pan in the oven and heat for 5 minutes.

4. Remove the pan from the oven. Pour the batter into the pan, swirling to evenly distribute the batter. Return the pan to the oven and bake until the *socca* is bubbly, colored a deep golden brown, and evenly dotted with little crater-like holes, about 18 minutes. Remove from the oven and sprinkle generously with the pepper. Tear the *socca* into pieces or scrap it with a scraper into ragged shards. Serve warm.

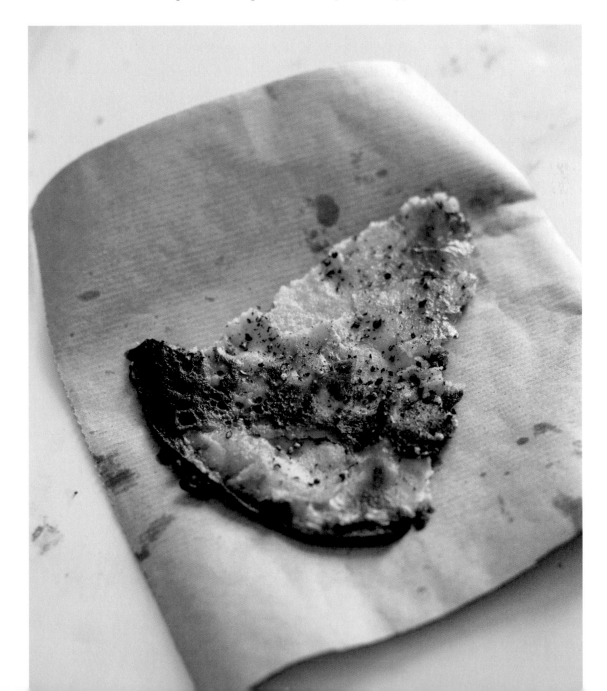

ALSATIAN ONION AND BACON TART: *FLAMMEKUCHEN*

This is a memory lane recipe for me: when researching The Food Lover's Guide to France *in the early 1980s, we found this fragrant onion and bacon tart on the menu everywhere in Alsace, and since then it has become a favorite bread tart. This is a lightened version, prepared with nonfat yogurt or* fromage blanc *rather than a richer heavy cream or* crème fraîche. *Likewise, the onions are steamed rather than cooked in fat, making for an ethereally light tart. Serve it with a simple green salad as a meal, with a glass of chilled Riesling.*

ONE **12**-INCH TART

EQUIPMENT: A BAKING STONE; A STEAMER; A WOODEN PIZZA PEEL; A METAL PIZZA PEEL OR A LARGE METAL SPATULA.

8 ounces large white onions, peeled and cut crosswise into 1/8-inch-thick rounds

4 ounces thinly sliced pancetta or bacon, cut into cubes

1/2 cup nonfat Greek-style yogurt or *fromage blanc*

1/8 teaspoon freshly grated nutmeg

Flour and polenta, for dusting

1 recipe Quick Whole Wheat Bread Tart Dough (page 285), shaped into a ball

Coarse, freshly ground black pepper

1. Place the baking stone on the bottom rack of the oven. Preheat the oven to 500°F.

2. Separate the onions into rings. You should have about 4 cups loosely packed onions.

3. Bring 1 quart of water to a simmer in the bottom of a steamer. Place the onions on the steaming rack. Place the rack over simmering water, cover, and steam until the onions are al dente, 5 to 6 minutes. Remove the basket from the steamer to drain the onions. (This can be done 2 to 3 hours before serving.)

4. In a large, dry skillet, brown the pancetta over moderate heat until crisp and golden, 3 to 4 minutes. With a slotted spoon, transfer the pancetta to several layers of paper towels to absorb the fat. Blot the top of the pancetta with several layers of paper towels to absorb any additional fat.

5. In a medium bowl, combine the yogurt, nutmeg, onions, and half of the pancetta. Stir to blend.

6. On a generously floured work surface, roll the dough into a 12-inch round.

7. Sprinkle the wooden pizza peel with polenta, and place the round of dough on the peel. Working quickly to keep the dough from sticking, assemble the tart: Spread the yogurt mixture evenly over the dough. Sprinkle with the remaining pancetta. Season liberally with pepper.

8. Slide the dough off the peel and onto the baking stone. Bake until the dough is crisp and golden and the top is bubbly, about 10 minutes.

9. With the metal pizza peel or large spatula, remove the tart from the baking stone. Sprinkle it generously with pepper. Transfer to a cutting board and cut into 8 wedges. Serve immediately.

NOTE: If you don't have a baking stone and a wooden peel, simply sprinkle the polenta on a baking sheet, place the round of dough on top, assemble the tart, and bake on the baking sheet.

WINE SUGGESTION: A young, fresh, dry Alsatian Riesling is in order here. Try one from the reputable firms of Ostertag or Zind-Humbrecht—crisp, dry, smoky wines with a saline touch of chalky minerality, an even match for the creamy onion and pancetta mixture offset with a hint of black pepper.

PARMESAN CROUTONS

Crispy, salty, cheese-covered croutons are thoroughly welcome additions to my kitchen cupboard. These are great to have on hand to toss into any salad or soup, or to munch on as a simple snack.

2 1/2 CUPS
EQUIPMENT: A BAKING SHEET; A PASTRY BRUSH.

Four 1/2-inch-thick slices Multigrain Sourdough Bread (page 270), about 6 ounces,
  crusts trimmed
Extra-virgin olive oil spray
2 tablespoons fresh, very finely grated Parmigiano-Reggiano cheese

1. Center a rack in the oven. Preheat the oven to 375°F.

2. Cut the slices of bread into 1/2-inch cubes. Place the cubes on the baking sheet. Spray with the olive oil, tossing to coat the bread cubes. Place the baking sheet in the oven and bake until the cubes are lightly toasted, about 5 minutes.

3. Transfer the bread cubes to a bowl and toss with the cheese, coating them lightly and evenly. Return the bread cubes to the baking sheet and continue baking until the croutons are a deep, even brown, about 10 minutes. Remove from the oven and let cool. (Store in an airtight container at room temperature for 1 week.)

TOMATO AND MUSTARD TART

So much of the joy and beauty of cooking lies in simplicity. Take a few basic top-quality ingredients and you realize there is no reason to turn yourself inside out to put something lovely, tasty, and tasteful on the table. I think this tart is a dream. Add a simple tossed green salad and you have a rapturous meal.

ONE **12**-INCH TART
EQUIPMENT: A BAKING STONE; A WOODEN PIZZA PEEL;
A METAL PIZZA PEEL OR A LARGE METAL SPATULA.

2 large tomatoes, peeled, cored, seeded, and chopped (about 2 cups)

Flour and polenta, for dusting

1 recipe Quick Whole Wheat Bread Tart Dough (recipe follows), shaped into a ball

1/2 cup sharp imported French mustard

1/4 cup mixed minced fresh chives, parsley, and basil

Extra-virgin olive oil spray

1. Place the tomatoes on several paper towel layers to drain.

2. Place the baking stone on the bottom rack of the oven. Preheat the oven to 500°F.

3. On a generously floured work surface, roll the dough into a 12-inch round.

4. Sprinkle the wooden pizza peel with polenta and place the round of dough on the peel. Working quickly to keep the dough from sticking, assemble the tart: Spread the mustard evenly over the dough. Arrange the tomatoes on top of the mustard. Sprinkle with the herbs.

5. Slide the dough off the peel and onto the baking stone. Bake until the dough is crisp and golden and the top is bubbly, about 15 minutes. With the metal pizza peel or large spatula, remove the tart from the baking stone. Spray it with olive oil. Transfer to a cutting board and cut into 8 wedges. Serve immediately.

NOTE: If you don't have a baking stone and a wooden peel, simply sprinkle the polenta on a baking sheet, place the round of dough on top, assemble the tart, and bake on the baking sheet.

VARIATIONS: Just like a pizza, the variations are endless here. We often make a tart topped with Baby Artichokes Marinated in Olive Oil (page 24), a shower of herbs, and freshly grated Parmigiano-Reggiano cheese.

WINE SUGGESTION: Almost any young, daily-drinking red from the Southern Rhône would be great here. Try the always reliable La Vieille Ferme Côtes-du-Ventoux from Perrin & Fils, a spicy, meaty wine with a touch of pepper.

QUICK WHOLE WHEAT BREAD
TART DOUGH

I doubt that a week goes by that I don't make this dough, and I am always happy to have it at the ready for a quick bread tart or pizza. The dough is foolproof, goes together instantly, and requires no proofing or rising. It makes a delightfully crisp and crunchy base for all of my bread tarts, including the Alsatian Onion and Bacon Tart (page 278), Tomato and Mustard Tart (page 283), and variations.

DOUGH FOR ONE **12**-INCH TART
EQUIPMENT: A FOOD PROCESSOR.

3/4 cup whole wheat flour

3/4 cup bread flour, plus extra if needed and for dusting

1 package (2 1/4 teaspoons) instant yeast

3/4 teaspoon fine sea salt

1/4 teaspoon sugar

2 teaspoons extra-virgin olive oil

In the bowl of the food processor, combine the whole wheat flour, bread flour, yeast, salt, and sugar, and pulse to mix. Combine 1/2 cup of hot water and the olive oil in a measuring cup. With the motor running, gradually add enough of the hot liquid for the mixture to form a sticky ball. The dough should be soft. If it is too dry, add 1 to 2 tablespoons more hot water. If it is too sticky, add 1 to 2 tablespoons flour. Process until the dough forms a ball. Transfer to a clean, floured surface and knead by hand for 1 minute. Cover with a cloth and let rest for at least 10 minutes before rolling. (The dough will keep, covered and refrigerated, for up to 4 days. Punch down the dough as necessary.)

PANTRY

I CAN'T IMAGINE CREATING SALADS AS A MEAL WITHOUT AN INVENTIVE PAN-
TRY AS A RESOURCE. A FINE REPERTOIRE OF SEASONED SALTS, PICKLED FRUITS
AND VEGETABLES, AND HOMEMADE STOCKS ARE ESSENTIAL TO THE SUCCESS OF
OUR SALADS.

Fresh capers growing on the bush

CAPERS IN VINEGAR

From May to October, my aging caper bush produces firm, tiny green buds—the bud of the whitish-purple flower that will bloom if the bud is not picked—which I pick and instantly drop into distilled vinegar for pickled capers. Unlike other sorts of pickling, this is pretty direct and simple, and the capers can be consumed in about 48 hours. I have a morning routine of walking out to my caper bush with a cup of espresso and a tiny jar filled with vinegar, to pick as many buds as have emerged that day. If you live in a Mediterranean climate, do everything you can to get a caper bush growing. They don't always "take," and you may have to plant several before you succeed, but perseverance and patience pay off. Nasturtium buds can also be pickled the same way, and though they are not as tasty as capers, they are definitely worth the effort.

EQUIPMENT: A SMALL JAR WITH A LID.

Fresh caper buds (or nasturtium buds)

Distilled white vinegar

Pick the caper buds when they are small and firm. Place them directly into a jar filled with distilled vinegar. The pickled buds can be used within 2 days. (Store the jar of pickled buds in the refrigerator for up to 1 year.)

CORNICHONS

I have grown the special miniature variety of cucumbers for making cornichons, but they seem to come in a handful at a time when I need an avalanche at a time. So I am content to grab them whenever I find them in the farmer's market and pickle a batch for year-round eating. I am a pickle lover, and nothing satisfies me more than to put my own homemade pickles on the table.

2 QUARTS

EQUIPMENT: TWO **1**-QUART CANNING JARS WITH LIDS AND RINGS.

1/4 cup coarse sea salt

2 pounds (about 70) 2-inch pickling cucumbers

3 cups distilled white vinegar

1 tablespoon sugar

4 large fresh tarragon sprigs

4 fresh or dried bay leaves

8 small fresh or dried hot red peppers

1/2 teaspoon whole black peppercorns

1. In a large bowl, combine the salt and 1 quart of cold water. Stir to dissolve the salt. Add the cucumbers and let stand in a cool place for 6 hours.

2. Sterilize the canning jars, lids, and rings by scalding them with boiling water. Drain well.

3. Drain the cucumbers, discarding the salt water.

4. In a medium saucepan, combine the vinegar, sugar, and 1 1/2 cups of water, and bring to a boil over medium heat. Remove from the heat.

5. Fill the jars with layers of the drained cucumbers, the herbs, and the spices, dividing the ingredients evenly between the jars. Pour the hot vinegar mixture into the jars, letting a bit of the liquid overflow the jars (this helps seal the lids well). Wipe the outside rim of each jar with a clean cloth, and seal with the lids and ring. Let stand until cool. Store in a cool, dry place for at least 3 weeks before opening the jars. (Once opened, store in the refrigerator for up to 6 months.)

HOMEMADE CURRY POWDER

The best way to ensure freshness with spices is to create your own concoctions. Be sure to date them and use them within 1 month for the most intense flavor. This is a favorite curry mix, one I keep on hand and use liberally during all seasons. Use this mixture when preparing Curried Pumpkin Seeds (page 9).

1/3 CUP

EQUIPMENT: A SPICE GRINDER OR A COFFEE MILL.

2 small, dried, whole red chile peppers

2 tablespoons coriander seeds

1 tablespoon cumin seeds

1 teaspoon black mustard seeds

1 teaspoon whole black peppercorns

1 teaspoon ground fenugreek

1 teaspoon ground ginger

1 teaspoon ground turmeric

In a small, dry skillet, combine the chile peppers, coriander seeds, cumin seeds, mustard seeds, and peppercorns, and toast over medium heat, shaking the pan often to prevent burning, for 2 to 3 minutes. Let cool. In a spice grinder or coffee mill, grind the toasted spices to a fine powder. Stir in the ground fenugreek, ginger, and turmeric. (Store the curry powder in an airtight container in a cool place for up to 1 month.)

PICKLED GARLIC

My friend Maggie Shapiro first introduced me to this recipe twenty-five years ago. As soon as fresh garlic appears in the markets in spring, I am sure to pickle some of the young garlic to use as I would any pickle or cornichons—in salads, in terrines, and as a flavorful accompaniment to a salad buffet.

1 1/2 CUPS
EQUIPMENT: A **1** 1/2-CUP JAR WITH A LID.

1 1/2 cups distilled white vinegar at 5% acidity (see Note)

2 tablespoons sugar

1/8 teaspoon fine sea salt

1 cup fresh young garlic cloves (about 24 cloves), peeled

In a small saucepan, combine the vinegar, sugar, and salt and bring to a boil over high heat. Add the garlic to the mixture and cook, uncovered, over high heat for 1 minute, stirring occasionally. Remove from the heat. Let cool. With a slotted spoon, transfer the garlic to the jar. Pour the vinegar over it and close the jar. (Store the pickled garlic in its jar in the refrigerator for up to 3 months.)

NOTE: Due to the low acidity in garlic, you need to use distilled vinegar with 5% acidity, otherwise the garlic may turn green or blue. Most distilled white vinegar, such as the Heinz brand, has a pickling and table strength of 5% acidity. It may not be marked on the label. Should your garlic turn color, you will know that the vinegar is not the proper strength.

FIGS IN VINEGAR

Especially in the winter months, I love looking into my pantry to find these pickled figs—with them come memories of the summer sun and breeze. I like to serve these with a smoked duck breast salad (see page 211), but they are also great with a cheese platter or simple roast poultry.

FIVE **12**-OUNCE JARS
EQUIPMENT: FIVE **12**-OUNCE CANNING JARS WITH LIDS AND RINGS.

1 1/2 pounds whole fresh figs, stemmed and rinsed

5 fresh tarragon sprigs

10 whole cloves

25 whole black peppercorns

5 fresh or dried bay leaves

1/8 teaspoon fine sea salt per jar

5 cups distilled white vinegar

1. Sterilize the canning jars, lids, and rings by scalding them with boiling water. Drain well.

2. Arrange the figs in the jars. Evenly divide the tarragon sprigs, cloves, peppercorns, bay leaves, and salt among the jars. Cover with the distilled vinegar. Seal with the lids and rings. Store in a cool place for at least 1 month before serving.

3. Serve as you would any pickles, with charcuterie or as a simple pickle with meats and poultry. (Once opened, store the jars of pickled figs in the refrigerator for up to 6 months.)

FIG CHUTNEY

We grow half a dozen varieties of figs in our garden, and a favorite is the tiny, purplish-black Ronde de Bordeaux. *It's a classic purple fig with flavors as deep and dense as its color. I prefer these miniature figs when preparing this chutney, shared with me by Raoul Reichrath, good friend and chef at the Provençal restaurant Le Grande Pré in Roaix. The chutney is delicious when served with Seared Pork Tenderloin Salad (page 252).*

FIVE **12**-OUNCE JARS
EQUIPMENT: FIVE **12**-OUNCE CANNING JARS WITH LIDS AND RINGS.

2 pounds whole fresh figs, stemmed and rinsed

1/3 cup white wine

1/3 cup best-quality Banyuls vinegar or sherry-wine vinegar

2 cinnamon sticks

4 whole cloves

1/2 teaspoon ground cayenne pepper or ground *piment d'Espelette*

1/2 cup honey

2 tablespoons extra-virgin olive oil

2 teaspoons coarse sea salt

1. Sterilize the canning jars, lids, and rings by scalding them with boiling water. Drain well.

2. In a large saucepan, combine all the ingredients. Bring to a boil over high heat. Reduce to a simmer and simmer for 1 1/2 hours, uncovered, stirring from time to time. Taste for seasoning.

3. Ladle the chutney into the sterilized jars. Seal with the lids and rings. (Store in the jars in the refrigerator for up to 3 months.)

QUICK LEMON CONFIT

Citrus confit is great to have on hand when preparing salads or appetizers, especially a freshly made Black Olive Tapenade (page 20).

2 CUPS

EQUIPMENT: A 2-CUP GLASS CONTAINER WITH A NON-METAL LID.

2 lemons, preferably organic

1/3 cup coarse sea salt

1/2 cup freshly squeezed lemon juice (from 3 to 4 lemons)

Scrub the lemons and dry them well. Cut each lemon lengthwise into 8 wedges. In a bowl, toss the lemon wedges, salt, and lemon juice to coat the fruit evenly. Transfer to the container. Close with the lid and let the lemons ripen at room temperature for 2 days. (Store the jar of confit in the refrigerator for up to 1 month.)

SPICED GRAPES

A cheese tray salad as a meal would not be complete without a few of these spiced grapes. I like to make them with a few of the Syrah grapes left on the vines at the end of the harvest in October, but any black grapes can be used here. If the grapes are large, separate them into single grapes rather than a cluster.

12 TO 16 SERVINGS
EQUIPMENT: A LARGE JAR WITH A LID.

8 ounces small black grapes

1 cup lavender honey

1/2 cup Banyuls red-wine vinegar or other best-quality red-wine vinegar

4 fresh or dried bay leaves

10 whole black peppercorns

3 whole star anise

1. Cut the grapes into small clusters, with just 6 or 8 grapes per cluster. Arrange them carefully in the jar.

2. In a small saucepan, combine the remaining ingredients and bring to a simmer over low heat. Stir and simmer for about 1 minute. Taste the sauce: if too tart, add more honey; if too sweet, more vinegar. Set it aside to cool slightly.

3. Pour the cooled sauce over the grapes. Secure the lid and refrigerate for 1 week before sampling. (Store the jar of grapes in the refrigerator for up to 6 months. The leftover sauce can be used to drizzle on cheese, especially young goat cheese.)

Espelette *peppers*

PICKLED PEPPERS

I grow hot peppers in my garden just to have a pantry full of pickled peppers all year long. I love the heat! I sprinkle minced peppers readily on fish and shellfish salads, on a toss of tomatoes, and on savory tarts, and serve them as a condiment in a cheese and salad meal. I grow jalapeño peppers as well as the French variety called piment d'Espelette, *a famed pepper from the Basque region, where it is dried and ground into a fine powder. When the Espelette peppers are fresh from the garden—either green or red—I simply pickle them. When fresh jalapeños are in the market, you can do the same. They can be pickled whole or cut into thin rounds.*

1 1/2 CUPS
EQUIPMENT: A **1** 1/2-CUP JAR WITH A LID.

4 ripe hot peppers (about 3 ounces total), whole or thinly sliced

4 fresh or dried bay leaves

1 cup distilled white vinegar

1/4 cup extra-virgin olive oil

1 teaspoon coarse sea salt

Fill the jar with the peppers and bay leaves. In a large saucepan, combine 1/4 cup of water with the vinegar, oil, and salt. Place the saucepan over high heat and bring to a boil. Pour the boiling liquid over the peppers in the jar. Wipe the rim with a clean cloth. Close with the lid. (Store the jar of peppers in the refrigerator for up to 6 months.)

BRINE-CURED BLACK OLIVES

If you can secure fresh olives, by all means try curing them yourself. I have been curing our Tanche variety of olives for more than twenty-five years, storing them in a large glass, wooden-framed crock especially designed for curing olives. Any glass or pottery crock could be used. Sample the olives as appetizers, make them part of a large salad buffet, and use them in Black Olive Tapenade (page 20) and as part of the Marinated Olive Quartet (page 19).

2 POUNDS

EQUIPMENT: A GLASS OR POTTERY CROCK LARGE ENOUGH TO HOLD THE OLIVES; A SLOTTED SPOON OR A PERFORATED WOODEN LADLE.

3/4 cup (3 1/2 ounces) fine sea salt

About 2 pounds ripe, uncured black olives

1. In a large saucepan, combine the salt and 1 quart of water, and bring to a boil. Stir to dissolve the salt. Let cool completely.

2. In the crock, combine the cooled brine and the olives. Cover and set aside at room temperature for several months, stirring from time to time. A scum will form on top, but it is harmless and can be stirred into the olives. Starting from a fresh brine, the olives will take 3 to 4 months of curing before they are edible. Once cured, they can be kept indefinitely in a cool, dry place. Never discard the salt brine, which will become black and inky. It can be used year after year, augmented with fresh brine as needed.

3. To serve, remove the olives from the brine with a slotted spoon or a specially designed perforated wooden ladle. Taste the olives. If they are excessively salty, they can be rinsed or soaked in cold water to remove some of the saltiness.

RENDERED DUCK FAT AND CRACKLINGS

We eat a lot of magret de canard, *or fatted duck breast, in our house. We love it sliced thin for carpaccio, smoked whole, or seared and cut into thin strips. When I am preparing smoked duck or carpaccio, I separate the fat from the meat and render it. In the winter months, I find all sorts of uses for this unctuous, fragrant fat, such as sautéing vegetables, especially potatoes.*

ABOUT **1** 1/2 CUPS
EQUIPMENT: A SLOTTED SPOON; A SIEVE; CHEESECLOTH.

1 pound duck fat (from 5 *magrets*, fatted duck breasts), cut into 1/2-inch cubes

Fine sea salt

1. In a large saucepan, combine the duck fat and 1/2 cup of water. Simmer over the lowest possible heat until the water evaporates, the skin pieces are crisp and browned, and all the fat has been released, 45 minutes to 1 hour.

2. With the slotted spoon, remove the crisp, brown pieces of skin—the cracklings— and transfer them to a double thickness of paper towels. Season with salt and serve the same day in salads, alongside sliced duck, or as an appetizer or snack.

3. Line the sieve with cheesecloth, set it over a bowl, and carefully strain the fat through the sieve. Use as you would butter or oil for searing or frying. (Store the duck fat in an airtight container in the refrigerator or freezer for up to 6 months.)

JAPANESE SESAME SALT: *GOMASIO*

While the flavorful mixture of fine sea salt and toasted sesame seeds known as gomasio *can be found in most health food stores, I prefer to make my own in small batches to ensure freshness. The mixture can be sprinkled on salads or used in baking, or combined with pumpkin seeds and tamari (see page 9) for a tasty snack.*

ABOUT 1/2 CUP
EQUIPMENT: A MORTAR AND PESTLE OR A SPICE GRINDER.

1 tablespoon fine sea salt

7 tablespoons toasted sesame seeds

If using a mortar and pestle, combine the salt and sesame seeds and pound to a coarse powder. Do not allow the mixture to form a paste. If using a spice grinder, grind the two ingredients to a powder, but do not let the mixture form a paste. (Store in an airtight container at room temperature for up to 1 month.)

FENNEL AND SAFFRON SALT

Once you try this on a simple fresh tomato salad, you will be sold! Fennel, saffron, and tomatoes make a perfect trio. Keep the salt on hand for any time you want to add sunny flavors. I use the less expensive ground saffron here. When sprinkled on tomatoes, the saffron bleeds a golden, reddish orange hue.

1/4 CUP

EQUIPMENT: A SPICE GRINDER; A SMALL JAR WITH A LID.

Pinch of ground saffron

3 tablespoons fine sea salt

2 tablespoons fennel seeds

Combine the ingredients in the spice grinder, and grind until the fennel seeds are fairly coarse. Transfer to the small jar, cover, and shake to blend. (Store the flavored salt in an airtight container at room temperature for up to 1 month.)

Red Hot Salt (page 307) and Fennel and Saffron Salt

LEMON ZEST SALT

Before slicing a lemon I always zest it, storing the zest in a tiny jar in the refrigerator to keep it from drying out. I then combine equal parts of zest and fine sea salt, grind it in a spice grinder, and store it in the refrigerator. I use this zest salt on virtually everything, for it adds color, texture and, yes, zest to the table.

2 TABLESPOONS
EQUIPMENT: A SPICE GRINDER; A SMALL JAR WITH A LID.

1 tablespoon grated lemon zest, preferably organic
1 tablespoon fine sea salt

Combine the lemon zest and salt in the spice grinder, and grind to a fine powder. Transfer to the small jar and close with the lid. (Store, sealed in the jar, in the refrigerator for up to 1 week. After that, the lemon flavor will begin to fade.)

RED HOT SALT

I love spice and color in my food, and this vibrant red salt provides a pleasantly smoky aroma, great color, and a fine, mysterious flavor. It will brighten up just about any salad, vegetable, meat, or poultry, and the combination is an essential ingredient in my Spicy Basque Mixed Nuts (page 8).

MAKES **2** CUPS

EQUIPMENT: A SMALL JAR WITH A LID.

2 teaspoons ground *piment d'Espelette* or other ground mild chile pepper

1/2 teaspoon hot-smoked *pimentón de la Vera* or other hot-smoked paprika

1/2 teaspoon mild paprika

1 teaspoon fine sea salt

Combine all the ingredients in the jar. Cover, and shake to blend. (Store the salt mixture, sealed in the jar, at room temperature for up to 1 month. After that, the flavors will begin to fade.)

NOTE: *Piment d'Espelette*, the mildly spicy pepper from France's Basque region and the *pimentón* from Spain, can be found on my Amazon Store on the home page of PatriciaWells.com.

FRESH TOMATO SAUCE

When my vegetable garden is in full production in July and August, I make this regularly trying to keep up with the tomatoes as they ripen. I make four different colors of sauce—red, green, yellow, and orange—for variety and a change of pace. The sauce can easily be frozen for winter pleasure. Serve it with the Ricotta, Parmesan, and Lemon Zest Terrine (page 48).

5 CUPS

EQUIPMENT: A FOOD MILL FITTED WITH THE FINEST BLADE.

1 tablespoon extra-virgin olive oil

3 pounds ripe heirloom tomatoes, cored and quartered

1 tablespoon coarse sea salt

Several fresh celery leaves

Several fresh or dried bay leaves

1 plump, moist garlic head, cloves separated and peeled

Hot red pepper flakes to taste (optional)

1. In a saucepan, combine all the ingredients. Cook, uncovered, stirring regularly, over moderate heat until the tomatoes have collapsed and are cooking in their own juices, about 15 minutes. Taste for seasoning. Remove and discard the celery leaves and bay leaves.

2. Place the food mill over a large bowl. Using a large ladle, transfer the sauce to the food mill and puree it into the bowl. (Store the tomato sauce in airtight containers in the refrigerator for up to 1 week or in the freezer for up to 6 months.)

HOMEMADE CHICKEN STOCK

Nothing gives me a greater sense of contentment than the aroma of chicken stock wafting from my kitchen. Chicken stock also gives me a sense of empowerment, knowing that no matter how bare the cupboard may be, I can always fashion a meal in a jiffy, using the golden stock as the base. This stock is rich and fragrant, and the preparation also means that I have plenty of super-tender poached chicken for making salads.

3 QUARTS

EQUIPMENT: A LONG-HANDLED **2**-PRONGED FORK; A **10**-QUART PASTA POT FITTED WITH A COLANDER; A FINE-MESH SKIMMER; DAMPENED CHEESECLOTH.

2 large onions, halved crosswise (do not peel)

4 whole cloves

1 large farm-fresh chicken (about 5 pounds)

2 teaspoons coarse sea salt

4 carrots, scrubbed and cut crosswise into 1-inch pieces (do not peel)

1 plump, moist garlic head, halved crosswise (do not peel)

4 celery ribs

1 leek (white and tender green parts only), halved lengthwise, cleaned, and cut crosswise into
   1-inch pieces

One 1-inch piece of fresh ginger, peeled

12 whole white peppercorns

1 bouquet garni: several bay leaves, fresh celery leaves, thyme sprigs, and parsley sprigs encased
   in a wire-mesh tea infuser or bound in a piece of cheesecloth

1. One at a time, spear an onion half with the fork and hold it directly over a gas flame (or directly on an electric burner) until scorched. Stick a clove into each of the onion halves. (Scorching the onions will give the broth a richer flavor, and the onion skin also gives the stock a rich, golden color.)

2. Place the chicken in the pasta pot and fill with 5 quarts of water. Add the onions, salt, carrots, garlic, celery, leek, ginger, peppercorns, and bouquet garni. Bring to a gentle simmer, uncovered, over moderate heat. Skim to remove any scum that rises to the surface. Add additional cold water to replace the water removed and continue skimming until the broth is clear. Simmer until the chicken is cooked, about 1 hour.

3. Remove the chicken from the pot. Remove the chicken meat from the carcass and reserve it for another use. Return the skin and carcass to the pot and continue cooking at a gentle simmer for another 2 1/2 hours.

4. Line a large colander with a double layer of dampened cheesecloth and place the colander over a large bowl. Ladle—do not pour—the liquid into the sieve to strain off any impurities. Discard the solids. Measure. If the stock exceeds 3 quarts, return it to moderate heat and reduce it. Transfer the stock to airtight containers and cover.

5. Immediately refrigerate the stock. Once chilled, spoon off all traces of fat that rise to the surface. (Store the stock in the refrigerator for up to 3 days or in the freezer for up to 3 months.)

NOTES:
- For a clear stock, begin with cold water and bring it slowly to a simmer. Never allow a stock to boil or it will be cloudy, since the fat will emulsify. Cold water also aids in extracting greater flavor.
- For the first 30 minutes of cooking, skim off the impurities that rise to the surface as the stock simmers.
- Use a tall pot, for it will limit evaporation. I always use a large pasta pot fitted with a colander, which makes it easy to remove the solid ingredients and begin to filter the stock.

VARIATION: Use 2 whole cooked chicken carcasses rather than a whole raw chicken. The resulting stock will not have the same clean, fresh flavor, but it is worthy nonetheless. One can also use about 4 pounds of inexpensive raw chicken necks and backs to prepare the stock.

HOMEMADE VEGETABLE STOCK

During my cooking class weeks in Provence, we often prepare the classic Provençal soup known as soupe au pistou. *It uses a kaleidoscope of summer vegetables, sauced with a light basil puree. The preparation creates a good deal of kitchen garbage, and one breathtakingly beautiful summer Monday as we made the soup, a student screamed out as she looked at the mounds of refuse: "Oh my goodness, even the garbage is beautiful!" Since then, we take all the "good" garbage and make a vegetable stock with the trimmings. This recipe is just a template. The possibilities are endless: use whatever peels, ends, and scraps you may have from any vegetables.*

3 QUARTS
EQUIPMENT: A LONG-HANDLED **2**-PRONGED FORK;
A **10**-QUART PASTA POT FITTED WITH A COLANDER; A FINE-MESH SKIMMER;
DAMPENED CHEESECLOTH.

2 large onions, halved lengthwise (do not peel)

4 whole cloves

1 teaspoon coarse sea salt

4 carrots, scrubbed and cut crosswise into 1-inch pieces (do not peel)

1 plump, moist garlic head, halved crosswise (do not peel)

4 celery ribs, with leaves

1 leek (white and tender green parts only), halved lengthwise, cleaned, and cut crosswise into
     1-inch pieces

One 1-inch piece of fresh ginger, peeled

6 whole black peppercorns

1 bouquet garni: several bay leaves, celery leaves, thyme sprigs, and parsley sprigs encased in a
     wire-mesh tea infuser or bound in a piece of cheesecloth

1. One at a time, spear each onion half with the fork and hold it directly over a gas flame (or directly on an electric burner) until scorched. Stick a clove into each of the onion halves. (Scorching the onions will give the broth a richer flavor, and the onion skin gives the stock a rich, golden color.)

2. Place all the remaining ingredients in the pot and fill with 5 quarts of water. Bring to a boil over moderate heat. Lower the heat and simmer, uncovered, for about 45 minutes.

3. Line a large colander with a double layer of dampened cheesecloth and place the colander over a large bowl. Ladle—do not pour—the liquid into the sieve to strain off any impurities. Discard the solids. Measure. If the stock exceeds 3 quarts, return it to moderate heat and reduce it. Transfer the stock to airtight containers and cover. Immediately refrigerate the stock. (Store the stock in the refrigerator for up to 3 days, or in the freezer for up to 3 months.)

HOMEMADE RED-WINE VINEGAR

When we purchased our home in Provence in 1984, an old wooden vinegar keg filled with homemade vinegar was part of the "dowry." Walter created a lovely oak stand to house it, and now it sits proudly in the corner of the kitchen. Use any kind of red here. Just make sure it is a wine that is good enough to drink. Do not add corked wine, which would certainly ruin the vinegar.

2 TO 3 CUPS
EQUIPMENT: A **2**-QUART WOODEN KEG,
A GLASS OR CERAMIC CROCK,
OR A LARGE BOTTLE WITH A WIDE OPENING
(DO NOT USE METAL, WHICH COULD IMPART A
METALLIC TASTE TO THE VINEGAR); CLOTH OR CHEESECLOTH;
A BOTTLE LARGE ENOUGH TO HOLD THE VINEGAR; A CORK.

1 cup unpasteurized red-wine vinegar

3 cups red wine

1. Place the vinegar and the wine in the vessel (which should hold at least twice the amount of liquid added to allow for plenty of air circulation). Cover the opening with a clean cloth or cheesecloth (to prevent the invasion of fruit flies) and secure it with a rubber band. Place in a warm place (about 70°F) where there is plenty of air circulation.

2. After about 2 weeks, check the mixture, giving it a good sniff. It should have a very distinct vinegary aroma. Continue to check from time to time. It should take anywhere from 6 weeks to several months to smell like real vinegar; the time will depend upon the quality of the vinegar used in the beginning, as well as the surroundings. It is best not to disturb the vinegar (shake it or move it around too much). A film will form on top of the mixture (if you are aging in wood, you may not be able to see it) and this film (sometimes called the "mother") will develop the formation of bacteria that will help turn wine into vinegar.

3. Once you have a liquid that smells of vinegar, drain off about 1 cup. If your vinegar has a fresh, though perhaps pungent, aroma, you do not need to reduce it. But if it has a strong aroma of glue, boil the 1 cup vinegar in a small pan over medium heat, reducing it by about one-third. As you boil the liquid, you may see flames as the remaining alcohol is burnt off.

4. Pour the vinegar into a clean bottle, cork it, and you've got your first batch! After that, add any bits and ends of red or white wine to the aging vessel, and wait at least 6 weeks or more to draw off more vinegar.

VARIATION: You can make white-wine vinegar and even Champagne vinegar (but who ever has leftover Champagne?) using this same method.

DRESSINGS AND SAUCES

DRESSINGS FORM THE BACKBONE OF ANY SALAD. I KEEP A BOTTLE OF MY CLASSIC VINAIGRETTE ON THE COUNTER AT ALL TIMES, SO THAT WHEN I WANT A SALAD, THE DRESSING IS AT HAND. I ALSO KEEP A JAR OF CREAMY LEMON-CHIVE DRESSING IN THE REFRIGERATOR MOST DAYS, FOR THE SAME REASON. VARIATIONS AND FLAVORINGS ARE ENDLESS. I ENJOY DRESSINGS SEASONED WITH TAHINI, AND ALSO LIBERALLY USE YOGURT IN PLACE OF OIL FOR A LIGHTER DRESSING. SOME SAUCES—SUCH AS THE VIETNAMESE DIPPING SAUCE—CAN ALSO DOUBLE AS DRESSINGS. AND ALWAYS REMEMBER TO GO LIGHTLY ON THE DRESSING—TOSSING, TOSSING, TOSSING TO EVENLY COAT THE SALAD INGREDIENTS.

BASIL-LEMON DRESSING

When I have a bumper crop of various basils in my garden, I prepare Basil Oil and this dressing. Serve this on your favorite vegetables or greens, such as blanched green beans, or on a favorite salad green, such as baby spinach or arugula.

ABOUT 1/4 CUP
EQUIPMENT: A SMALL JAR WITH A LID.

1/4 cup Basil Oil (recipe follows)

1 tablespoon freshly squeezed lemon juice

Fine sea salt

In the jar, combine the oil and lemon juice. Cover with the lid and shake to blend. Taste for seasoning. The dressing can be used immediately. (Store the dressing in the refrigerator for up to 10 days. Shake to blend again before using.)

BASIL OIL

I smile when I open the refrigerator and find a bottle of this oil. Offering fragrance, color, and flavor, this all-purpose oil can be used as is, drizzled on grilled eggplant or sliced fresh tomatoes, as a garnish for soups, or in place of mayonnaise in a sandwich. I blanch and refresh the basil so it keeps its brilliant green color. I make enough of this in the summer to freeze it for a needed pickup during the winter months.

1/2 CUP

EQUIPMENT: A 5-QUART PASTA POT FITTED WITH A COLANDER; A FINE-MESH SIEVE; A FOOD PROCESSOR OR A BLENDER, A SMALL JAR WITH A LID.

3 tablespoons coarse sea salt

2 cups loosely packed fresh basil leaves

1/2 cup extra-virgin olive oil

1/2 teaspoon fine sea salt

1. Prepare a large bowl of ice water.

2. In the pasta pot, bring 3 quarts of water to a rolling boil over high heat. Add the coarse salt and the basil leaves and blanch for 15 seconds. Drain the basil and transfer the leaves to the fine-mesh sieve. Dip the sieve into the ice water to refresh the basil and help it keep its bright green color. Transfer the basil leaves to a thick kitchen towel. Roll the towel and squeeze to dry the leaves.

3. In the food processor or blender, combine the basil leaves, oil, and fine salt and process until pureed and well blended. The oil should be tinged with green, with tiny green flecks of basil floating in it. Transfer the oil to the jar. Close with the lid. The oil can be used immediately. (Store in the refrigerator for up to 10 days. Remove from the refrigerator at least 10 minutes before using if the oil has congealed. Shake to blend again before using. Store in the freezer for up to 3 months.)

BUTTERMILK—LEMON ZEST DRESSING

Buttermilk is a fine, protein-rich liquid that is perfect for a light salad dressing. Here an added touch of lemon juice and zest makes for a quick and easy dressing.

ABOUT 2/3 CUP
EQUIPMENT: A SMALL JAR WITH A LID.

1/4 teaspoon fine sea salt

1/2 cup buttermilk, shaken to blend

Grated zest of 1 lemon, preferably organic

2 tablespoons freshly squeezed lemon juice

In the jar, combine all the ingredients. Cover with the lid and shake to blend. Let stand for 1 hour to allow the flavors to blend. (Store the dressing in the refrigerator for up to 3 days. Shake to blend again before using.)

CAESAR SALAD DRESSING

While this is the *essential dressing for a classic Caesar salad, it is also excellent on other greens, with or without additional "frills," such as croutons, tomatoes, or cheese.*

ABOUT **1** CUP

EQUIPMENT: A FOOD PROCESSOR OR A BLENDER.

1 ultra-fresh large egg

1/4 cup freshly squeezed lemon juice

3 plump, moist garlic cloves, peeled, halved, green germ removed, and minced

4 anchovy fillets in olive oil, drained

6 drops Worcestershire sauce

1/2 cup mild-flavored vegetable oil, such as grapeseed or safflower

1/4 cup freshly grated Parmigiano-Reggiano cheese

Fine sea salt

Freshly ground black pepper

In the food processor or blender, combine the egg, lemon juice, garlic, anchovies, and Worcestershire. Process to blend. With the machine running, slowly add the oil, processing until the mixture is emulsified. The dressing should be thinner than mayonnaise. Stir in the cheese. Season to taste, and serve immediately.

CLASSIC VINAIGRETTE

This has been my signature vinaigrette for decades, and it's the best all-purpose dressing for greens as well as vegetables. I like to use two kinds of vinegar to create a true symphony of flavors.

ABOUT 1 1/4 CUPS
EQUIPMENT: A SMALL JAR WITH A LID.

2 tablespoons best-quality sherry-wine vinegar

2 tablespoons best-quality red-wine vinegar

Fine sea salt

1 cup extra-virgin olive oil

In the jar, combine the vinegars and salt to taste. Cover with the lid and shake to dissolve the salt. Add the oil and shake to blend. Taste for seasoning. The dressing can be used immediately. (Store the vinaigrette at room temperature or in the refrigerator for several weeks. Shake to blend again before using.)

CREAMY LEMON-MUSTARD DRESSING

Sometimes a dish needs a touch of mustard to wake it up, and this is when I call on a creamy dressing with a nice hit of mustardy punch.

1 1/4 CUPS

EQUIPMENT: A SMALL JAR WITH A LID.

Grated zest of 1 lemon, preferably organic

2 tablespoons freshly squeezed lemon juice

1/2 teaspoon fine sea salt

1 cup light cream

1 tablespoon imported French mustard

In the jar, combine the zest, lemon juice, and salt. Cover with the lid and shake to dissolve the salt. Add the cream and mustard. Shake to blend. Taste for seasoning. The dressing can be used immediately. (Store the dressing in the refrigerator for up to 1 week. Shake to blend again before using.)

CREAMY LEMON-CHIVE DRESSING

Salad dressings do not need to be rich or calorie-laden to be delicious, and this dressing drives home the point. With the lactic touch of light cream, the gentle acidity of the lemon juice, and the hit of color and pungency of the chives, this all-purpose dressing is a standard in our kitchen. Use it to dress a simple green salad, a couscous salad, a potato salad, or a light green bean salad.

1 1/4 CUPS
EQUIPMENT: A SMALL JAR WITH A LID.

2 tablespoons freshly squeezed lemon juice

1/2 teaspoon fine sea salt

1 cup light cream

1/3 cup finely minced fresh chives

Lemon zest

In the jar, combine the lemon juice and salt. Cover with the lid and shake to dissolve the salt. Add the cream, chives, and lemon zest. Shake to blend. Taste for seasoning. The dressing can be used immediately. (Store the dressing in the refrigerator for up to 1 week. Shake to blend again before using.)

But will it curdle? Given the right circumstances, such as the addition of acids or heat, any milk or cream product will curdle (meaning the curd protein coagulates and forms clumps). The greater the fat content of the milk or cream, the more it will resist curdling. I use a light cream with a 12% fat content, much like what is also called half-and-half, and have never had a problem with curdling when adding lemon juice to the cream.

Bee on a lime blossom

LIME AND VANILLA DRESSING

This incredible dressing will shake your world! I sprinkle this on fresh garden tomatoes,
and it is the essential ingredient in any simple fish tartare.

1/4 CUP

EQUIPMENT: A SMALL JAR WITH A LID.

2 plump, moist vanilla beans

1/4 cup extra-virgin olive oil

1/2 teaspoon fine sea salt

Grated zest and juice of 2 limes, preferably organic

1. Flatten the vanilla beans and cut them in half lengthwise. Using a small spoon, scrape out the seeds and place them in the jar. Reserve the pods for another use. (I dry the pods, then store them in a jar of sugar to make vanilla sugar for baking.) Add the oil and salt to the jar. Cover with the lid and shake to blend. Let the mixture steep for several hours before using.

2. At serving time, add the zest and juice.

LEMON AND OLIVE OIL DRESSING

Along with a classic vinaigrette made with sherry vinegar and red-wine vinegar, this is an all-purpose dressing I turn to time and again.

ABOUT 1/4 CUP

EQUIPMENT: A SMALL JAR WITH A LID.

1/4 teaspoon Lemon Zest Salt (page 306), or fine sea salt to taste

1 tablespoon freshly squeezed lemon juice

1/4 cup extra-virgin olive oil

In the jar, combine the salt and lemon juice. Cover with the lid and shake to blend. Add the oil and shake once more. Taste for seasoning. The dressing can be used immediately. (Store the dressing in the refrigerator for up to 3 days. Shake to blend again before using.)

YOGURT AND LEMON DRESSING

I think we all play favorites in the kitchen; I know I do. One day I am all over the Tahini-Lemon-Yogurt Dressing and Dipping Sauce (page 332), dreaming up salads and dishes that would marry well with its salty tang. Then, suddenly, I abandon it in favor of another dressing and another direction. At this writing, this is my most loved dressing, and I drizzle it on everything I can get my hands on!

ABOUT 3/4 CUP

EQUIPMENT: A SMALL JAR WITH A LID.

1/2 cup plain low-fat yogurt

2 tablespoons freshly squeezed lemon juice

1/4 teaspoon Lemon Zest Salt (page 306) or fine sea salt

In the jar, combine the yogurt, lemon juice, and salt. Cover with the lid and shake to blend. Taste for seasoning. The dressing can be used immediately. (Store the dressing in the refrigerator for up to 1 week. Shake to blend again before using.)

TAHINI-LEMON-YOGURT DRESSING AND DIPPING SAUCE

This sauce is on my list of greatest hits of salad dressings: light, tangy, and rich without being heavy. What more could one ask?

1 CUP

EQUIPMENT: A FOOD PROCESSOR OR A BLENDER.

2 plump, moist garlic cloves, peeled, halved, and green germ removed

1/4 cup tahini (sesame paste)

1/2 cup plain low-fat yogurt

2 tablespoons freshly squeezed lemon juice

1/2 teaspoon fine sea salt

In the food processor or blender, mince the garlic. Add the tahini, yogurt, lemon juice, and salt and puree to blend. Taste for seasoning. The dressing can be used immediately. (Store the dressing in the refrigerator for up to 1 week. Shake to blend again before using.)

HOMEMADE MAYONNAISE AND FRIENDS

Homemade mayonnaise is so far superior to anything one can find in the supermarket, I can't imagine why one would not make one's own, especially when the food processor deals with it in a few seconds. Try to use the small *insert bowl of a food processor or a mini food processor. Sometimes the large bowls are simply too big for the task.*

ABOUT 2/3 CUP

EQUIPMENT: A GLASS MEASURING CUP WITH A POURING SPOUT; A WHISK, A FOOD PROCESSOR WITH A SMALL INSERT BOWL, OR A MINI FOOD PROCESSOR.

1/2 cup organic grapeseed, peanut, or safflower oil

1 ultra-fresh large egg yolk, at room temperature

2 teaspoons imported French mustard

1/4 teaspoon fine sea salt

1 teaspoon freshly squeezed lemon juice

To make the mayonnaise by hand

Place the oil in the measuring cup. In a medium bowl, whisk the egg yolk, mustard, and salt until light and thick. While continuing to whisk, gradually add just a few drops of the oil, whisking until thoroughly incorporated. Do not add too much oil at the beginning or the mixture will not emulsify. As soon as the mixture begins to thicken, add the remaining oil in a slow and steady stream, whisking constantly. Work in the lemon juice. Taste for seasoning. The mayonnaise can be used immediately. (Store the mayonnaise in an airtight container in the refrigerator for up to 3 days.)

To use the food processor

Place the oil in the measuring cup. In the *small* bowl of the food processor or in a mini processor, combine the egg yolk, mustard, and salt and pulse until well blended. With the motor running, very slowly add just a few drops of the oil, processing until the mixture begins to thicken. With the motor still running, slowly add the remaining oil in a slow and steady stream. Add the lemon juice and pulse again. Taste for seasoning. The mayonnaise can be used immediately. (Store the mayonnaise in an airtight container in the refrigerator for up to 3 days.)

VARIATIONS: There are many classic ways to doctor homemade mayonnaise. Here are the instructions for three favorites.

SAUCE RÉMOULADE

To 2/3 cup mayonnaise, stir in:

1 tablespoon Capers in Vinegar (page 289)

1 tablespoon minced Cornichons (page 290)

2 tablespoons minced fresh herbs, including parsley, tarragon, and chives

Ground cayenne pepper

SAUCE GRIBICHE

To 2/3 cup mayonnaise, stir in:

1 hard-cooked egg (page 69), white and yolk chopped

2 tablespoons minced fresh herbs, including parsley, tarragon, and chives

SAUCE TARTARE

To 2/3 cup mayonnaise, stir in:

1 hard-cooked egg yolk (page 69), chopped

1 tablespoon Capers in Vinegar (page 289)

1 tablespoon minced fresh chives

VIETNAMESE DIPPING SAUCE

I keep this sauce on hand at all times. I am a fanatic for anything Vietnamese and find that this salty, spicy, all-purpose sauce can uplift any kind of spring roll or salad. My favorite fish sauce from Vietnam is the Phu Quoc brand. This is the perfect dressing for the Vietnamese Chicken and Green Papaya Salad (page 198).

1 CUP

EQUIPMENT: A SMALL JAR WITH A LID.

1/4 cup Vietnamese fish sauce, preferably Phu Quoc brand

1/4 cup freshly squeezed lime juice

1/4 cup water

1/4 cup sugar

2 plump, moist garlic cloves, peeled, halved, green germ removed, and minced

2 fresh red bird's-eye chiles, minced

1/4 cup carrot julienne

In the jar, combine all the ingredients. Tighten the lid and shake well to dissolve the sugar. Taste for seasoning. (Store in the refrigerator for up to 3 days.)

AVOCADO-CHILE SALSA

This is a quick, easy, versatile "from the garden" salsa that is great on fish or chicken or dolloped on the Rancho Salad (page 96).

3/4 CUP

1 ripe avocado, halved, pitted, peeled, and cut into 1/4-inch cubes

2 plum tomatoes, cored and cut into 1/2-inch cubes

1 jalapeño pepper, seeded and minced

1/2 cup minced fresh cilantro

3 tablespoons freshly squeezed lime juice

1/2 teaspoon fine sea salt

In a large bowl, combine all the ingredients, mixing gently with a spoon. (Store in an airtight container in the refrigerator for up to 1 day.)

PATRICIA'S PANTRY

These are some of my favorite pantry products, all available on my web site, www.patriciawells.com through my Amazon Store. Come visit me and stock your pantry.

Jean Leblanc pure first-pressed extra-virgin olive oil

Jean Leblanc oils are the finest! I am never without them.

Jean Leblanc stone-milled cold-pressed walnut oil

Drizzle this on warm shellfish and you are in heaven.

Huilerie J. Leblanc pistachio oil

Yes, this is expensive, but a few drops on avocado and zucchini will change your world.

Jean Leblanc nut oils set: hazelnut, almond, and walnut

The perfect starter collection of Leblanc oils.

Jean Leblanc nut oils set: almond, walnut, pistachio, truffle, and hazelnut

The Leblanc luxury collection.

Gianfranco Becchina olio verde al limone extra-virgin olive oil

This lemon-infused olive oil is always in my pantry. Try drizzling it on mozzarella and summer, vine-ripened tomatoes. It's a triple threat.

Gourmet Goods To You sherry vinegar

For a perfect vinaigrette: 1 part vinegar to 3 parts oil.

La Piana 20 year aged balsamic vinegar

Drizzle this on the best Parmesan you can find.

Chefshop sel gris—fine sea salt from Noirmoutier

The salt I use every day for cooking and baking.

Le Paludier *fleur de sel*—sea salt from Guérande

Caviar from the sea! Use just a finishing touch to transform every dish.

Brittany Sea Salt—coarse gray sea salt from Guérande

If salt can be elegant, this is it!

Das Salt gourmet finishing salt

What a lovely way to sample a variety of salts.

Maldon sea salt

British Maldon salt is a great finishing salt, leaving a wonderful sensation on the tongue.

Spicy World whole black Tellicherry peppercorns

Now this is real pepper, the finest in the world.

Edmond Fallot Dijon mustard

The finest artisanal mustard in the world, from Beaune.

Edmond Fallot Dijon mustard crock

More Fallot, here in a reusable porcelain crock.

Edmond Fallot Dijon mustard, authentic imported jar— traditional mustard

You can't beat tradition, and this one is delicious.

Edmond Fallot mustard crock—whole grain

Walter's favorite whole-grain mustard.

Boxed Edmond Fallot mustard selection: Dijon, grain, peppercorn, gingerbread, and basil

What a great way to test all the varied flavors.

Edmond Fallot tarragon Dijon mustard

Tarragon mustard for a thin slice of beef, heaven!

Edmond Fallot French cornichons (gherkins)

I use these cornichons in my popular potato salad.

Terre Exotique Espelette pepper powder (*piment d'Espelette*), AOC

A French Basque region treasure: not too hot but with personality. Sprinkle on chocolate desserts, your favorite tomato soup, pasta, rice, you name it.

Fieschi Mostarda di Cremona

Cremona's legendary sweet-tart chutney. Mostarda and cheese is a marriage made in heaven—but be careful, it can blow your head off!

Roland nonpareille capers

I always have capers on hand for potato salads, pastas, and so on.

Mustapha's Moroccan caperberries

An instant treat—serve with olives at cocktail time.

Mustapha's Moroccan Provençal green olives

Crisp, firm Provençal green olives.

Le Mas des Abeilles lavender honey

Lavender honey from Provence is the only honey I use.

Nielsen-Massey pure Madagascar Bourbon vanilla extract

The finest pure vanilla you can find.

JR Mushrooms & Specialties premium Bourbon-Madagascar vanilla beans

The best vanilla beans! Never too many.

Frontier Natural Brands Vietnamese cinnamon powder (5% oil)

Wait until you experience the aroma of this powerful cinnamon.

Valrhona "Caraibe" dark chocolate (66% cacao)

I keep of tin of these in my purse and snack drawer. Just in case.

Valrhona organic dark chocolate (70% cacao)

Hard to beat this chocolate! In my pantry for all chocolate desserts.

Valrhona cocoa powder

The finest for cocoa drinks and baking.

Rustichella spaghetti

This is the best brand of pasta in Italy. My pantry bulges with it.

Rustichella bucatini

Serve bucatini with pancetta, pecorino, and black pepper! Yes!

Rustichella fusilli col buco

Fusilli with garlic and walnut sauce, fantastic.

Rustichella organic whole wheat orecchiette

Their whole wheat pastas will change your life.

Rustichella d'Abruzzo penne pasta

Penne, my favorite with a great homemade tomato sauce.

Rustichella d'Abruzzo napole-tana pasta sauce

My go-to sauce when I don't have time to make my own.

Selezione Egidio Cremonesi carnaroli rice

For perfect risotto, every time.

Moretti Bramata polenta

We love polenta in our house.

Tenuta Castello whole farro grain

A wonderful, crunchy grain for salads or risotto.

Tenuta Castello farro flour

I use this flour in all my sourdough breads for added color and flavor.

SAF perfect rise instant yeast

The best yeast for baking.

Garbanzo bean flour

The essential flour for a great chickpea flour crepe, or socca.

Mutti Italian tomato paste concentrate

This is the pure *tomato paste concentrate from Italy that I use in my soups. Be sure to read the labels: This contains nothing but tomatoes and salt.*

Fresh Kaffir lime leaves

Oh, are you in for a treat! I make fresh kaffir lime leaf "dust" and use it in soups, shrimp salad, and even make a sorbet with it.

Pure fish sauce from Phu Quoc Island, Vietnam

This is the real deal! Cannot prepare Vietnamese food without it.

Thai fresh lemongrass

In love with lemongrass! Mince it and freeze any leftovers and use as fresh.

Fresh green papaya

An essential ingredient in many Vietnamese salads.

Fresh Thai chile peppers

I sure do like the heat! These can be dried, ground, and stored.

Tête de Moine cheese

The tangy cow's milk cheese made by monks in Switzerland.

Saint Marcellin cheese

An all-time favorite cow's milk cheese, pungent and creamy.

Chaource cheese

A cow's milk cheese that makes you stand up and take notice.

Brie cheese

The king of cow's milk cheeses.

Montrachet goat cheese

Tangy, lactic, delicious goat's milk cheese.

EQUIPMENT: ITEMS FOR A DREAM KITCHEN

Here is a list of my kitchen essentials, along with items for the dream kitchen. I am the gadget girl, though I know that out of one hundred maybe only two will change your life. But that's enough for me. All are available on my web site, www. patriciawells.com through my Amazon Store.

All-Clad stainless 12-quart multi cooker with steamer basket

We eat pasta several nights a week and could not live without this! And we steam almost all our veggies.

Cuisinart ICE-30BC Pure Indulgence 2-quart automatic frozen yogurt, sorbet, and ice cream maker

Sorbets are on our menu with nearly every meal, and this machine does the job.

Nordic Ware 9-inch leak-proof springform pan (10 cup)

One of the top essentials in my kitchen. I bake everything in this pan.

Peugeot Elis electric salt and pepper mill combo

Peugeot electric mills changed my life! You can grind the salt and pepper with a single hand, and they are made to last a lifetime.

CM International Camerons Cookware stainless steel stovetop smoker

Truly essential! We smoke poultry, fish, meat, veggies, and it totally transforms a meal.

Soehnle Page digital kitchen scale

One of the best kitchen tools—fast, tiny, and efficient.

Progressive International lettuce keeper

Brilliant! Salads stay crisp and fresh! I could have a dozen in my refrigerator, for veggies and greens.

Amco Swing-A-Way S2062 easy-release grease separator

I was so happy to find this gadget! Brilliant design, and it's red.

StainlessLUX fine stainless steel juicer / fruit squeezer

The best citrus juicer in the world.

Old Stone Oven 14 × 16-inch baking stone

I could not live without a baking stone for pizzas or breads.

EXO Products Super Peel pizza peel in solid ash

A must-have for pizzas and breads.

Kitchenaid Artisan 5-quart stand mixers

I've used mine almost every day for more than forty years . . .

Mario Batali The Italian Kitchen Collection pizza peel

Foolproof pizza is on its way.

Zyliss all cheese grater, fine and coarse drum set

A drum grater is essential, especially for Parmesan and Gruyère.

Norpro ceramic compost keeper

We compost in the country. Love that this is ceramic and red.

Kyocera double-edged mandoline slicer

I confess to being a mandoline addict! I've tried dozens, and this one is great.

Kyocera wide julienne slicer

Long live mandoline addiction! And it's red.

Rösle zester

I never toss lemon or lime peel— fragrant zest is a free addition to any dish.

Prepara herb savor

This gadget works! *Herbs stay fresh forever. I only wish it were a bit larger.*

Black & Decker 1-tier food steamer/rice cooker

A rice cooker makes perfect rice every time.

Lekue silicone super-flexible oven mitt

Not everyone cottons to silicone mitts, but I no longer have burns up and down my arms.

Siliconezone grid pot holder

I adore these pot holders.

KitchenAid all-purpose scraper

A dozen of these would not be enough—not just for pastry but also for scraping bits of food off a cutting board.

Oxo Good Grips silicone pastry brush

Good riddance to old-fashioned pastry brushes! These are so easy to keep clean.

Le Creuset silicone spatula

You will want a dozen.

All-Clad stainless measuring cup set

Measure, measure. Never too many sets around the house.

All-Clad stainless measuring spoon set

Essential!

All-Clad stainless roasting pan with rack and turkey forks

A must for roast chicken and turkey. Be sure to add a bit of water so the drippings don't burn.

All-Clad 6-piece stainless steel tool set

Great tools! Will last forever.

Iittala all steel bowl set

I am a huge fan of anything that stacks.

HIC porcelain 24-ounce 7 1/4-inch *coeur à la crème* dish

Love these for making homemade yogurt cheese.

Emeril pre-seasoned cast-iron 14-inch open flat-bottom wok

I use a wok for everything, even making risotto.

Typhoon cast-iron pestle and mortar

The next best thing to an antique stone pestle and mortar . . .

Typhoon signature 10-inch bamboo steamer

I love the texture of these steamers, so light and efficient.

Chef's Choice 662 international professional electric food slicer with 8.6-inch diameter blade

Great to slice almost anything— homemade sourdough bread, thin meats for carpaccio, as well as sausages and hams.

All-Clad copper-core porcelain double-boiler insert

Essential for melting chocolate.

All-Clad Master Chef 2 seven-piece cookware set

A great starter set.

Cuisipro Accutec box grater

Another excellent choice for grating cheese.

Swiss Diamond cast-aluminum nonstick 11-inch fry pan with lid

A great nonstick with a glass lid.

All-Clad food mill

Perfect for making homemade tomato sauce.

Calphalon Everyday nonstick 8-inch omelet pan

Walter makes the best omelets with this pan.

Le Creuset enameled cast-iron 10 2/3-inch crepe pan

Egg crepes are one of my favorites, and so versatile.

All-Clad flavor infuser

Stuff the infuser with Parmesan rinds for soup, all manner of herbs for stocks.

All-Clad stainless slotted spoon

There are never enough slotted spoons in my world!

All-Clad stainless-steel nonstick sauté pans

I use nonstick pans to cut down on the amount of fat in a dish.

Rösle apple cutter

For perfect apple slices.

All-Clad stainless balloon whisk

Whisk away! The design of this sturdy whisk is not only beautiful but efficient. It's also easier to clean than a classic whisk.

All-Clad stainless nonstick frittata pan (11.75-inch)

Frittatas are the most versatile food in the world.

All-Clad stainless 9-inch locking tongs

Everyone needs at least three of these in the kitchen. Hang them on the stove so they are handy.

BonJour Monet 8-cup French press coffee maker

Truly makes the best coffee.

Taylor 9842 commercial waterproof digital thermometer

Ideal for meats, and I also use it on my sourdough bread to make sure it is baked through.

Presto 05420 Frydaddy electric deep-fryer

So good, so fast, so great for testing just a tiny bit of food.

Oxo Good Grips 4-inch pizza wheel

For perfect pizza slices.

Harold Import Company stainless-steel fish turner (13 3/4 inches)

Handy for fish and everything else. In a pinch, can serve to pull a pizza from the oven.

Laguiole French olive wood spatula with drainage holes

Beautiful and practical.

Sunbeam 91640 99-minute, 59-second digital count up/ count down timer

Perfect timing is essential in the kitchen.

MIU commercial oven thermometer

All ovens are different. Don't bake or roast without an oven thermometer.

CDN TR3-R digital timer on a rope

How perfect: On a rope, digital, and it's red.

M.V Trading Co. large 12-inch bamboo steamer

I love the size and texture of these steamers. So simple.

KitchenAid KHB100ER hand blender

Hand blenders are, well, handy.

KitchenAid KPRA pasta roller attachment for stand mixers

The flat roller is fabulous for making delicious light flatbreads.

Calphalon Classic Bakeware Special Value 12 × 17-inch rectangular nonstick jelly roll pans

Jelly roll pans are not just for jelly rolls.

Chicago metallic nonstick petite broil and roast pan

A nice size for roasting or broiling.

Leifheit Pro Line triple-plated chrome over zinc cherry/olive pitter

Dual purpose, for perfect pitting of cherries and olives.

Nesco FD-75PR 700-watt food dehydrator

I use a dehydrator to dry cherries and sliced apples and to make my own raisins.

Paderno World Cuisine 20-imprint 15.5 × 5.5-inch nonstick madeleine sheet

Miniature madeleines . . . I can smell them now.

Pyrex Prepware 2-cup measuring cup, clear with red measurements

What would we do without Pyrex measuring cups? I only wish they didn't drip so much.

Pyrex Prepware 1-cup measuring cup, clear with red measurements

Measure, measure . . . and the numbers are in red.

Rösle shaker

Come summer, we make coffee and iced Shakerados! (Espresso coffee, shaker half-filled with ice, shaken vigorously for 15 seconds, strained into cocktail glass.) Yum!

Bormioli Rocco Pompei 6-piece stacking bowl set

Never enough stacking bowls in my kitchen.

J.A. Henckels Twin L kitchen 2-piece set

A cool duo . . . a small knife and a scissors.

Vic Firth maple rolling pins

What a cool trio! Bake, bake, bake! I like the large size for pastries and smaller sizes for smaller uses, such as cookies.

Cuisinart DLC-10S Pro Classic 7-cup food processor

Use this twenty times a day.

Foodsaver Pro III vacuum sealing kit

Never throw away leftovers again—essential!

Thermos Nissan 26-ounce travel companion stainless-steel insulated bottle

Nothing is better than your own home-brewed coffee when on a journey.

Oxo Good Grips apple corer and divider

We love apples in our house, and this gadget makes a perfect cut each time.

Calphalon apple corer with plunger

Perfect cored apples, every time.

Cuisinart ICE 40 Flavor Duo Frozen Yogurt Maker

We recently added this duo ice cream maker to our kitchen. Great when you want two different flavors.

New Metro Design Beater Blade for KitchenAid

This is revolutionary! My bread is made in a fraction of the time it takes with KitchenAid's own blade.

Kitchen Crop Sprouter—3 Tray

I always have three sprouting trays at my kitchen window. Amazing what flavor tiny sprouts can offer.

Soda-Stream Soda and Seltzer Maker Starter Kit

No more hauling bottles from the store! Open the fridge and have bubbly water at your fingertips.

Maxi-Matic EWM-900BK Elite Cuisine Waffle Maker

This is the waffle iron I use at home. Easy. Just don't fill it with too much batter.

Lock & Lock HPL343S16, 16-piece Polypropylene Food Storage Container Set

I adore these containers: They manage to keep food fresh longer than any other system. Great for cheese.

Cuisipro 4-Piece Stainless Steel Oval Measuring Cups

These oval measuring cups are sturdy, beautiful, and practical.

Cuisinart CBT- 700 Die Cast 700-Watt Blender

I love this blender! It's powerful, has great capacity, and I use it daily for soups and sorbets.

Crockpot 3060-W 6-quart round slow cooker

People laugh, but I make southern pork barbecue in my crockpot. Can also be used for making duck confit.

INTERNET FOOD SOURCES

Not everyone can walk out the door and find the freshest and most exotic ingredients in the world. This is where the Internet comes in. Because inventories and service fluctuate, check to see what is currently available.

FISH AND SHELLFISH

Browne Trading Company

Portland, Maine
Ships overnight anywhere in the United States.
800-944-7848
www.brownetrading.com
Rouget barbet (red mullet), scallops, halibut, snapper, ahi tuna. There is a web site, but you need to call to order fish, according to availability. They supply Le Bernardin in New York City.

Dirk's Fresh Seafood Products

Chicago, Illinois
773-404-3475
www.dirksfish.com
Huge selection of sustainable fresh fish and shellfish.

Farm-2-Market

Roscoe, New York
800-477-2967
www.farm-2-market.com
Mussels, spiny lobster, Dungeness crab, sea scallops, and more, shipped to the United States.

Great Alaska Seafood

Soldotna, Alaska
866-262-8846
www.great-alaska-seafood.com
Halibut and halibut cheeks, shipped to the United States and Canada.

Heritage Foods USA

Brooklyn, New York
718-389-0985
www.heritagefoodsusa.com
Alaskan wild salmon (seasonal, late summer) as well as pork, shipped to the United States.

Monterey Fish Market

Berkeley, California
510-525-5600
www.webseafood.com or www.montereyfish.com
Fresh Pacific seafood including wild Pacific salmon, Dungeness crab, calamari, shrimp, and sand dabs, shipped overnight.

Pacific Seafood Group

Clackamas, Oregon, and stores nationwide
503-905-4500
www.pacseafood.com
Mussels from New England, Washington State, New Zealand, and Canada.

Penn Cove Shellfish, LLC

Coupeville, Washington
360-678-4803
www.penncoveshellfish.com
Mediterranean mussels farmed in Washington State.

Taylor Shellfish Farms

Shelton and Bow, Washington
360-426-6178
www.taylorshellfishfarms.com
Mediterranean mussels, Dungeness crab.

MEAT

D'Artagnan

Newark, New Jersey
800-327-8246
www.dartagnan.com
Fresh and frozen truffles, duck confit, foie gras, duck, guinea hens, quail, squab, poussin, rabbit, and duck fat.

Golden Gate Meat Co.

San Francisco, California
415-861-3800
www.goldengatemeatcompany.
com
Angus beef, baby veal.

Grimaud Farms

Stockton, California
800-466-9955
www.grimaudfarms.com
Muscovy duck, guinea hens,
duck fat.

Heritage Foods USA

Brooklyn, New York
718-389-0985
www.heritagefoodsusa.com
Pork as well as seafood, shipped
within the United States.

Johnston County Hams

Smithfield, North Carolina
919-934-8054
800-543-HAMS (4267)
www.countrycuredhams.com
Dry-cured ham (American
prosciutto) made in North
Carolina.

Nueske's

Wittenberg, Wisconsin
800-392-2266
www.nueskes.com
Applewood-smoked bacon.

Polarica

San Francisco, California
800-426-3872
www.polaricausa.com
Fresh and frozen truffles, duck
confit, foie gras, duck, guinea hens,
quail, squab, poussin, pheasant,
rabbit, and duck fat with overnight
delivery in the United States.

Preferred Meats

Oakland, California
800-397-6328
www.preferredmeats.com
Grass-fed beef, Berkshire pork,
lamb, applewood-smoked bacon.

Zingerman's

Ann Arbor, Michigan
888-636-8162
www.zingermans.com
Cured meats as well as oils,
vinegars, spices, porcini powder,
olives.

CHEESE

Fromages.com
www.fromages.com
Huge selection of excellent
unpasteurized French cheeses,
delivered worldwide within 24 to
48 hours.

PANTRY

Adriana's Caravan
New York, New York
800-316-0820
www.adrianascaravan.com
Huge international selection of
spices, oils, and vinegars, as well as
fresh and dried mushrooms.

Dean & Deluca

Stores nationwide
800-221-7714
www.deananddeluca.com
Artisanal oils, vinegars, cheeses,
Valrhona chocolate, spices.

Earthy Delights

DeWitt, Michigan
800-367-4709
www.earthy.com
Fresh and frozen peeled chestnuts,
artisanal oils and vinegars, fresh
wild mushrooms, foie gras.

Kalustyan's

New York, New York
800-352-3451
www.kalustyans.com
International selection of spices
and condiments, especially Middle
Eastern foods.

La Tienda

Williamsburg, Virginia

888-331-4362

www.tienda.com

Spanish products, including *lomo,* piquillo peppers, sherry vinegar, saffron, *pimentón* paprika.

Marky's

Miami, Florida

800-522-8427

www.markys.com

Huge selection of international fresh and cured products, including Spanish white anchovies in vinegar, olive oils, and sauces.

Penzey's Spices

Wauwatosa, Wisconsin

800-741-7787

www.penzeys.com

Spices and herbs.

Spanish Table

Berkeley and Mill Valley, California; Santa Fe, New Mexico; Seattle, Washington

510-548-1383 (Berkeley)

www.spanishtable.com

Spanish products, including squid ink, *lomo embuchado,* artisanal sherry vinegar, saffron, piquillo peppers, *pimentón* paprika.

Zingerman's

Ann Arbor, Michigan

888-636-8162

www.zingermans.com

Oils, vinegars, spices, porcini powder, cured meats, olives.

MUSHROOMS AND TRUFFLES

Adriana's Caravan

New York, New York

800-316-0820

www.adrianascaravan.com

Fresh and dried mushrooms, as well as oils, spices, and vinegars.

D'Artagnan

Newark, New Jersey

800-327-8246

www.dartagnan.com

Fresh and frozen truffles, duck breasts, as well as specialty meats.

Earthy Delights

DeWitt, Michigan

800-367-4709

www.earthy.com

Fresh wild mushrooms as well as pantry products.

Fresh and Wild

Vancouver, Washington

800-222-5578

www.freshwild.com

Wild mushrooms and dried Red Flame seedless grapes, with expedited shipping.

Plantin America, Inc.

Weehawken, New Jersey

888-595-6214

www.plantin.com

Black truffles (fresh, frozen, canned, or jarred), dry mushrooms, sea salt, truffle slicers. My supplier.

Urbani Truffles

Norwalk, Connecticut

718-433-1560

www.urbanitrufflesonline.com

Fresh and preserved black and white truffles and truffle products.

PRODUCE

Farmer's markets information and locations nationwide.

www.ams.usda.gov/farmersmarkets

Produce and other products direct from the source.

Frieda's

Los Angeles, California

800-241-1771

www.friedas.com

Specialty produce, including exotic Asian fruits and vegetables, edible flowers.

Jacob's Farm / Del Cabo, Inc.

Pescadero, California

650-879-0580

www.delcabo.com

Cooperative growers of organic tomatoes, fruits, vegetables, herbs.

Phipps Ranch

Pescadero, California

650-879-1032

www.phippscountry.com

Heirloom and exotic dried beans, spices, and organic rices and grains.

CHOCOLATE

Chocosphere

Portland, Oregon

877-992-4626

www.chocosphere.com

All kinds of chocolates, including Valrhona.

Dean & Deluca

Stores nationwide

800-221-7714

www.deananddeluca.com

Valrhona chocolate as well as specialty produce and products.

KITCHEN EQUIPMENT

Amazon.com

Raytek Mini Temp MT4 and 6, infrared thermometer for ovens.

BIA Cordon Bleu

www.biacordonblu.com/biaweb/
Archive/Giftware/giftware.html
Porcelain cheese markers.

Bridge Kitchenware

Roseland, New Jersey

973-287-6163

www.bridgekitchenware.com

Extensive selection of professional equipment.

King Arthur Flour (The Baker's Store)

Norwich, Vermont

802-649-3361

800-827-6836

www.kingarthurflour.com

Everything a baker could want, including equipment such as individual pie tins and ingredients such as hazelnut paste.

Mugnaini

Watsonville, California

888-887-7206

www.mugnaini.com

Wood-fired bread ovens.

PCD Professional Cutlery Direct

North Branford, Connecticut

800-792-6650

www.cookingenthusiast.com

Professional equipment.

ACKNOWLEDGMENTS

My most sincere thanks go to Cédric Ganachaud, our indefatigable gardener, who provides us with a welcome bounty of multicolored heirloom tomatoes and endless varieties of peppers, eggplant, herbs, and greens all summer long. I also want to thank all the farmers and conscientious merchants in both Paris and Provence whose produce allows me to wave a magic wand and transform a simple herb, a tomato, a melon, into pure pleasure on the plate.

Friends and family have also been a big part of this book, as we gathered together, feet under the table, toasting and feasting all the salads in our lives: Thank you, Susan Herrmann, Rita and Yale Kramer, Andrew Axilrod and Alyson De Groot, Todd Murray and Douglas Sills, Jeffrey and Katherine Bergman, Juan Sanchez, Ina and Jeffrey Garten, Dorie and Michael Greenspan, Johanne Killeen and George Germon, Jean-Claude and Colette Viviani. Thank you Jeff, Sue, and Dana Kauch for your special talents and friendship.

Restaurateurs have provided endless inspiration here, and special thanks go to Raoul and Flora Reichrath at Le Grand Pré and Préface, to Marlies and Johannes Sailer at Les Abeilles, and to all the Paris cafés and bistros that manage to turn simple salads into very special meals.

Thanks to Jane Sigal, who helped dot the i's and cross the t's; to Harriet Bell, who first said "Yes!" to the salad idea; to Emily Buchanan for keeping everything tidy and on target; to my agent, Amanda Urban, who is always there when I need her. At HarperCollins and William Morrow, a big thank you to Jonathan Burnham for believing in me, to Cassie Jones for jumping in at the last moment to put a shine and polish on the manuscript, and to designer Lorie Pagnozzi. Thanks also to Liate Stehlik, Lynn Grady, Tavia Kowalchuk, Carrie Bachman, Andy Dodds, Shawn Nicholls, Joyce Wong, Ann Cahn, Mary Schuck, and Karen Lumley.

But my biggest thank you is reserved for my husband and lifetime partner, Walter Wells, with respect and gratitude for this most perfect life.

INDEX

Iceberg, Tomato, Avocado, Bacon, and
  Blue Cheese (My Cobb Salad),
  67, 67–68
Iceberg Lettuce Salad with Bacon and
  Roquefort, 90, 91
Italian Salad: Celery, Fennel, Spring
  Onion, and Radish with
  Bocconcini, Prosciutto, Olives,
  and Marinated Artichokes, 106–7
Italian Salt and Sugar–Cured Beef:
  Carne Salada, 229–31, 230

Japanese Sesame Salt: *Gomasio*, 304
Jellied Chicken Salad, Franck's, 201–2

Kaffir Lime(s)
  about, 37
  Dust, Shellfish Velouté with, 36–37
  Dust, Warm Asian Shrimp Salad
    with, 168–69
  Thai Beef Salad, 238–39
Kumquat, Fig, Sheep Cheese,
  Pomegranate Seed, and Arugula
  Salad, 97–98

Lamb
  Roast Leg of, Thyme-Marinated,
    244–45
  Salad with Potatoes, Peppers,
    Tarragon, and Cherry Tomatoes,
    242–43
  Sausages, Spicy, from Bordeaux,
    240–41
Lemongrass and Lime–Cured Beef
  Salad, Walter's, 217–18
Lemon(s)
  -Basil Dressing, 319
  Caesar Salad Dressing, 323
  Capers, Cornichons, and Mint,
    Poached Turkey Breast Salad
    with, 207–8
  -Chive Dressing, Creamy, 326
  Confit, Black Olive Tapenade
    with, 20
  Confit, Quick, 297
  and Hazelnut Oil Dressing, 209
  -Mustard Dressing, Creamy, 325
  and Olive Oil Dressing, 330
  -Tahini-Yogurt Dressing and
    Dipping Sauce, 55, 332
  and Yogurt Dressing, 331
  Zest–Buttermilk Dressing, 322
  Zest Salt, 306, 306
Lettuce
  Bacon, and Tomato *Tartines*, 83
  Chicken Salad with Peas, Feta, and
    Mint, 184–85

A Deconstructed Club Sandwich
  Salad with Purple Potato Chips,
  80–81
Iceberg, Salad with Bacon and
  Roquefort, 90, 91
Lamb's, and Potatoes, Warm
  Parmesan-Crusted Sole Salad
  with, 174–75
My Caesar Salad with Polenta
  Croutons, 63–64
My Cobb Salad: Iceberg, Tomato,
  Avocado, Bacon, and Blue
  Cheese, 67, 67–68
Salad Niçoise, 75–76, 77
Lime(s)
  and Avocado, Crab Salad with,
    124–25
  Cream, Tangy, Smoked Trout, and
    Trout Eggs, Scallop Ceviche with,
    162–63
  and Lemongrass–Cured Beef Salad,
    Walter's, 217–18
  and Vanilla Dressing, 329
  Vietnamese Dipping Sauce, 336
Liver, Chicken, Terrine with Black
  Peppercorns, 203–4
Lobster Salad with Green Beans, Apple,
  and Avocado, 131–32, 133

Mackerel
  Home-Smoked, 134–35
  Marinated in White Wine, 138–39
Manchego, Chorizo, and Tomatoes,
  Scrubbed Bread *Tartines* with,
  246
Mayonnaise, Homemade, and Friends,
  333–35
Meat. *See* Beef; Lamb; Pork; Veal
Mint
  Braised Salmon with Cucumber
    Ribbons, Herb Salad, and Ginger
    Dressing, 148–49
  Broccoli Soup with, 31
  Capers, and Spring Onions, Potato
    Salad with, 136–37
  Chilled Yogurt, Herb, and Jalapeño
    Soup, 42
  and Goat Cheese, Zucchini Blossom
    Frittata with, 52–53
  Lemon, Capers, and Cornichons,
    Poached Turkey Breast Salad
    with, 207–8
  Peas, and Feta, Chicken Salad with,
    184–85
  Rosemary, and Tarragon, Rare-
    Roasted Beef with, 219–20
  Thai Beef Salad, 238–39

Multigrain Sourdough Bread: *Pain au
  Levain*, 270–73, 271
Mushrooms
  Mixed Nuts, Cracklings, and
    Chestnuts, Smoked Duck Breast
    with, 211
  and Spinach, Egg Crepes with,
    46–47
Mussel *Tartine* with Chorizo,
  Tomatoes, and Basil, 140–42, 141
Mustard
  -Lemon Dressing, Creamy, 325
  Sorbet, 249
  Spicy, and Tuna, Penne Salad
    with, 57
  and Tomato Tart, 282, 283–84

Noodles
  Glass, Ginger and Sesame Chicken
    Salad with, 194–95
  Soba, and Chicken with Ginger-
    Peanut Sauce, 192–93
Nuts. *See also* Almond(s); Hazelnut(s);
    Peanut(s); Pistachios
  Mixed, Mushrooms, Cracklings, and
    Chestnuts, Smoked Duck Breast
    with, 211
  Mixed, Spicy Basque, 8, 9
  Toasted, Green Beans, and Cured
    Olives (Summer Salad), 103–5

Oil, Basil, 320
Olive(s). *See also* Tapenade
  Black, Brine-Cured, 302
  Bocconcini, Prosciutto, and
    Marinated Artichokes, Celery,
    Fennel, Spring Onion, and
    Radish with (Italian Salad),
    106–7
  Cured, Green Beans, and Toasted
    Nuts (Summer Salad), 103–5
  Greek Salad, 78, 79
  Green, Celery, and Anchovy Salad,
    112
  Ham and Cheese Bread, 266–67,
    267
  Marinated, Quartet, 18, 19
  Picholine, with Toasted Cumin and
    Paprika, 21
  Scrubbed Bread *Tartines* with
    Chorizo, Manchego, and
    Tomatoes, 246
  Spring Onions, Capers, and Parsley,
    Veal and Potato Salad with,
    256–57
Onion and Bacon Tart, Alsatian:
  Flammekuchen, 278–80, 279